The Winemaker's Encyclopaedia

The Winemaker's Encyclopaedia

by
BEN TURNER
and
ROY ROYCROFT

FABER & FABER · London and Boston

First published in 1979
by Faber and Faber Limited
3 Queen Square London WC1N 3AU
Printed in Great Britain by
Redwood Burn Limited
Trowbridge and Esher
Phototypeset in V.I.P. Palatino by
Western Printing Services Ltd, Bristol

British Library Cataloguing in Publication Data

Turner, Ben
    The winemaker's encyclopaedia.
    1. Wine and wine making - Dictionaries
    I. Title   II. Roycroft, Roy
    641.8'72'03   TP546

    ISBN 0-571-11418-0
    ISBN 0-571-11420-2 Pbk

ABONDANCE   Wine well diluted with water. Sometimes given in French schools to children.

ACETALDEHYDE   Formed during fermentation as a step in the production of alcohol. The enzyme zymase reduces acetaldehyde to alcohol, but acetic acid can be produced if the fermentation temperature is too high or if there is an infection by spoilage organisms. The presence of a large quantity of sulphite will prevent acetaldehyde being reduced to alcohol, and glycerol or acetic acid is then the major product. Excess oxygenation during racking can also result in glycerol being produced instead of alcohol, but 50 to 100 ppm of sulphite will prevent this oxidasive reaction.

ACETAMIDE   The product of spoilage bacteria that causes the unpleasant flavour known as 'mousiness'.

ACETIC ACID   The monobasic acid that gives vinegar its characteristic sour taste. It is produced when alcohol is oxidized by bacteria. It is also formed, in very small quantities, by the redox reactions during maturation. But, far from causing spoilage, these very small quantities add to the matured quality of the wines. (*See also* ACETIFICATION.)

ACETIFICATION   This is the production of acetic acid in a wine. It is perhaps the most common ailment of wine and is caused by the vinegar bacillus—*Acetobacter mycoderma aceti*—which floats invisibly in the air and clings to fruit and winemaking vessels. The first sign of infection is an oily sheen on the top of the wine which is followed by the smell of ethyl acetate and then the sour vinegar smell. When a wine is strongly attacked, nothing can reduce the distinctive vinegarish taste. The remedy lies in cleanliness, sulphiting and good cellar work. All vessels should be washed in sulphite solution before use and the must and the wine should be kept closely covered at all times. The storage containers should be kept full and well corked so that no air can enter.

 Sour wine is sometimes produced by lactic acid bacillus but the taste is not very pleasant. (*See also* VINEGAR and LACTIC ACID BACTERIA.)

ACETOBACTER   *See* VINEGAR BACTERIA.

ACETOIN   Produced by lactobacilli, it causes an off-flavour in the wine. It is prevented by cleanliness and the use of sulphite.

ACID COMPARISON TABLES

Comparative parts per thousand (ppt) of various acids when measured as:–

Sulphuric	Citric	Tartaric	Malic
0·5	0·72	0·77	0·68
1·0	1·43	1·53	1·37
1·5	2·14	2·29	2·05
2·0	2·86	3·06	2·73
2·5	3·57	3·83	3·42
3·0	4·29	4·59	4·10
3·5	4·99	5·36	4·78
4·0	5·71	6·12	5·47
4·5	6·43	6·89	6·15
5·0	7·14	7·65	6·84
5·5	7·86	8·42	7·52
6·0	8·58	9·18	8·20
6·5	9·28	9·95	8·88
7·0	9·98	10·72	9·56

Addition of acids: parts per thousand as sulphuric for different acids of a given weight added to 1 U.K. gallon and to 5 litres

1 U.K. gallon		5 litres	Citric	Tartaric	Malic
⅛ oz	3·5g	3·85g	0·55	0·51	0·57
¼	7·0	7·7	1·09	1·02	1·14
⅜	10·5	11·8	1·64	1·53	1·71
½	14·0	15·4	2·18	2·04	2·28
⅝	17·5	19·3	2·73	2·55	2·85
¾	21·0	23·1	3·27	3·05	3·42
⅞	24·5	27·0	3·82	3·56	3·99
1	28·0	30·8	4·36	4·07	4·56
1⅛	31·5	34·7	4·91	4·58	5·13
1¼	35·0	38·5	5·45	5·09	5·69
1⅜	38·5	42·4	5·99	5·60	6·26
1½	42·0	46·25	6·54	6·11	6·83

For experimental purposes: 2½ oz (70 g) of acid crystals dissolved in 19 fl. oz (0·54 litres) of water makes 20 fl. oz (0·566 litres) of solution. Thus 1 fl. oz (28 ml) equals ⅛ oz (3·5 g).

The following are examples of the *average* range of acidity of some commercial wines:

	ppt tartaric
Bordeaux (red)	5·2 to 6·0
Burgundy (red)	5·5 to 6·5

Burgundy (white)	6·0 to 7·0
Val de Loire	7·0 to 7·5
Madeira	5·0 to 5·5
Hock	5·4 to 6·2
Côte du Rhone	4·6 to 5·4
Sauternes	7·2 to 7·6

ACIDIFICATION   The increase of acidity in a must or wine either by the addition of acids or by infection from spoilage micro-organisms.

Acid is added to a must to correct a deficiency. Without the additional acid the wine would lack balance and freshness and would not keep. It would also be susceptible to spoilage by micro-organisms. It is not a chemical process but simply the addition of natural substances which are already present but not in sufficient quantity. Acidification by spoilage organisms is the increase of a wine's acidity by the reduction of non-acids to acids, so raising the total acidity. It is prevented by the use of sulphite.

ACIDIMETRIC OUTFIT   Equipment used to check the total acid content of a solution. *See* under TITRATION for details.

ACIDITY (FIXED)   The acidity of the combined acids, i.e. malic, tartaric, citric etc. which is measured by titration.

ACIDITY (REAL)   The degree or intensity of a must's or wine's acidity which is measured by pH.

ACIDITY (TOTAL)   The overall acidity of a wine from combined and volatile acids.

ACIDITY (VOLATILE)   Volatile or free acids are those which can be separated from wine by distillation. Only very small amounts, from 0·3 to 0·4 g per litre, are present in wine. Larger amounts usually signify infection by micro-organisms, hence the French law which prohibits the sale of wine containing 0·9 g of free acid per litre from the vineyard and 1g from the shops. Volatile acidity increases with the age of a wine and when it reaches about 0·7 g per litre, it becomes quite noticeable as a sour taste on the palate.

ACIDS and ACIDITY   Acids are compounds which have a dissociated hydrogen ion that, when in solution, is available for reduction reactions. Acids are divided into two categories—weak and strong. The weak, which are plant or organic acids, play an important part in the series of chemical changes that occur during plant respiration (called Kreb's cycle). They are also important in winemaking. The strong acids, hydrochloric, nitric and sulphuric, have no part in winemaking, although the units of measure used in the titration of free acids are often expressed as if of sulphuric acid.

The principal acids of grapes are tartaric and malic. Depending on the grape variety, the soil and the weather during growth and ripening, the ratio can vary from 1 tartaric/1 malic to 10 tartaric/3 malic. In addition to these principal acids, the following acids have also been found in grapes: caffeic, chlorogenic, cis-asonitic, citric, fumaric, galacturonic, glucuronic, glyceric, glycolic, glyoxylic, isocitric, lactic,* oxalic, oxaloacetic, α-oxoglutaric, pyruvic, quinic, shikimic, succinic (Kliewer 1966).

The major acids of fruits other than grapes are citric and malic. Minor acids are as quoted for grapes plus others in varying combinations.

The individual effects in a wine's aroma/bouquet and flavour are mostly unknown as yet. Acidity is, however, essential to a wine's quality and well-being. If the acidity is too high it has to be reduced (*see also*, BENTONITE, CALCIUM CARBONATE, POTASSIUM CARBONATE and MALO-LACTIC FERMENTATION), or if it is too low it has to be increased, because a wine derives many benefits from the correct range and balance.

(1) Yeasts thrive and ferment best in an acid solution between 3·0 and 3·4pH.
(2) Spoilage organisms are inhibited by an acidity of 3·4 pH or below.
(3) Production of glycerol is stimulated by an adequate quantity of tartaric acid.
(4) Esterification is assisted by malic and succinic acids.
(5) Acids play an essential part in the redox reactions of maturing, and although higher acidity can increase maturation time, the wine is the better for it.
(6) If a wine contains too little acid it tastes insipid; if it contains too much it tastes sharp and acidic. The correct balance imparts freshness and cleanliness and adds to the individuality, personality and quality of a wine.

The real acidity is measured by pH and the optimum for wine is between 3·1 and 3·4, but this does not reflect the fixed or total acidity, due to the presence of salts which act as buffers. Fixed acidity is measured by titration and varies between 3·5 and 6 ppt (parts per thousand) as sulphuric acid equivalent, depending on the type and style of the wine. As the fixed acidity is masked on the palate by sugar, it normally has to be higher in a sweet wine to obtain the right balance. When it is necessary, one or more of the following acids may be used for acidification.

(a) CITRIC ACID The principal acid of citrus fruits from which it gets its name, but it is also found in grapes as a minor acid. The juice of one small

---

* The presence of lactic acid may be due either to the action of micro-organisms or to the reactions with ion exchange resins used in the separation of acids.

lemon approximates to 3·5 g of citric acid crystals. The crystals are readily soluble in water, help to promote rapid fermentation and have good antiseptic properties. Citric acid is not utilized in ester formation and so does nothing to promote bouquet or flavour, but a high content can prolong maturation. It is therefore of more benefit in balancing a must than in balancing a finished wine.

(b) MALIC ACID This is the principal acid of apples (*Malus*) and is present in some other fruits. It is also one of the principal acids of grapes and gives unripe berries their characteristic sour taste. As the fruit ripens malic acid plays a part in the respiratory process and decreases in quantity. The decrease is accelerated by rising temperatures, which is the reason why grapes contain too much acid after cold summers and too little after very hot summers.

Malic acid promotes a reasonably rapid fermentation and its use by the yeast can reduce by up to 30% the malic content during fermentation. It very freely enters into ester-forming reactions, thus developing bouquet and flavour.

(c) TARTARIC ACID The principal acid of ripe grapes and no other fruit. Alone in a must it will cause slow fermentation. It can impart a harsh taste to a young wine but is invaluable during maturation as it readily participates in esterification. It is less soluble in alcohol than in water and it readily combines with potassium. Chilling or the addition of potassium carbonate will, therefore, cause precipitation of cream of tartar. This is useful in reducing the acidity of a too acid wine.

(d) MIXED ACIDS Each acid has its advantages and disadvantages and it is now considered that a mixture of all three acids is preferable when adjusting the acidity of a must. The possible best mixture for general use would appear to be one part citric, two parts malic and two parts tartaric acids. A better practice would be to have each acid separate and make adjustments for the natural acids present in the must so as to give an overall ration of 1 : 2 : 2. For example if an apple must in which nearly all the natural acid was malic contained two parts per thousand as sulphuric acid, then an adjustment to five parts acid per thousand would be to increase the total acidity by one part per thousand with citric acid and two parts per thousand with tartaric acid. (*See* ACID COMPARISON.)

Yeast must have an acid solution in which to live and multiply. During fermentation and maturation, chemical reactions occur which result in some acids being produced in the wine, that were not in the must. These are butyric, carbonic, lactic, nucleic, phosphoric, propionic, pyruvic, succinic and valerianic plus certain others which are sometimes present in such minute quantities as to be virtually unmeasurable. Some winemakers consider the presence of succinic acid to be so important that they add a little to improve the wine's bouquet.

9

ACIDS IN FRUIT Total acid content of any ingredient cannot be stated accurately because it depends on the cultivar, growth factors (soil, fertilizer, climate, micro-environment etc.), the stage of ripeness and length of storage. Likewise there can be variations in the amounts of individual acids comprising the total content. The table on pages 12 and 13 gives the probable content as a ratio of the individual acids. From a titration of a must the content of individual acids can be calculated and adjusted as required, e.g. an apricot must with 4 parts per thousand would contain 3 ppt citric and 1 ppt malic.

ACID/SUGAR BALANCE This critical factor varies from wine to wine, from one grape variety to another and from year to year. It is also the determining factor on just when to harvest the ripening grapes, on whether de-acidification is necessary and, in part, on how much sugar to add during fermentation. (*See* CHAPTALIZATION.) A reasonable guide for the balance is 1 g of acid for every 10 units of gravity per litre of unfermented fruit juice or must to be fermented into table wine. (*See also* ACIDS.)

AEROBIC/ANAEROBIC Yeast cells have the dual ability to live in the atmosphere where oxygen in the air is readily available to them, and also in a must from which free air has been excluded. In the stage in which oxygen is readily available from the air, the yeast is said to be living in its aerobic state. When the yeast has to live in the state in which it is denied free oxygen it lives in an anaerobic condition, i.e. without air. Many moulds, spoilage yeasts and bacteria are able to live only in an aerobic state and when wines or musts are left in contact with air, these micro-organisms are able to develop. They cannot develop on or in musts and wines from which air is properly excluded. Lactic acid bacteria, however, are anaerobic organisms and can grow despite the absence of free oxygen.

AFTERTASTE When a wine is swallowed, new feelings of pleasure or dislike are experienced by the taste-buds on the part of the tongue beneath the uvula, which are normally resident in the throat rather than the mouth. These taste buds are extremely sensitive and a wine which otherwise seems pleasant, sometimes has a fault which shows up when swallowing several times after the wine has left the mouth. On the other hand, the really good wines taste smooth and round and pleasant in the aftertaste, or farewell, as it is more elegantly called. Any imbalance or contamination or disease is sure to show up here. It is a crucial part of wine evaluation to pass the wine around the mouth and uvula, to spit it out and then to swallow several times. This is the final test as it were; a wine that does not get good marks here is no prize winner!

AGE The age of a wine is the period of time which has elapsed since the wine was made. Beer usually needs only a few weeks to mature,

10

cider only a few months, but wine often needs years. Light white wines age or mature more quickly than red and heavy wines, but most need first a period in bulk storage, followed by another in bottle. Each wine has a different requirement. Generally speaking, wines that have a high content of acid, tannin, alcohol and sugar take longest to mature. Delicate and fragrant white wines are sometimes bottled straight from their lees as soon as they are crystal clear in order to retain the bouquet and flavour. There is no short cut to ageing a wine once made since the process of maturation is still not completely understood. Some winemakers marginally reduce the acid, tannin and sugar content of a must by blending of ingredients deficient in these constituents when they wish to produce a quick-maturing wine. Others make wine with a tartaric acid content of 8 to 9 ppt (5·5 to 6 ppt as sulphuric) and leave them to mature for at least 10 years.

AGRAFE A metal clip used on Champagne and sparkling wine bottles to hold stoppers firmly in place during the secondary fermentation. It is easily and quickly removed at the moment of disgorgement and subsequently replaced by a wire cage called a muselet. (*See also* DISGORGEMENT and SPARKLING WINE.)

AIR CONTROL It is essential for wine to be exposed to air and for air to be excluded from wine. This appears to be a contradiction but is not so, for air is both beneficial and harmful depending on the stage, age, condition, type and alcohol content of the wine and the length of time they are in contact. The well-being and improvement of wine is therefore directly related to the control of air.

A must is sulphited to inhibit the action of micro-organisms and to prevent oxidation. The vessel is then covered and air excluded to prevent loss of the sulphur dioxide and re-contamination from the air.

Alcoholic fermentation can take place either with (aerobic) or without (anaerobic) the presence of air. Carbon dioxide produced during fermentation is heavier than air and forms into a layer between the wine and the air, provided it is not disturbed. This acts as an inhibitor of infection. Even so, during and immediately after fermentation there are differences in the control of air according to the type of wine being produced.

For light table wines the colony of yeast cells added to a must is normally sufficient to ferment it fully without a further supply of oxygen. The yeast cells can live and cause fermentation without oxygen but most spoilage organisms need air. Air is therefore excluded during fermentation.

Light wines generally require little or no oxidation and being low in alcohol are susceptible to spoilage. To minimize the spoilage risk, it is only necessary to rack at the end of fermentation when the wine is clearing and again when a deposit forms. Some oxygen is induced during the racking process, but oxidation can be prevented and spoilage

FRUIT OR VEGETABLE	Citric	Malic	Tartaric	Succinic	Isocitric & Lactone	Oxalic	Quinic	Other
Apples		18					1	citric + succinic + tartaric = 1 trace shikimic in peel
Apricots	3	1						
Bananas	1	1					trace	
Blackberries								
cultivated	trace	1		trace	1			
wild		8			13			
Black currants	30	4				2		
Boysenberries	20	3		trace	trace			
Cherries	trace	all						
Damsons		all						
Elderberries	all	1						
Figs	all	1						
Gooseberries	1	1			trace	trace		shikimic trace
Grapes	from 1 to	3	1 to 10					some varieties contain a very little citric
Grapefruit	all							
Greengages	all							

Lemons	20	1		
Limes	all			
Loganberries	4	1		
Nectarines	all			
Oranges	7	1		
Peaches ripe	1	3		
Peaches unripe	higher ratio of citric			
Parsnips	1	3		
Pears	2	1		
Pineapple from 7	1			
to 4	2			
Plums	all			
Prunes	all			
Raisins	as for grapes			
Raspberries	5	2		
Red currants	9	1	trace	
Rhubarb	5	16	2	
Rowanberries	all			
Strawberries	36	4	2	1
Sloes	all			
Sultanas	as for grapes			
Tangerines	5	1		
White currants	14	5	trace	trace

organisms inhibited by the addition of sulphur dioxide (SO_2) at the rate of 50 ppm. In larger wineries, receiving vessels and the pipelines thereto are also pre-filled with nitrogen or carbon dioxide so as to exclude air and thus prevent oxidation.

Before and after racking the vessels must be kept tightly closed and only the minimum space between wine and closure is permitted. Air is always excluded during bottle maturation.

For heavy and dessert wines the crop of yeast cells produced in a must is rarely sufficient for complete fermentation. Oxygen is therefore required by the yeast for reproduction and this is supplied by early rackings. A pulp fermentation is usually strained after four days or so and the air so induced assists the formation of further yeast cells. Juice or extract fermentations are usually racked seven days after the visible ferment begins. Either is racked again if the fermentation slows down with the sugar content still high. (*See also* SYRUP METHOD.)

At all times during the fermentation of these wines air is not permitted to be in contact with the wine and the air is excluded by means of an airlock.

After fermentation, heavy wines are stored in bulk and a controlled amount of oxidation is permitted according to the individual wine (*see* OXIDATION). This is achieved by one of two methods:

(1) The wine is stored in casks, from which there will be some loss of wine through evaporation, and there will be some contact with air seeping through the wood. The casks should be topped up every four weeks to prevent the wine standing on ullage.
(2) The wine is stored in non-porous vessels tightly closed with the minimum air space between closure and wine. These wines should be racked at intervals appropriate to the style of wine until they are sufficiently oxidized.

Care has to be exercised with both methods so that the wine does not become over-oxidized.

After a period of bulk maturation, wines are bottled to permit the most important stage of maturing to take place, i.e. oxidation and reduction (redox reactions) of the wines' components in the absence of air. The bottles are therefore filled as full as practical and corked as tightly as possible. Sealing of the corks is also an advantage. Air is excluded. (*See also* MATURATION.)

AIRLOCK Sometimes called a fermentation lock. Although it has been customary for several hundred years to keep fermenting wine covered to exclude dust, only in more recent years has it been realized that by excluding air, contamination is minimized. Some water and glycerine, or a metabisulphite solution, is placed in the lock. The pressure of escaping carbon dioxide builds up so that a lozenge of gas passes through the water, at first rapidly at thirty or forty times a minute and then steadily more slowly, until the completion of fermentation, when all activity ceases.

The glass airlock is extremely fragile and plastic airlocks are now available which perform the same task equally effectively and last very much longer. They become brittle after some years, however, and need replacing at intervals. If airlocks are not available, a plug of clean unmedicated cotton wool or a loose-fitting cover may be used instead. As long as the excess gas can escape, carbon dioxide being heavier than air will remain on the surface of the wine during fermentation and prevent infection.

In addition to keeping out all dust, germs, moulds and wild yeasts, the airlock, by restricting the flow of fresh air containing oxygen, inhibits the growth of further cells already present. The yeast continues to live in its anaerobic condition and the formation of alcohol is encouraged.

ALBUMEN, ALBUMINOUS PROTEIN   Used as blood or white of egg for fining wine. *Refer to* BLOOD, EGG WHITE and FINING for details.

ALCOHOL   Pure alcohol is a colourless liquid that has a burning taste, spirituous odour and only approximately four-fifths the weight of water with which it will mix in any proportion. It burns with a hot non-luminous flame and its vapour is explosive when mixed with air.

The fermentative production of alcohol is the basis of winemaking, and without alcohol a liquor would not be a wine. At first, alcohol was known as the spirit of wine, but this has since been renamed ethyl alcohol. Today, however, we know of many alcohols most of which have no connection with wine, yet all have an affinity to ethyl alcohol. The *Concise Oxford Dictionary* states, alcohol is (chemically) a 'large class of compounds of [the] same type as spirits of wine', and yet the word 'alcohol' derives from the ancient word for the eye-black and face paint associated with Jezebel the Sideon princess. The early Assyrian word *guhlu* meaning 'eye-stain' or 'eye-paint' was adopted in the Arabic as *Kuhl* (*Koh'l*). With *al* meaning 'the' it became *al kuhl* the name given to fine powders, mainly dyes. Such a powder was the native antimony sulphide which was used by Eastern women in the dual role of protective face covering and eyebrow and eyelash black. Thus it was that Jezebel 'painted her face and tied her hair and looked out of the window' at the coming of Jehu the son of Nemshi to Jezreel.

Generally, powders which were purified by sublimation were known as al-kuhl. Then at a much later date, possibly in the ninth or tenth century, a fairly pure spirit was produced in Italy by a somewhat similar distillation of wine. This sublimated spirit of wine became known as the alcohol of wine and so to the alcohols of today.

The alcohols which can be expected to be present in wines, if only in minute quantities are:

Ethyl alcohol This is the alcohol of wine which comprises from 8 to 18% of the wine's volume according to type. Its chemical formula is C_2H_5OH and its very presence gives to wine and other alcoholic drinks their characteristic flavour. Although it has only a very slight odour itself, alcohol is an excellent solvent for odorous materials, has a sweet taste and moderates the acid tastes of fruits. When reference is made to the alcoholic strength of wine, it is the ethyl alcohol content which is intended. Alcohol in its vinous sense at least, is synonymous with ethyl alcohol. It is formed by the reduction of sugar in the presence of the zymase complex of enzymes which is secreted by the living yeast cells. (*See also* ZYMASE, FERMENTATION and YEAST.)

Ethyl alcohol is a colourless liquid much lighter than water and with a specific gravity of about 0·796 at 15 °C (59 °F) and a boiling point of 78·3 °C (173°F). It has a strong affinity for water which dilutes it. It has long been known as a volatile anaesthetic and acts by dulling the nerve centres of the brain. A century ago it was a valuable aid in surgery. In small quantities it releases the inhibitions which restrain the activities of most people, and this accounts for the certain boisterousness and garrulity affected by those who have had a drink or two. Physiologically it dilates the blood vessels and arteries and so lowers the blood pressure for a time. Body heat is the more readily given off and care should therefore be taken not to catch cold after over-indulging.

Ethyl alcohol is a food and moderate quantities can be used by the body to produce energy. It is best, however, to take food at the same time as alcohol, since the speed of the digestion of the alcohol is consequently slowed down to that of the food, and entry to the blood stream is spread over a longer period. This reduces the effect of the alcohol to the consumer without diminution of its pleasure.

Methyl alcohol (CH_3OH) The simplest of all alcohols and very poisonous. It can cause blindness and even death if consumed in sufficient quantity. Methylated spirit is an impure form of this alcohol. Its boiling point is 68 °C.

A small quantity of methyl alcohol is formed during the fermentation of potatoes and was believed to be due to the fermentation of the starches, but this is not so. It is primarily derived from the hydrolysis of pectins but may actually be present in some fruits and other ingredients. The small amount produced in wine has no harmful effect but when wine is distilled the methanol (methyl alcohol) becomes concentrated and therefore dangerous.

Glycerol (glycerine) A thick, syrupy, hygroscopic, colourless liquid, produced by the fermentation of glucose in the presence of sodium sulphite which reacts with the aldehydes formed and so liberates a larger quantity of glycerine. It is one of the higher alcohols and can be observed in strong wines by swirling the wine in the glass and watching the colourless folds of glycerine slide down the sides of the glass to the wine. It adds slightly to the sweet taste and in small quantities helps to mask acidity and make a wine taste smoother.

Fusel oils The name given to a mixture of higher alcohols which include amyl, isoamyl, butyl, isobutyl, hexyl, propyl etc. These higher alcohols are mainly formed from the amino acids which are derived from the proteins in the must, but some of their formation parallels that of ethyl alcohol. The formation of fusel oils can, however, be minimized by providing the yeast with a readily assimilable nitrogen in the form of ammonium phosphate, one of the yeast nutrients.

The minute quantities generally present in wine are harmless and help to produce fragrant esters and vinosity. But fusel oils are highly poisonous in concentration and for this reason distillation by amateurs is prohibited by law. In commercial distilling there are certain processes to remove the fusel oils.

Other alcohols Other alcohols have been isolated as being produced in wine but of their source and effect little is known. Acetylmethylcarbinal has practically no odour and is always present in wines fermented at a high temperature; it is found in increased quantities in wines which have been attacked by vinegar bacteria. Diacetyl is found in only very small amounts but has an odour of butter. Mannitol is only present when the wine has been attacked by spoilage bacteria and is the result of laevulose reduction. There are also sorbitol, from certain fruits particularly apples, and finally mesoinositol and butylene-glycol.

ALCOHOLIC STRENGTH The quantity of alcohol by volume in a given quantity of an alcoholic drink. In beer the range is approximately 3% to 5%. Cider contains about 7%. In wine the range is usually from 8% to 14%. It is possible to ferment stronger wines up to 18% in ideal conditions, but this is not common. Fortified wines are between 17% and 22% alcohol, and spirits are from 30% to 40% alcohol in general, though some can be purchased with a content of up to 80% by volume.

ALDEHYDES A group of chemical compounds which may be regarded as products of the partial oxidation of alcohol and are in fact compounds of dehydrogenated alcohols (*see* OXIDATION). There are various forms, many of which have their own odour ranging from the pleasant to the very unpleasant. Many occur naturally, such as benzaldehyde in the kernels of bitter almonds, apricots and peaches; citral which imparts the characteristic aroma of lemon oil; and acetaldehyde in grapes. Others are produced from other alcohols such as formaldehyde from methyl alcohol and acetaldehyde from ethyl alcohol. Acetaldehyde is of course produced during yeast fermentation of a must and contributes to the bouquet and characteristic flavour of wines and other alcoholic drinks distilled from them.

17

Acetaldehyde reacts with sulphite; and in the early stages of fermentation of a must, if there is a high sulphur dioxide concentration, acetaldehyde, carbon dioxide and glycerol are the main products, and alcohol is merely a by-product. As the acetaldehyde builds up it reacts with a co-enzyme to produce ethyl alcohol.

ALKATHENE *Refer to* PLASTICS.

AMATEUR WINEMAKER The phrase 'amateur winemaker' applies to everyone who makes wine for personal use but not for sale. It was first used in 1835 by W. H. Roberts in his excellent book *The British Winemaker and Domestic Brewer*. There are thought to be 20 million amateur winemakers around, many of them making outstanding wines.

AMBER A term used to describe the colour of an old white wine. (*See* COLOUR.)

AMER, AMERTUME The name of a disease which causes a bitter taste in wine. (*See* MANNITOL.)

AMINES The name given to a group of chemicals which are produced by spoilage organisms. They are identified by their fishy smell.

AMINO ACIDS Esters of fruit volatiles that unite in chains to form protein which is required by yeasts to maintain their viability. When protein is not available, yeast cells de-aminate the amino acids and produce fusel oils in the process. This is followed by loss of yeast activity and stuck ferments can result. Except in the making of sparkling wine and Sherry, the autolysis of yeast cells releases amino acids with detrimental effect on the bouquet and flavour.

AMMONIUM PHOSPHATE/SULPHATE In common with all plants, the wine yeast needs nitrogen to live, and musts should therefore contain ingredients that will release nitrogen for their use. Ammonium phosphate or sulphate are two readily available sources of nitrogen and are therefore used as nutrients. Approximately 5 g per 5 litres are required. The addition of ammonium phosphate is preferable since the phosphate radical is also required as an energy transferer, conducive to vigorous fermentation. In the absence of nitrogen, yeasts de-aminate the amino acids from dead yeast cells thus producing fusel oils.

AMPELOGRAPHY The scientific description of the vine and especially of its fruit—the grape.

AMYLOZYME 100 A trade name for the enzyme amylase which is used in the conversion of starch into fermentable sugars. It is used according to the supplied instructions to clear starch hazes from finished wines and to convert starch to sugars in musts containing starchy materials such as potatoes, rice and other grain.

ANEURINE HYDROCHLORIDE *See* VITAMINS.

ANTHOCYANINS Anthocyanins are the red, blue and purple pigments of flowers, fruits and other parts of plants which are water-soluble and easily extracted in winemaking. The colour and hues that appear in nature, as on the cheek of an apple, are the result of several factors, such as concentration, mixture, the presence of tannin, absorption on colloidal particles and the pH. In the latter lies the interest of winemakers. At the higher pH encountered in plants, anthocyanins pass through violet, then blue and, at very high pH not encountered in plants, some turn yellow. But at low pH all anthocyanins are red, although of different hues. Thus in wines with a low pH, purple and blue tints cannot be held and all wines are red from anthocyanins or white from anthoxanthins or flavones. It therefore follows that a purplish colour or tint in a bright red or rosé wine indicates a high pH although a purplish tint in the rim of a fully robed red wine indicates that it is still young.

ANTHOXANTHINS and FLAVONES These are the important group of pigments in plants that are responsible for yellow colourings which include orange. The anthocyanins are the pigments responsible for red, purple and blue colours.

ANTI-OXIDANT Any chemical which prevents fruit, must or wine from oxidizing. (*See also* ASCORBIC ACID and SULPHITE.)

APERITIF A beverage drunk just prior to a meal to induce appetite. Perhaps the most common in England is a dry Sherry, but gin-based drinks are also popular. On the continent of Europe, Vermouth-flavoured drinks are in vogue. Just how the appetite is stimulated is not understood for certain, but alcohol relaxes all the nerves including those of the stomach and possibly the natural hunger is thus able to assert itself.

In general terms any clean-tasting, moderately well-flavoured wine, not too dry, serves very well as an aperitif. Very sweet wines can cloy the palate, very dry wines sometimes taste harsh on a bare palate.

APPEARANCE OF WINE A wine's appearance is a matter of attraction. If the wine is well bottled, corked and capsuled, with an attractive label squarely fixed, then it has eye appeal! If in addition it is brilliant and of good colour and is displayed before serving in a plain and colourless decanter or carafe, then it has even more eye appeal. White wines vary from the faintly tinted to pale yellow and golden amber, but not brown (except for Sherry or Madeira types and wines that are naturally brown). Red varies from bright red to a robe of deep red. The appearance gives the beholder a feeling that the wine is good, and one sometimes feels that it has more quality than it actually has. A hazy wine of poor colour, even a brown wine, badly presented will have no eye appeal. It gives the impression of being inferior and no matter how high the quality may in fact be, the wine will be at a disadvantage. The best that will be said of it is: 'Not as bad as it looks'. On the other hand, a mediocre wine that is of good colour, brilliant and well presented will always be considered better than a top quality wine of poor colour that is hazy and badly presented.

To the experienced judge, or taster, the appearance of a wine has much to tell of its quality and state.

Acid affects the colour of anthocyanins, the higher the acidity the brighter the red. Whether the red is light or dark, it should be a distinct red if the acid content is of the correct concentration. The lower the acidity the more bluish the tint, and if the acid content is very low the red may assume a purplish tint. Age also has an effect. The older the wine, the more the red assumes a brownish tint, and ultimately it becomes completely brown.

When a white wine assumes a brownish tint it denotes great age, but when it has become quite brown the colour denotes that the wine has over-oxidized through redox reaction and will have an over-age odour. If a young wine takes on a brown tint or becomes brown, the browning is due to enzymic oxidation. Odour and taste are not affected.

A silky sheen or oily appearance in either red or white wines clearly indicates that the wine has suffered bacterial spoilage. (*See also* ROPI-NESS.)

APPLE JACK A spirit distilled from cider. Not very well known in England but more widely made and drunk in Canada.

APPRAISAL OF WINE and APPRECIATION OF WINE *See* JUDGING WINE. Also concerned in appraisal or appreciation of wine are AROMA, BOUQUET, FLAVOUR, SMELL, TASTE/TASTING and TEXTURE. Acidity, alcohol, sugar and tannin are also important factors affecting appreciation.

AROMA In the general sense, aroma is a fragrant or sweet smell with subtle persuasive qualities. Used specifically in reference to wine the aroma is the odour derived from the fresh ingredients, e.g. the smell of fresh grapes in a Riesling wine. It originates from substances in the skin. Although technically each grape or fruit cultivar has its own particular aroma, some have so little that it is not detectable in the wine. This is one of the reasons for blending together a number of different grape varieties, or similar ingredients in fruit wines. When wine is made with ingredients that have little or no natural aroma the finished wine cannot have an aroma.

A young wine will have aroma provided the ingredients were suitable, but will have little bouquet. As the wine ages the aroma slowly decreases and the bouquet increases but in a wine of quality there should be a combination of both aroma and bouquet. In judging a wine both qualities must be assessed.

ASBESTOS PULP Asbestos pulp, in appearance, is rather like unevenly broken wads of light grey Kapok, though it is in fact crushed asbestos which is a mineral that is inert to acids and alkalis. It is used for filtering wine and a handful is usually sufficient to clear several gallons. Before use it should be freed from its natural 'cardboard' taste.

A handful of pulp is covered with two pints of hot water and thoroughly whisked. Then the water is run off through a fine strainer and the pulp squeezed 'dry'. This is repeated once more with hot water and twice with cold water. Water is run through the pulp first and then tasted. If it is tainted, further washing of the pulp is required until water run through it is quite free from any taint or flavour.

Cellulose powders and pads that are non-toxic are now available and preferred for filtering wines.

ASCORBIC ACID More commonly known as vitamin C, it is used in winemaking as an anti-oxidant. It is anti-oxidant only and has no bactericidal properties. Commercially, it is added in relatively large amounts to wines of high acidity in which it is hoped to induce a malo-lactic fermentation. The winemaker relies on the high acidity of a must to provide some protection against spoilage organisms since sulphite cannot be used when a malo-lactic fermentation is required.

Ascorbic acid is also added to some wines just prior to bottling. If wines have to be stored in bottles standing upright, the corks can shrink and thus permit some air to leak into the bottle while the sulphur dioxide decreases. Ascorbic acid is then used at the rate of 50 ppm in conjunction with a low level of sulphur dioxide. If the wine is likely to be unstable, the ascorbic acid is added in conjunction with both sorbate and sulphite. If the wines can be stored in bottles lying on their sides, 50 ppm sulphite will prevent oxidation, as well as providing other benefits and there is no need of ascorbic acid.

It is best to prepare a stock solution of 10% pure ascorbic acid for use at the rate of 5 ml per litre of wine.

Although ascorbic acid is effective as an anti-oxidant it can itself cause darkening or browning by being broken down in the absence of sulphur dioxide and especially if traces of metal are present in the wine.

ASTRINGENCY The term used in wine evaluation to describe the effect of dryness in the mouth caused when tasting certain wines. When it is pronounced, astringency can be unpleasant. It is due to excess tannin.

ATTENUATION The diminution of density is the sense in which the word attenuation is used. It refers to the reduction of the specific gravity due to fermentation. The thickish, sticky must is thinned or attenuated by fermentation.

AUTOLYSIS Autolysis is the destruction of the cells of a body by the action of its own serum. Yeast autolysis was defined by Joslyn (1955) as 'an enzymatic self-destruction of yeast cells and essentially involves hydrolysis of the protoplasmic constituents and their excretion into the surrounding medium'.

When wine is left standing on the dead yeast cells in the sediment at the bottom of a wine, the cells decompose by autolysis. This is encouraged by storage in a high temperature. The results are a low redox potential, possible formation of hydrogen sulphide, and the release of the products of autolysis, including certain amino acids, which are used as growth factors by bacteria. The final result can be not only off-flavours in the wine but also complete spoilage. Early and regular racking is therefore important in helping to prevent bacterial spoilage by restricting yeast autolysis and thereby minimizing the growth factors required by spoilage bacteria.

Wines of too high an acidity, in which there is a substantial proportion of malic acid, can be left on the yeast sediment to induce autolysis resulting in a malo-lactic fermentation and the reduction of the wines' acidity. This is practised commercially with dry wines only, never with sweet wines (*see* MALO-LACTIC FERMENTATION). It is conducted under controlled conditions requiring regular analysis. Amateurs are not advised to attempt it. Furthermore, no matter how high the acidity of a wine, only spoilage will result from excessive yeast autolysis if the wine does not contain malic acid.

It has been said that the autolysis of dead yeast cells provides matter for growth and reproduction of live yeast cells. It is an unnecessary and dangerous practice. In addition it has been suggested that autolysis induces specific wine yeast flavours in a wine. This is doubtful except in bottle-fermented Champagne and Sherry produced under a flor.

It is generally accepted that if Champagne, after bottle fermentation, is allowed to age for some years on the yeast sediment it develops a more pleasing 'Champagne' flavour.

With flor Sherries the old yeast falls from the flor to form a deposit as it is replaced by new cells and again it is thought that flavour produced by autolysis has some importance. In neither instance has the effect been measured and it should be noted that in both instances autolysis occurs under conditions restrictive to bacterial infection.

Apart, therefore, from malo-lactic fermentation under controlled conditions, ageing of bottle-fermented Champagne and production of Sherry under a flor, to permit yeast autolysis is dangerous and off-flavoured or spoilt wines are most likely to result.

BACCHUS *See* DIONYSUS.

BACTERIA IN WINE The bacteria that infect wines are micro-organisms which are present everywhere and on everything. Some could be beneficial to wine but most cause spoilage in many different forms. They are divided into two types; the aerobic and the anaerobic. The aerobic require air to live and multiply, e.g. on the surface of a wine. The anaerobic thrive in the absence of air, e.g. in a must or in wine. Both, however, are inhibited by sulphite, by a pH of 3·4 or lower, by heat or by alcohol when the content reaches 12 to 14% by volume. During fermentation the carbon dioxide layer acts as an inhibitor of infection. Danger times are both before fermentation and afterwards, if the alcohol content is less than 12% by volume. Must should therefore be sulphited at the rate of 50 to 150 ppm and kept covered. Low-alcohol wine should be sulphited at the same rate and protected from air by being kept in containers with the minimum of air space. Even with high-alcohol wines it is advisable to exclude air as far as is practicable.

The most common aerobic bacteria in winemaking are those that cause acetification. The major anaerobic bacteria that spoil wine are the lactic acid bacteria (lactobacillus).

All bacterial infection is more easily prevented than cured.

Cleanliness, the use of sulphite, the correct degree of acidity and the exclusion of air will prevent infection.

Malo-lactic fermentation by lactobaccilli is sometimes encouraged and this is dealt with separately as are several other diseases.

BACTERIAL HAZE Wines that become hazy after having been clear for a time are usually infected with bacteria. If the hazing is noticed before a taint occurs, the immediate use of sulphite at the rate of 150 ppm, inhibits the bacteria and clears the wine. A hazy wine is tested for bacteria by pouring a small quantity into a glass and adding a little sulphite. If the wine clears after standing for 24 hours then bacteria is the cause of the haze.

BACTERICIDE A substance that can kill bacteria. If too low concentrations are used, however, there is always a danger of the bacteria not being inhibited or killed, and they may then become tolerant to the particular bactericide or even develop new metabolic pathways and thrive on it.

The best bactericide for musts, is sulphite reinforced by the acid in the must; for wines, sulphite and/or alcohol and for equipment, sulphite reinforced with acid. It is always safer to exceed the required concentration slightly than to use too little.

BALANCED MUST One in which all the factors, acid, sugar, tannin, body, flavour etc., are in the right proportions to produce a harmonious wine in which no single factor is dominant. It is achieved by first assessing the type of wine for which the available grapes or other ingredients are most suited and balancing the must for that type. (*See also* ACIDS, BODY, CORRECTION OF WINE, FLAVOUR, SUGARS, TANNINS.)

BAUMÉ Differently graduated hydrometers are used in other countries for various purposes. Baumé was the Frenchman who gave his name to a scale on a hydrometer so graduated as to indicate immediately the potential alcohol content of a given must; thus 12 degrees Baumé in a must fermented to complete dryness would produce 12% of alcohol by volume. (*See also* BRIX, HYDROMETER, TWADELL.)

BEAD The bubbles in sparkling wine. The smaller the beads and the longer they continue to rise in the glass, the better the quality of the wine. Bottle fermentation produces the smallest beads and the most continuous. The German transfer system produces the next smallest, the French Chamant (Cuve closed) somewhat larger, and carbonation, the largest and most quickly dispersing, like fizzy lemonade. (*See also* CHAMPAGNE, SPARKLING WINE.)

BEESWINE or BEE WINE A name at one time used for honey wine or mead; but long since discontinued.

A home-made wine that was once very popular and is still occasionally made, is Bee Wine, also known as Beeswine, Californian Bees or Australian or Brazilian Wine. The 'bees' are yeast and bacteria which clump together, forming lumps like tapioca or pieces of white bread and live in partnership. When fermenting they move up and down in the solution. The common 'bee' is *Saccharomyces pyrifirmis* and *Bacterium vermiforme*, but there are other strains. To produce a wine, it is only necessary to make up slightly acid and weak sugar solution, add the yeast culture (the 'bees') and wait for the fermentation to begin and end. Sometimes a little ginger is added for flavouring.

The old method was to take a glass jar, nearly fill it with water, add a teaspoonful of sugar or syrup and the 'bees'. One spoonful of sugar or syrup was added each day for a fortnight, then the liquid was strained and bottled. The largest clump of 'bees' was discarded and the smaller ones used to start another brew.

BEESWING A slight sediment or crust, consisting of shiny, filmy scales of tartar formed in wines after long keeping and which does not settle against the sides or bottom of the bottle. It is quite harmless to the wine and may at one time have been considered a sign of authenticity, particularly for Port. There is a record of an old silver wine label engraved 'Beeswing Port' and Tennyson wrote of someone fetching 'his richest beeswing from the bin reserved'.

BEET SUGAR This is obtained from a variety of beet which originally grew wild on the sea shores of France. Marggraf originally discovered in 1747 that it had a high sugar content compared with other plants, about

4%. At the time of the Napoleonic wars it was exploited for sugar production in France because of the possibility that sugar supplies from the West Indies might be cut off by naval blockade. Not until the early part of the present century were beets used for sugar in the United Kingdom. Careful selection and cultivation have resulted in the beets now yielding up to 18% of sugar.

When refined and sold as 'white sugar' the 'beet sugar' is chemically and visually the same as 'cane sugar', i.e. 99·95% pure sucrose.

Although some winemakers prefer to use only cane sugar, it is not always possible to obtain it, and in any case the belief that there is any difference in finished wines resulting from the sugar is only an illusion. There may have been some difference years ago when the sugars were less pure, but with the purity of today there is absolutely no difference.

BENTONITE   This substance was first used by Lothrop and Paine in 1931 for fining honey. Later, Saywell used it for fining vinegar. It is now widely used for fining wines. Bentonite is a clay consisting mainly of montmorillonite which is a hydrated silicate of magnesium produced from decomposition under water of volcanic glass. It has an unusual ability to combine with proteins and tremendous swelling properties in water. It causes no harm to wine, even when used to some excess. The one disadvantage when using bentonite is its formation of bulky lees. This can be partly overcome by combining the lees from several wines that have been fined. After standing for a few days, the sediment will settle and leave a clear but blended wine. Because of its ability to combine with protein, bentonite is sometimes used after a first fining with egg white or gelatine, to remove any over-fining. For use *see* FINING.

BENZOIC ACID   The only chemical legally permitted to be used commercially to stop fermentation and prevent a wine fermenting to dryness. (*See* SODIUM BENZOATE.)

BIBLIOGRAPHY   The following titles are mostly in print at the time of going to press, but those that are out of print can usually be obtained through a public library. The list consists of books of general interest as well as those specific to the making of wine:

Amateur Wine Making, by S. M. Tritton, Faber & Faber, 1968
American Wines and Wine Making, by P. G. Wagner, Knopf, 1956
Applied Wine Chemistry and Technology, by Anton Massel, Heidelberg Publishers, 1969
Aroma and Flavour in Winemaking, by J. G. Carr, Mills & Boon, 1974
Australian Wine: The Complete Guide, by Dan Murphy, Sun Books, Melbourne, 1970
Biochemistry of Fruits and their Products, by A. G. Hulme, 2 vols., Academic Press, 1970–1.
Check List of Books and Pamphlets on Grapes and Wines and Related Subjects,

1938–48, by M. A. Amerine and L. B. Wheeler, University of California Press, 1951

Cider Making, by A. Pollard and F. Beech, Rupert Hart-Davis, 1957

Classification of Australian Wines, by Dan Murphy, Macmillan, Australia, 1974

Compleat Home Winemaker and Brewer, by Ben Turner, W. Luscombe, 1976

Dictionary of Drinks and Drinking, by O. A. Mendelsohn, Macmillan, 1965

Dictionary of Wines, Spirits and Liqueurs, by A. Simon, Barrie & Jenkins, 1958

Dionysus: Social History of the Grape, by E. Hyams, Thames & Hudson, 1965

Estate Wines of South Africa, by Graham Knox, David Philip, Cape Town, 1976

Growing your own Wine, by Ben Turner, Pelham, 1977

Home Winemaking, by B. A. Chatterton, Robert Hale, 1973

Judging Home Made Wine, by Amateur Winemakers National Guild of Judges (U.K.), 1964

Larousse Dictionary of Wines of the World, by Gerard Debuigne, Hamlyn, 1976

Larousse Gastronomique (in English), ed. by N. Frood and P. Montagne, Hamlyn, 1965.

Making Mead, by B. Acton and P. Duncan, Amateur Winemaker, 1965

Micro-organisms and Fermentation, by A. Jørgensen and A. Hansen, Griffin, 1948

Modern Sensory Methods of Evaluating Wine, by M. A. Amerine, University of California Press, 1975

Plain Man's Guide to Wine, The, by R. Postgate, Michael Joseph, 1976

Progressive Winemaking, by P. Duncan and B. Acton, Amateur Winemaker, 1967

Science and Technique of Wine, by L. Frumkin, P. Stephens, 1974

Science of Wine, by Cedric Austin, University of London Press, 1968

Sherry, by J. Jeffs, Faber & Faber, 1971

Table Wines: The Technology of their Production in California, by M. A. Amerine, University of California Press, 1970

Technology of Wine Making, by M. A. Amerine and W. V. Cruess, Avi (U.S.A.), 1967

Vivat Bacchus, by Rudolf Weinhold, Argus Press, 1978

Wine, by Hugh Johnson, Mitchell Beazley, 1974

Wines and Spirits, by L. W. Marrison, Penguin, 1970

Wines and Vineyards of France, The, by L. Jacquelin and R. Poulain (translated by T. A. Layton), Hamlyn, 1966

Wines for All Seasons, by G. Fowles, published quarterly by G. Fowles of Reading

Wines of the U.S.A.: How to Know and Choose Them, by S. Murray, Wine Press, 1957

Wine Tasting, by J. M. Broadbent, Christie, Manson & Woods, 1974
World Atlas of Wine, by Hugh Johnson, Mitchell Beazley, 1971

BINARY FISSION   A method of reproduction more common to bacteria but which can be used by yeasts. A cell forms a dissepiment through the middle and divides along this into two similar daughter cells.

BINS   Originally, bins were always kept in a cellar for the storage of bottles of wine laid one on top of the other. Nowadays, a bin is a storage rack in which bottles of wine can be laid on their sides in any room. Sometimes made of shaped No. 3 gauge (6 mm) wire, sometimes of oblongs of wood about 50 mm × 25 mm joined together by metal strips into a framework. Bins come in sizes from 12 bottles upwards or can be made to measure to fit any particular storage space, e.g. under the stairs. A bin able to hold up to 100 bottles is of tremendous value in laying down wine long enough to mature. In the cellar of the House of Commons, and no doubt elsewhere, earthenware drainpipes are stacked and the bottles of wine are stored in them. Bottle cartons stored on their sides make effective bins in a damp-free store.

BISULPHITE   *See* SULPHITE.

BITE   A certain hardness that may be due to tannin. Without tannin a wine tastes soft and flabby, without anything to bite on. On the other hand, wine with an excess of tannin has too much bite and can be astringent. (*See also* MORDANT and TANNINS.)

BITTER DISEASE   Sometimes called TOURNE, it is caused by a member of the lactic acid bacteria family and usually occurs only in sweet wines that are low in alcohol. The wine tastes extremely bitter. It can be prevented by the proper use of sulphite. (*See also* MANNITE INFECTION.)

BITTERNESS   A barely perceptible bitterness in a finished wine due to tannin is desirable, though it should not linger on the palate. It helps to enhance the wine's qualities. In some wines, particularly of the aperitif type, a noticeable but palatable bitterness is induced as a characteristic of the wine, by the addition of herbs including wormwood and orange peel. Even so, the wine should be clean in the mouth and the bitterness should not remain on the palate.

Some of the unpleasant kinds of bitterness are due to spoilage of the wine by the activities of micro-organisms. Other causes of bitterness are the use of wrong ingredients in the must, such as the white pith of citrus fruit or the inclusion of stems or stalks of the fruit. The inclusion of fruit stones or crushed pips also causes an unpleasant bitterness. Another and common cause of bitterness is due to the infrequent or inefficient removal of the sediment from the wine (racking) and the omission of sulphite.

As long ago as 1873 Louis Pasteur proved that the development of bitter spoilage in finished wines was the result of micro-organisms. Pasteur sterilized a number of bottles of Burgundy and kept a similar number unsterilized. All the unsterilized wines ultimately became cloudy and bitter whilst the pasteurized ones remained clear and untainted. It is now known that the production of mannite from sugars by lactic acid bacteria fermentation is a cause of bitterness, but it is thought that its production is also associated with tannin.

BLEACH Domestic bleach is an excellent cleaning agent for equipment which removes stains and taints when used in a solution of 12 ml in 5 litres of water. In other than minute traces it is toxic, and it is therefore essential that all equipment that has been cleaned by a bleach solution be thoroughly rinsed with copious quantities of water.

Also, it must be used only on non-porous material such as glass, stainless steel, stoneware etc. It is not advisable to use it for cleaning plastic containers because of the danger that some smell may be retained in the plastic and so taint the wine.

Strong bleach contains sodium hyperchloride which is a powerful germicide, but there are hazards in handling it.

BLENDING The importance of blending, so widely known and practised by the commercial winemaker, is still largely ignored by others. The professional winemaker grows a number of different varieties of grapes which he blends together before pressing them, some grapes being used for their colour, some for their bouquet, some for their flavour, some for their acidity, some for their tannin, some for their sugar content and so on. Subsequently, many winemakers and especially merchants, blend together wines from a variety of vintages, or wines from the same vintage but from other vineyards or both. This is to enable them to reproduce year after year a fairly standard and acceptable wine, which the consumer can readily recognize and remember.

In the field of domestic winemaking, far too many people expect to make a quality wine out of a single ingredient every time, regardless of the condition of ripeness of the fruit, its cultivar, the soil in which it was grown or the climate affecting its growth. Grapes from the same vine, or fruit from the same bush or tree, can vary enormously from year to year and the same variety grown in one part of the country can vary enormously from that grown in another. For this reason alone, new winemakers should be extremely critical of their standards and if they have no opportunity to blend grapes or fruit before making their wine, then they should consider carefully their opportunities of blending wines subsequently.

It is not sufficient to mix together two poor wines and hope for the best. Each wine should be studied critically for its virtues as well as for its failings, and whilst it is quite impossible to give firm guidance on how such wines should be blended, a general rule of thumb which will be found advantageous is to blend opposites. By this it is meant that a wine with a very pronounced flavour, should be blended with one lacking in flavour; a wine that tastes too acid should be blended with one clearly short of acid; a too thin wine should be blended with a too fat wine; and in such proportions as will result in a balanced wine.

When blending, it is even permissible, although not necessary, to include one wine which is either still fermenting or which has not yet cleared to brightness. A further fermentation will fully integrate the different wines into one, new, homogenous wine. In these circumstances there is little point in trying to blend different wines in a glass beforehand, because the result obtained will be considerably varied by the subsequent fermentation and necessary maturation. Stable wines are unlikely to re-ferment and so trial blendings are advisable and recommended. Clearly, after wines have been blended or re-fermented, it is necessary to mature the new wine in just the same way as you would treat any other new wine, by racking and a period in a cask or jar and then in bottle. Winemaking is both a science and an art. Blending is all art and you need to use your imagination in deciding which wines to blend together.

It cannot be too strongly emphasized that, especially with poor quality wines, blending and/or re-fermentation and a further period of maturation, nearly always result in a wine greatly superior to the sum of all of its original parts. Although a wine may be of poor quality, it is imperative that it be at least sound and free from disease, if it is to be blended. Blending a wine that suffers from some disease, will only pass on that disease to the other wines and the resultant blend will become contaminated.

BLOOD Ox blood is used by some winemakers for fining. It is a source of albuminous protein that reacts with tannin resulting in an insoluble deposit. It not only clears a wine but also reduces acidity and astringency.

BLOOM The waxy dust coating on grape and other fruit skins is called the bloom. It is more noticeable on black than white grapes and fruit, although it can be on either. It consists of the indigenous wine yeast, plus wild yeasts, bacteria, moulds and dust. Certain of the wild yeasts are capable of producing some alcohol and varying side effects, whilst others simply cause spoilage. Unless sulphite is used in the must these organisms will cause infection.

BLUE FININGS The fining of wines contaminated with metals is done by adding potassium ferrocyanide. The process is highly dangerous since hydrocyanic acid may be produced. This is the very poisonous prussic acid. It is forbidden to use this process except in Germany and then only under the control of a specialized chemist. Inexperienced winemakers are expressly warned, for their own sake, not to attempt to use potassium ferrocyanide.

BODY   A term used to describe the 'thickness' of a wine. Wines are said to be thin (have little body) or fat (full-bodied). Body is the wine's content of fruit extract which varies with the water content of the fruit, due to soil, sunshine, temperature, variety and ripeness at the time of picking. In general terms, the cooler the climate, the thinner the body and the hotter the climate, the fatter the body. Generally, the riper the fruit, the fuller the body, but other factors such as glycerol, have an effect. Body can be increased or decreased by the quantity of pulp fermented, by partial drying of the grapes before processing—and by the growth of *Botrytis cinerea* on grapes.

BOILING and BOILING WATER   Except in the making of a 'wine' from vegetables it is never desirable and should rarely be necessary to boil ingredients for a must. Whilst boiling admittedly assists in the fuller extraction of colour and other solutes it destroys the vitamins, reduces and varies the flavour and introduces so much starch or pectin that the wine may prove difficult to clear. In the making of fruit wines, hot water is often poured over the ingredients and this clearly has the advantages of extracting colour, flavour, juices, sugar etc., usually without extracting too much pectin. When the must is cool, however, it is still advisable to add pectin-destroying enzymes to secure a good extraction and a clear wine in due course. For certain ingredients with delicate or over-strong flavours and for soft fruits generally, cold water should be used. It reduces the loss of essences and flavours, or reduces pungent flavours and does not cause too great a breakdown of the pulp. Cold water extraction is considered by some winemakers to be the best method for all fruit wines. (*See also* HEAT TREATMENT.)

BOTRYTIS CINEREA   A fungus disease of fruit that as the 'noble rot' is welcome but as the 'grey rot' is disastrous on grapes.

As 'grey rot' *Botrytis cinerea* attacks immature green grapes after a lengthy period of humidity. The fungus rapidly multiplies, covering the grapes with a grey powder. The grapes then darken and fall. Wine from affected grapes is of poor quality, can taste mouldy and ages rapidly. Prevention is by spraying with fungicide. To encourage 'noble rot', however, grapes should not be sprayed with fungicide.

As the 'noble rot', the fungi attacks ripe grapes when the temperature and humidity are right. First, small brown spots appear on the grape skin which gradually becomes covered with a furry, grey bloom. Finally the grape becomes a dark, purplish-brown and shrivels. During the growth of the fungi, the mycelia penetrate the skin and in feeding, particularly if the weather is dry, take water from the grapes which then shrivel. The result is an overall decrease in the acids, the formation of citric and glutinic acid, gums and a concentration of the sugars.

Fermentation of such grapes is very slow, sometimes taking several months, because the high sugar content partly inhibits the yeast. A considerable quantity of glycerine is formed giving an exceptional smoothness to the wine, which, when bottled, at about 3 years, is an exquisite and rare, naturally sweet white wine. The classic European examples are fine Sauternes, Trockenbeerenauslese and Tokay, but the condition is found in all wine growing areas. The effect of *Botrytis cinerea* on fruits other than grapes used for winemaking does not appear to have been studied. (*See also* FUNGI, MILDEW and MOULDS.)

BOTTLES   The word 'bottle' has a wide range of meanings, but here we are only concerned in its connection with wine. The early wine bottles were mainly of goats' leather, though other materials were probably used. In the New Testament—Mark 2: 22—it says 'else the new wine doth burst the bottles, the wine is spilled, and the bottles will be marred', which rather suggests that the bottles were more valuable than the wine!

The making of glass vessels is an ancient craft dating from before the fifteenth century B.C., yet they do not appear to have been made in Britain until the seventeenth century A.D., a span of 32 centuries.

Until the seventeenth century A.D. wine was served from the storage vessel, usually a cask, direct into the drinking vessel or by means of jugs and similar containers. Then crude potash, or soda glass vessels began to be used and were called 'bottle-decanters', 'decanting-bottles' or 'serving bottles'. From these developed the glass storage bottle of today and also the decanter. The first 'serving bottles' were shaft and globe in shape, rather like a Chianti bottle without the straw jacket, but as with later bottles they had a kick in the bottom (*see* PUNT). As binning was unknown in the seventeenth century, the bottles must have been laid in sand or sawdust.

Early in the eighteenth century, bottles with partially straight sides, sloping outwards from the shoulder and curving in at the base, were produced. By 1730 serving bottles with straight, or near straight, sides were made with very short necks. Later the length of the neck was extended and the straight-sided bottles were used more and more for storage. The kick, or punt, in the bottom became traditional and even considered essential by some. It is retained in many wine bottles of the present day.

In recent years the emphasis, in general, has been on eye appeal, and modern packaging has had its influence on wine bottles as much as on anything else, producing unusual shapes. Nonetheless, certain traditional coloured and shaped bottles are predominantly used.

BURGUNDY (red wine)   Green/black in colour, cylindrical with sloping shoulders and holds 70–75 centilitres. It has a punted bottom.

BURGUNDY (white wine) Greenish or white in colour, otherwise identical to the red wine bottle.

CHAMPAGNE Lightish black in colour, cylindrical with sloping shoulders and punt as Burgundy bottle but made with very much thicker walls to withstand an internal gas pressure, which may rise to 6–7 kg per cm^2 (90 or 100 lb per sq in) when new and unblemished. Use weakens them, however, and second-hand bottles should not again be subjected to the full pressure. It usually holds 75–80 centilitres.

CLARET Lightish black in colour, cylindrical with square shoulders, punted bottom. Holds 70–75 centilitres. This type of bottle was first used in 1798 by Chateau Lafite.

BORDEAUX (white wine) Colourless glass, otherwise as Claret bottle.

PORT and SHERRY Dark brown/green/black in colour, square shoulders, flat bottom, and usually more squat than the Claret bottle.

RHINE WINE (Hock) The tall flute which holds 72 centilitres, is reddish brown in colour, without shoulders as it tapers from the neck to the base, which is flat without a punt.

MOSEL (Moselle) Green in colour, otherwise the same as Rhine wine bottles though sometimes taller.

ALSACE Varies in shades of green and blue, otherwise the same as Rhine wine bottles.

STEINWEIN The Steinwein flagon or Bocksbeutel was also adopted by the Australians for their Emu wines and by Portugal for the well-known Mateus Rosé. Dark in colour, it is of flattened shaft-and-globe shape but with a short shaft and with sloping shoulders. It has a flat bottom.

CHIANTI known as a fichi. Light green in colour, it has the original shaft-and-globe shape and the bottom is left rounded, which necessitates the straw jacket and base, sometimes fancifully patterned and coloured.

Of all the types of wine bottle in use today, the most common and regarded as the standard wine bottle is the bottle used for Bordeaux wine. It nominally holds 75 cl (26 2/3 fl. oz or 1/6 gallon). Litre bottles are now beginning to be used by British bottlers for cheaper wines, and half-litres are also being introduced. These latter are being found to be more satisfactory for two people than the standard half-bottle. Sometimes a full bottle is more than can be comfortably consumed at one sitting, yet a half-bottle is not enough for two.

Other bottle sizes are magnum—2 bottles, flagon—3 bottles, double-magnum or Jeroboam—4 bottles, Rehoboam—6 bottles, Methuselah—8 bottles, Salmanazar—12 bottles, Balthazar—16 bottles,

Nebuchadnezzar—20 bottles. With the exception of the magnum and flagon the other sizes are only likely to be found in use for show purposes.

Bottles should never be stored in a dirty condition, but should be thoroughly washed, drained and dried before being put away. New wine should not be put into bottles which have contained wine and have not been thoroughly cleaned first. A freshly emptied spirit bottle could be immediately filled with wine without harm, but even an empty spirit bottle that has stood empty should be cleaned before re-use. All bottles before being filled with wine should be rinsed inside with a strong sulphite solution.

It is not essential for a bottle to have a punt at the bottom to be called a wine bottle.

BOTTLE AGEING   Most wines improve during a period in bottle, before serving them, but there are exceptions to this. Some light, ordinary wines, low in alcohol and tannin content, can be drunk immediately they have become clear and bright. Whilst such a wine will keep for a year or two in bottle it will not improve and will then rapidly deteriorate. Certain good quality, light and delicate wines are also bottled immediately fermentation has finished and as soon as the wines have been cleared. Bulk maturation is omitted and the wines develop their fine bouquet and flavour in the bottle. The best known French examples are *Beaujolais Nouveau* and *Muscadet sur lie*. In Australia and elsewhere it is also a fairly common practice to bottle fine Rieslings within six weeks of crushing the grapes. These wines have all the appeal of youth, being exceptionally clean, fresh and well balanced. But, like the ordinary wines already mentioned, these wines do not keep for long.

Thin and medium wines made in the home, from fruits and other ingredients, often have a much higher alcohol content than commercial wines and may be somewhat acid, depending upon the fruit from which they were made. Some such wines need at least one year in bottle for the further interaction of the acids and alcohol to produce ethers and esters and so develop bouquet and flavour. The wines also mellow and improve in character. Others may require several years in bottle to reach their peak. Full-bodied and heavy dessert wines require even longer and may remain in peak condition for from ten to fifteen years.

Cylindrical corks should always be used and the bottles laid down on their sides to keep the corks moist and therefore swollen and tight fitting. During bottle ageing the chemical reaction takes place without air, which must be excluded from the bottle. If circumstances prevent the storing of wines on their sides and they have to be stored upright, the top of the corks should be sealed with a paraffin wax or similar sealant.

Nearly always, whether the wine be white or red and no matter how bright it was when bottled, some new sediment will be thrown, indicating that activity has occurred in the bottle. Generally speaking, the higher the alcohol, acid and tannin content of the wine, the longer it should be aged in bottle. During bottle ageing the sugar content of a wine will decrease due to chemical action and not fermentation. This has been described in the past as 'the wine feeding on the sugar'. It is also sometimes described as 'the wine drying out'.

Sherry-type wines should not be bottled until they are ready for drinking, since all their maturation goes on in the presence of air. For this reason they are often bottled with a screw cap or flanged cork and are stored upright. Vermouths are similarly bottled.

BOTTLE BRUSH   This consists of a 45 cm wire handle, in one end of which some bristles are intertwined with the wire, so as to stick out in a cylindrical form some 10 cm long and 5 cm in diameter. Other bristles are worked into the end pointing downwards so that the punt can be adequately cleaned. A bottle brush should be part of the standard equipment of every winemaker and all bottles cleaned with it immediately after use. Mechanical and bench models are also available.

BOTTLE CRADLE   *See* CRADLE.

BOTTLE FERMENTATION   This is the fermentation induced in a bottle of still wine to produce a sparkling wine. Details are given under CHAMPAGNE.

BOTTLE RIPE   When wine has been matured in a jar or cask for a while, it is necessary to store it for a period of time in bottles so that it can acquire a state known as 'bottle ripeness'. The length of time depends on its composition. The wine steadily improves by redox reactions until it reaches its peak. At this point it is said to be 'bottle ripe'. The condition is held for a time, and thereafter declines, or goes downhill. Hence the term 'over the hill' for a wine that has passed its best.

Storage in bottle to acquire final maturity is, after correct balance of the must, the most important factor in producing quality wine, but it does require judgement of the period necessary for storage from an appraisal of the wine, particularly as to acid and tannin content which tend to prolong the storage time.

BOTTLE SICKNESS, or BOTTLE FEVER   Newly bottled wine that has not been sulphited occasionally develops a flat taste that takes from 1 to 3 weeks to disappear. Known as bottle sickness, it is the result of the wine absorbing oxygen during bottling with the consequent formation of acetaldehyde and loss of bouquet.

BOTTLING   When wine has been matured sufficiently in cask or jar it should be bottled. For red wines, a dark glass bottle should be used so that the light does not reduce the colour of the wine. For golden and white wines, clear glass bottles may be used. The bottle should be thoroughly cleaned, if need be with the aid of a bottle brush, and finally rinsed with a sterilizing solution of sulphite. The bottle should then be drained and shaken dry of loose drops of solution and filled to within 2 cm (¾ in) of where the bottom of the cork will reach. A cylindrical cork softened in the same solution of sulphite should then be inserted until flush with the top of the bottle neck. A capsule or foil should be fitted over the top and neck of the bottle, which should finally be labelled with the name and year of the wine.

The best commercial bottling is done by equipment that first fills the bottle with carbon dioxide or nitrogen to replace the air. Automatic bottling machinery of varying sizes from 6 bottles upwards may now be bought. When such equipment is not available the absorption of oxygen can be minimized by running the wine gently down the side of the bottle to avoid any splashing. If the wine is being siphoned, the delivery end of the tube should nearly touch the bottom of the bottle.

BOTTOMS Winemakers' slang for the wine mixed with sediment which is left over after racking. It is common among the 'careful' to mix several lots of 'bottoms' together and when the wine separates from the dregs to rack and bottle it. Surprisingly, it frequently produces a quite passable drink, which is referred to as 'Bitsa'!

BOUQUET Originally a French word meaning a bunch of flowers or nosegay and adapted as such into the English language early in the eighteenth century. It is also used with a second meaning, of perfume exhaled by wine. This is the perfume or odour developed by a wine through esterification, oxidation, and redox reactions during normal ageing. The bouquet and aroma are damaged if the fermentation is conducted at 27 °C (81 °F) or higher and the finest bouquet and flavour are attained by slow oxidation and ageing. It can only be produced and given off if there has been sufficient acid, tannin, residual sugar and alcohol in the wine to produce ethers and esters, particularly during bottle ageing.

Whilst there are differing opinions whether selected wine yeasts have more than a slight effect on bouquet, some wild yeasts affect it by producing various ethers and esters. These can be beneficial to the wine bouquet in the right proportions, but will spoil it unless controlled. Control is difficult, however, and wild yeast should therefore be inhibited in the must. Exceptions to the slight effect of selected wine yeasts on bouquet are the Sherry yeast under flor conditions and the bottle bouquet of Champagne, produced during the bottle fermentation and storage for a period on the yeast sediment before disgorgement.

An experienced taster can tell much about the age of a wine by its bouquet, and bouquet is probably the most important single factor in assessing the flavour or quality of a wine.

BRANDY This was earlier known as 'brandwine' or 'brandewine' from the Dutch *brandewijn* which means burnt wine, the 'burnt' referring to the heating of the wine on a fire to distil it. Brandy is now a spirit distilled from grape wine and usually a simple wine of about 8% alcohol is used for the purpose. There are two methods which produce different types of brandy. For the one a pot-still is used. From the initial wine, liquid containing about 20% of alcohol is distilled. This is distilled again and then a third time with the quality depending on the skill of the distiller during the last two distillations. The resultant spirit which contains about 60% alcohol is then matured in oak casks for five to fifty years during which time it loses an average of 2% of its alcohol each year, due to evaporation through the pores of the staves.

The second method is by the use of a continuous still which produces the higher alcoholic liquid direct in one operation. The spirit is matured in wood but not for so long and the quality is generally not so good as that produced by a pot-still. Eventually the brandy is blended and diluted with water to about 40% alcohol, bottled and then offered for sale.

Fruit brandies are also widely made, and some have achieved a well-deserved place in the variety of drinks available. Not all are made in the same way as grape brandy, although many are. Some, however, consist of an undistinguished brandy to which fresh picked and selected fruits are added so that the fruit essences are mingled with the brandy to give it a superior bouquet and flavour.

BREATHING When a cork is drawn from a bottle of wine and the bottle allowed to stand open, the wine breathes. Whilst breathing it reacts with oxygen and the bouquet develops. If there is any sulphur dioxide in the wine its smell will disappear. How long a wine should be left to breathe before serving it depends on the individual wine, but up to one hour is normal for most wines, with even longer for young wines. Gently pouring a wine into a decanter also helps this process.

BRILLIANCE The term used to describe the clarity of a wine. A brilliant wine is one that has no impediment at all in its clarity and is absolutely limpid. A very attractive visual quality, sometimes referred to as star-bright or crystal clear.

BRIX The Brix hydrometer is so graduated as to record the percentage of sugar by volume in must or wine. Thus, 18% Brix indicates that there is 18% sugar by volume in a must. This would record as a specific gravity of 1·075, equivalent to a potential alcohol content of 10%. (*See also* BAUMÉ, HYDROMETER and TWADELL.)

BROACH To broach a cask is to tap it and remove some of the wine. It is beneficial to store red wine for six months in a small cask and up to two years in larger casks before bottling. When the time comes for bottling, the cask is broached. The cork in the tap hole is wiped clean with a sulphite solution, and the neck of the tap which has been thoroughly washed in the same solution is placed against the cork and held in position with one hand. A mallet is taken in the other hand and brought smartly down on to the face of the tap, so that the cork is driven into the wine, and its place taken by the neck of the tap. A second hit with the mallet will ensure a tight fit. The spile is loosened or withdrawn from the bung, and the handle of the tap is turned so that the wine will flow. The cask is then efficiently broached.

BROWNING   There are two causes of darkening or browning of fruit or wine. The most common is caused by oxidation through the enzyme polyesterase. The enzymes derived from the use of over-ripe or rotten fruit act upon the tannins with free oxygen when air is in contact with the wine. This browning can be prevented by the addition of sulphite or with ascorbic acid, if the must contains a high degree of acidity, but ascorbic acid can itself darken a wine if too much is used. Browning can also be caused by contaminating the wine with metal, especially iron.

BUCHNER FILTER   A straight-sided funnel fitted with a perforated porcelain plate. The funnel fits, by means of a rubber bung, into a conical flask with a side outlet for a tube to a vacuum pump, to speed filtration.

BUFFER   A term used for certain salts which suppress the degree of acidity in relation to the actual acid content of a liquid. Thus, a liquid which is buffered will require a greater quantity of acid for a given pH than one that is unbuffered. The buffers which can be present in solution have great variation which is the reason why, from solution to solution, the parts per thousand figure of acid varies for the same pH. The degree of acidity remains constant. Hence the need for titration to check the actual quantity of acid present in a must.

BUNG   A bung is the stopper fitted into the hole in the centre of a stave in a barrel. Mostly made from wood with a 1 cm hole bored in the centre, it is, however, sometimes made from cork. It is through the bunghole that a cask is filled. Bungs usually measure about 5 cm in diameter. The hole in the bung is for a spile.

   A bung is also a closure for wide-necked vessels such as jars. For this purpose the bungs are normally made from cork, although plastics are now occasionally used and both are without a hole in them. Rubber bungs are used for vessels with smaller diameter necks.

BURETTE   A calibrated glass or plastic tube fitted with a stopcock and used in the titration of musts.

BURGUNDY (red)   Dry, full-bodied, table wine of superb colour, with an alcohol content that is usually around 12%. The tannin content is not harsh and so the wine matures more quickly than Claret. It is usually at its best after five years. Except for the very finest wines, Burgundies are blended wines from different vineyards. Most years the lack of sunshine necessitates chaptalization. The popular grape varieties are the Pinot Noir for the finest wines and the Gammay for the Beaujolais and other wines.

BURGUNDY (white) A dry, full-bodied, firm—even flinty—table wine that is a pale to medium straw colour, in which there is often a touch of green. It is usually ready for drinking after two or three years in cask and bottle. The finest wines are of superb character and individuality and easily earn the title of the best dry white wines in the world. They are made from the Chardonnay grape.

CAKE When fruit or grapes are squeezed dry in a press, either before or after they have been fermented, the resultant wad of residue is called the 'cake'.

CALCIUM CARBONATE Commonly known as chalk and used in winemaking to reduce or remove acidity. BP quality 'Precipitated chalk' is used at the rate of 8 g per 5 litres and will reduce acidity by approximately 1·5 ppt expressed as sulphuric. Carbon dioxide is released during the formation of calcium salts which are insoluble, and foaming therefore occurs.

CALCIUM SULPHATE Better known as plaster of Paris or gypsum, calcium sulphate is sometimes used to increase the acidity of a wine, a practice that was old in the time of Pliny. The calcium sulphate combines with potassium bitartrate, which is always present in grape wines. Calcium tartrate precipitates and settles as a sludge at the bottom of the vessel, while free tartaric acid and potassium sulphate form in the wine. It is most widely used in southern Spain in the making of Sherry, and it is permitted by law in France. The practice is known as 'plastering'. It lowers the pH giving increased protection against infection and in some way aids the formation of the flor.

CAMPDEN TABLET The proprietary name for a small tablet of potassium or sodium metabisulphite which when dissolved in 5 litres of must or wine releases around 50 parts per million of sulphur dioxide. Campden tablets are commonly added to musts and wines to act as an inhibitor of micro-organisms and, in solution with acid, used to rinse bottles, jars and all equipment before and after use. One to three Campden tablets are added per 5 litres of must, according to the acidity, to inhibit the growth of moulds, bacteria and spoilage yeasts, until an active wine yeast can start the fermentation. Many winemakers add one tablet per 5 litres of wine when racking to retard further yeast or bacterial growth and prevent oxidation. Malo-lactic fermentation cannot take place in wines so treated. (*See also* SULPHITE.)

CANDIDA MYCODERMA This yeast has erroneously been called *mycoderma vini*, and was first identified by Persoon in 1822. It is an aerobic, film-forming yeast that grows on low-alcohol wines, forming a chalky-white pellicle on the surface. It can also be found on pickling brines. The cells vary in shape and length but are generally cylindrical and up to 13 microns (μm) in length. They can utilize ethyl alcohol as a source of carbon and are strongly oxidative. They oxidize the alcohol to carbon dioxide and water.

This spoilage organism can be readily controlled by the use of sulphite in the must and the sulphiting or exclusion of air from stable, low-alcohol wines. When a stable wine is attacked, further spoilage can be prevented by pouring a drop or two of oil on to the wine to form a protective film on the surface. Olive oil is excellent for this purpose. The oil excludes from the wine the atmospheric oxygen that the *Candida* require for life and reproduction.

CANE SUGAR This is the sugar extracted from the sugar canes grown in the West Indies, Australia and elsewhere. For all winemaking purposes there is no difference between cane sugar and beet sugar. Chemically the two sugars are identical and when purchased are 99·95% pure. Therefore, there are no advantages to be gained from using cane sugar as opposed to beet sugar. Ordinary white granulated sugar is the cheapest and best form of sugar to use in winemaking.

CAP When pulp is present in a must which is fermenting, the gas forms in bubbles around the solid matter and lifts it to the top of the fermentation. There it forms into a solid layer which floats on the top of the liquid with a large proportion above the surface. This layer of pulp is known as the 'cap'. It is essential that this 'cap' be frequently roused or broken up, and the pulp submerged in order to obtain the maximum extraction and to prevent the growth of moulds or other contamination. Rousing the 'cap' twice to three times a day is regarded as sufficient and it should be strained out as soon as possible. A SINKER is sometimes used to hold the pulp below the surface.

CAPSULES Thimbles of material which are fitted over the corks on to the necks of bottles. Firstly, they seal the cork and therefore the wine from air and bacteria. Secondly, capsules give a neat finish and improve the appearance of bottles of wine. They can be obtained quite cheaply and in several forms. One variety consists of a soft plastic material, packed in an airtight container holding just enough moisture to keep the capsules soft. Another variety is made from coloured metal foil, often with a design stamped upon it. These can be bought in any number and colour and merely have to be slipped over the top of the bottle and gently pressed to the sides. The plastic capsules are also available in a variety of colours, but a little more care has to be exercised when fitting them on to the neck of the bottle. They fit quite snugly, but air which gets pushed up into the cap as it is slipped on to the bottle has to be gently expelled. As the capsule dries it clings closely to the glass. Both these and other forms give an improved appearance to the finished bottle, and no bottle of wine should go on exhibition or be offered as a gift unless it is properly finished.

CARAMELIZED The term used to describe the flavour of Madeira wine which acquires a 'toffee' taste due to the heating process that is employed in its production. It is also the characteristic of the Marsala flavour.

CARAMELS These were once the semi-purified forms of sucrose—white granulated sugar. They are now specially produced and are in fact white sugar plus other matter which alters the physical characteristic and adds distinctive flavours. The different types of caramels are sold as Demerara, Barbados, Foot, Moist, Coffee sugar, Pieces etc. All are fermentable by wine yeasts and could be used in winemaking, but they impart to the wine a distinctive caramel flavour and affect the colour. Unless the caramel flavour is especially required, as in Madeira-type wines, only white granulated sugar should be used. Sucrose heated above its melting point loses its structure and turns brown. This substance is also known as caramel and has a 'toffee' colour and flavour.

CARBOHYDRATES These compounds of carbon, hydrogen and oxygen occur widely (*inter alia*) in fruits, grains and roots, as sugars, starch and cellulose. They are readily broken down by the various enzymes into simple sugars which are fermented into alcohol and when consumed, in wine for example, they supply energy to the body. If the energy is not used it is stored in the form of fat. Some low-carbohydrate, weight-reducing diets prohibit the consumption of alcohol since alcohol itself is a carbohydrate, but dry wines which contain no residual sugar are not forbidden, if only a small quantity is consumed from time to time. Such wines are also permitted to diabetics.

CARBONATED WINE One which is given a sparkle by having carbon dioxide injected into it in the bottle to create an effervescence when poured.

CARBONATION A cheap and effective method of making a sparkling drink by adding a dose of carbon dioxide gas to it while it is cool. Fizzy lemonade and similar drinks are commonly carbonated. Some inexpensive sparkling wines are also carbonated under low pressure. Champagne is expensive because each bottleful is virtually handmade, as far as the sparkling effect is concerned, by the méthode champenoise. A carbonated wine soon loses its sparkle and quickly goes flat as the carbon dioxide is only in solution. (*See also* CHAMPAGNE.)

CARBON DIOXIDE   Carbon dioxide (CO_2) is the gas given off during the process of fermentation. The molecules of glucose and fructose ($C_6H_{12}O_6$) are split by enzymes called the apo-zymase complex, secreted by the yeast, into two molecules of carbon dioxide ($2CO_2$) which come off as gas and two molecules of ethyl alcohol ($2C_2H_5OH$) which remain in solution. Of any given quantity of sugar, approximately 47% is converted into carbon dioxide during fermentation and 48% into alcohol.

The carbon dioxide gas is formed throughout the body of the must and does not come solely from the bottom of the fermentation vessel. The small bubbles rise to the surface and burst with a hissing noise; this is the visible and audible form of fermentation. Silent and invisible fermentation continues subsequently in the highly complex chemical processes which continue throughout a wine's life. Sometimes, when a bottle has been stored for some period, the pressure of carbon dioxide will blow a cork or worse still burst a bottle. Sometimes, it is noted that when a cork is drawn, a ring of bubbles appears around the neck of the bottle of wine, indicating that further fermentation has occurred and that carbon dioxide is now being released. This may be the result of a malo-lactic fermentation in which carbon dioxide is the by-product of the conversion of malic acid into lactic acid.

Carbon dioxide is also, of course, the sparkling agent in Champagne wines. The sparkling bubbles which generate such good wine are, chemically speaking, only an excess of carbon dioxide which has been imprisoned in the wine and now finds escape to the air. Carbon dioxide can be pumped into a still wine but the wine soon goes flat after pouring, whilst when the CO_2 is produced by a bottle fermentation, it continues to come off all the while the wine is in the glass.

Being inert, carbon dioxide is one of the gases used commercially from cylinders for pressurizing wine through filters and for flushing containers, connecting pipes etc. This is not practicable when only small volumes of wine are produced, although carbon dioxide from a fermentation is sometimes used. Being heavier than air, the gas will fill a container like water and remain in it if left undisturbed. Receptacles used for filtration are first filled by being coupled to a vessel containing a strong fermentation. This helps to prevent over-oxidation of the wine during the process. If sulphite is also added to the wine, it considerably assists the carbon dioxide.

CARBONIC ACID   A weak acid formed by carbon dioxide being soluble in water and partially dissociating. The acid helps in the buffering of wine and in the prevention of oxidation during racking. It disappears with the loss of carbon dioxide at the end of fermentation. Hence the reason for heating before titrating a sample that contains carbon dioxide, i.e. during fermentation.

CARBONIC MACERATION   The method of obtaining a more

aromatic wine than by normal vinification. It is widely used in the making of Beaujolais especially Beaujolais Nouveau, also in the Rioja region of Spain and in California. The process involves placing the uncrushed grapes in a suitable container which is then sealed. Under the weight of the uppermost grapes, a quantity of those at the bottom are crushed and the juice is fermented by the previous addition of a yeast culture. Carbon dioxide is given off and this stimulates an intracellular fermentation that converts part of the sugar to alcohol in the unbroken grapes. This causes extracts of colour and flavour from the skins to spread throughout the grape pulp, resulting in aromatics which would not be present from normal vinification. After macerating in this way for up to seven days or so, the grapes are crushed and fermentation continued on the pulp for just a day or two or pressed and fermented in the absence of skins and pips. The result is fragrant wine with a low content of volatile acid and tannin. Maturation is quicker and a smooth, well-flavoured wine is ready for drinking sooner than by traditional methods.

CARBOXYLASE An enzyme secreted by wine yeasts that removes the carbon from pyruvic acid reducing it to acetaldehyde. This is one of the few non-reversible reactions in the production of alcohol.

CASEIN This is a protein containing amino acid and is the principal constituent of milk and cheese. In its pure form, it is virtually insoluble in water or wine and can only be dissolved in an alkali. The salt, potassium or sodium caseinate, is soluble in water. Both forms are used for fining but the salt is less readily obtainable. They replace the very old practice of fining with milk, more particularly for the larger volumes of wine.

A sample test should be made before treating a bulk quantity of wine. Into each of five bottles pour 100 ml wine, then add 0·1, 0·2, 0·3, 0·4 and 0·5 ml of casein solution per bottle respectively. The bulk wine should be treated with the same ratio of casein solution as the sample showing brilliancy with the lowest concentration of the solution.

Casein lightens the colour of the wines, particularly that of red wines and in wines known to be low in tannin it is advisable to add half as much tannin as casein.

The addition of ordinary milk to wine as a fining agent has long been practised. The recommended quantity to use is 2 ml per litre of wine, well stirred in. It is not quite so effective, however, as the casein solution detailed above. Skimmed dried milk is equally effective and has the advantage of not containing butter fat.

CASK A cask is a wooden container in which wine is stored to mature. It is sometimes used as a fermentation vessel but it is difficult to remove the deposits and a vat is more suitable for the purpose.

Originally wine was kept and carried about in goat skins which are still used today in some of the Atlantic islands and in part of northern Africa.

In the lands under the civilization of Greece and Rome, pottery wine jars were used, the most common of which was the amphora. When full of wine the mouth of the amphora was sealed with wax, probably beeswax. Even in these modern times, a large version of the amphora, which the Spaniards call a tinja, is used for Manzanilla Sherry.

Wine casks are sometimes made from chestnut, cherry or redwood but nearly all, and certainly the best, are made from oak. The particular variety of wood affects the wine stored in it, and there are also variations within the same variety. Some winemakers refer to the 'personality' of a cask and know that certain of their casks can produce better wine than others. Casks have always been made in various sizes from as small as a few gallons (10 litres) to as large as several hundred gallons (1,000 litres) and each size has its own name, such as pin—4½, firkin—9, barrel—36, hogshead—usually 52½, pipe—115, butt—108, and tun—210 gallons. The metric equivalents are: 20, 41, 164, 238·5, 491, 523 and 955 litres, but they are rarely quite so precise in size. The Bordeaux tonneau (tun), for example, contains 900 litres.

Wine in a cask slowly oxidizes by being in contact with air. The smaller the cask the quicker the wine becomes over-oxidized and spoiled. This is because of the larger surface area of wine, in ratio to its volume, that is in contact with air through the staves of the cask. The smallest size that can safely be used is six gallons. Even in this size, the wines should be regularly checked for oxidation by removing samples with a pipette, or wine thief, inserted through the bunghole. In these small casks the average period for storage appears to be not more than six months for white wines and only slightly longer for red, provided the wine has 12% alcohol or more. Wines containing less than 12% alcohol should not be stored in cask in damp or humid places, since in these circumstances the alcohol evaporates as well as some of the water. The larger the casks, the longer can be the storage period, but, even in butts, only from two to four years is customary, according to the wine. Small casks can also produce a woody taste in the wine.

In the belly of the cask is a bunghole about 5 cm in diameter through which the cask is filled. Since the cask is always stored on its side, it is positioned so that the bunghole is at the top and the cask is supported at each end in such a way that the belly of the staves is not in contact with any surface, otherwise the cask is liable to leak through the joins in the staves under pressure from the weight above.

In one end of the cask is a small hole about 2·5 cm in diameter and this is the tap-hole which, during wine storage, is normally plugged with a cork cut off flush with the end boards. When a cask is broached after an adequate period of storage, a wooden tap is placed against the cork in the tap-hole and the tap is hit firmly with a mallet so that the cork is driven into the wine and the tap fills the hole tightly. The wine cannot be drawn off through the tap unless air can enter the cask to take the place of the wine. For this purpose the bung can be loosened, or if a spile has been driven through the bung, the spile is removed to admit air and afterwards replaced. If the cask is used for fermentation (not advised) a gas release is fitted through a hole made in the bung. For storage after fermentation the gas release is removed and a spile inserted in the hole.

It is important to keep the cask quite full during the storage of wine to minimize the possibility of spoilage. The wine level should be checked at intervals not exceeding a fortnight, and the wine topped up, if necessary, to replace the loss by evaporation. The amount of evaporation depends upon the environment in which the cask is stored, and on the porosity of the wood. Sometimes several bottles of wine may be required to top up even a small cask during a period of six months.

Misunderstanding has occurred as to whether it is alcohol or water that evaporates from a cask. In actual fact both seep through the walls of a cask and evaporate from its outer surface, but in ratios depending upon the atmosphere. If the temperature is high and the air is dry, the water evaporates faster than the alcohol and the wine in the cask becomes stronger, as with Sherries in Spain. If the temperature is low and the air is laden with moisture, the alcohol evaporates faster than the water and the wine in the cask becomes weaker. Unfortunately, the latter frequently applies in the British Isles. Nevertheless, almost all strong wines benefit by a period of storage in a cask, though the actual reason has not yet been isolated. Probably it is a combined effect of slow oxidation by air and chemical reactions between wood and wine.

When a cask has been emptied, the tap cork should be removed through the bunghole. The tap should also be removed and a fresh cork fitted. If the cask is to be used again immediately, it should be thoroughly flushed with clean water, rinsed with a sulphur dioxide solution (10 g potassium or sodium metabisulphite and 10 g citric acid dissolved in 5 litres water), flushed with clean water again, drained and filled with new wine of a similar colour to that last stored in it. It is advisable to keep separate casks for white wines and for red wines, since white wines stored in casks which have previously held red can extract red colouring matter that has permeated the wood. If a cask is to be stored empty of wine for a period, then after cleaning and sterilizing it, it should be filled with water and kept filled until required for use, changing the water at frequent intervals. Before use again, drain the cask, pour in a sulphite solution, roll it about, flush it with clean water and drain it.

A new cask will require soaking with water for a few days to swell the timber and make it liquid tight. The water will at first leak from the cask and should be replaced, but slowly the loss will decrease as the timber swells. Wet sacks laid over the cask are an aid to the soaking. When the timber has swollen sufficiently the water is emptied and the cask filled with hot soda solution, 100 g soda dissolved in each gallon of water, and left twenty-four hours. This reduces the tannin content of the oak and removes woody flavours. After the twenty-four hours' soaking, the soda solution is emptied and the cask flushed out with clean water, then a sulphur dioxide solution is added and rolled about to neutralize any residual soda solution. Finally the cask is flushed out with clean water and drained before filling with wine.

A second-hand cask should first be inspected carefully to see that it is not damaged in any serious manner, such as a cracked stave. The inside should be examined and all loose solid matter removed. If it has been kept dry for some time it will require soaking with water to swell the timber as with a new cask. Some second-hand casks, if they have been stored dry for too long, will not completely seal themselves and continue to leak no matter how long they are soaked. Such a cask should be returned to a cooper to be re-made. If the cask has been recently emptied it will not require soaking but only flushing out with clean water. After emptying, it is half-filled with a hot soda solution and vigorously rolled at intervals until it has cooled, when it is again emptied. Alternatively it can be filled with a solution of 50 ml of domestic bleach (hypochlorite solution) to each 25 litres of water and left for twenty-four hours before emptying. It is then flushed out with clean water several times. This must be done thoroughly to remove all traces of the bleach which is, of course, toxic. A sulphur dioxide solution is then added and the cask rolled thoroughly. After emptying, it is flushed out again with clean water and drained. It is then ready for filling with wine.

When a cask is ready for filling, it is placed on its cradle with the bunghole uppermost and the tap-hole facing outwards. The wine is run in to fill it completely and then the bung is inserted. Bungs are often difficult to remove if fitting correctly, but this difficulty can be mitigated by first wrapping the bung in a piece of clean hessian or the like before ramming it home. The ears of the hessian then provide a grip for removing the bung. Details of the wine with dates should be written on a label which should be pinned to the cask.

Some winemakers paint the metal rings of their casks with an anti-rust solution and coat the upper half of the staves with polyurethane to close the pores in the wood. Epoxy resin, cerevaisin wax and paraffin wax are also used.

CASSE The name given to a 'break' in the clarity of a wine. The cloudiness is often caused by the presence of an excess of metallic salts in a wine. Many vegetables and fruits contain traces of iron extracted from the soil by the growing plant. In combination with the acids also present, ferric salts are formed and if the quantity is at all excessive the wine becomes cloudy and difficult to clear. Commercially such wines can be cleared by using an exact amount of potassium ferrocyanide but for the amateur the risk of poisoning is so great as not to be recommended to anyone other than a person trained and qualified in this branch of chemistry. Casse can also be caused by allowing the must or wine to come into contact with iron or copper. Oxidasic casse caused by using fruit that is over-ripe can be prevented by adding 50 ppm SO_2 during fermentation.

CATECHOL   A simple structured tannin, or polyphenol, found in fruits. It is one of the tannins that cause astringency in wine.

CELLAR   Even a few bottles of wine stored for maturation nowadays constitute a cellar and the word does not normally imply a dark basement with rough walls and an earth floor. A cellar of wine can be as few as a dozen bottles stored in a bin in the larder or under the stairs. When bottles are kept for any length of time, it is necessary to store them on their sides and a properly made bin is most effective for this purpose. The bin can be made to fit any store place and possess any number of bottle openings. The storage place should be free from vibration, dry, dark and of even temperature, preferably 12 °C (55 °F). It should be kept clean and any spilt wine should be immediately wiped up with a cloth soaked in a sulphite solution.

CELLARCRAFT   This is the work of maturing wines in any hygienic manner so as to improve them and serve them in the peak of condition. Wines should be racked when deposits have been thrown, sulphited as may be necessary to keep them free from infection, bottled in clean sterile bottles, corked with clean sterile corks, capped, labelled and stored at the right temperature, until they are suitable for drinking.

Cellarcraft includes the fining, filtering and blending of wines when necessary, and in general the improvement of wines, from after fermentation until they are served.

CELLULOSE   One of the higher sugars comprising long chains of glucose. The connective tissue of plants is composed mostly of cellulose. Enzymes secreted by wine yeasts are incapable of breaking down cellulose but a commercially prepared product, Rohament P, will do so. Added to fruit pulp, Rohament P can therefore increase the yield of juice.

Powders allied to cellulose are used both in powder and in pad form when filtering. They can replace, and are sometimes preferred to, asbestos pulp. They are also non-toxic and are used in a similar way to asbestos pulp. Like asbestos pulp they should be washed before filtering wine and the washing water should be discarded.

CEREALS   Grains contain starch which is reduced by diastase to make a fermentable must from which spirits are distilled. Some winemakers add cereals to their musts to give body to their wine. Unless diastase is also present the starch will not be converted into fermentable sugars and the most that can be hoped for is some mucilage.

When cereals are malted, the starch is converted to maltose which is readily fermentable by yeast. Normally used for ales, beers and spirits, it is only rarely used for wine.

CEREVAISIN WAX *See* WAX.

CHALK *See* CALCIUM CARBONATE.

CHAMBRÉ The recommended temperature for serving most red wines. It simply means 'at room temperature'. But the temperature of the room can vary so much that the phrase 'free from chill' is sometimes more precise. This is because red wines, high in tannin, are slow to release their aroma, bouquet and flavour at low temperatures and if they are taken straight from a cold cellar to the table, it is necessary to warm the wines for full appreciation. A temperature between 15 and 20 °C (59 and 68 °F) is preferable. This can best be achieved by standing the wine for some hours in the room where it will be drunk. The bottle should not be dipped in hot water nor placed on a hot stove, since the rapid change in temperature will be deleterious to the wine. Neither should the bottle be plunged into tepid water nor stood near a warm radiator, as the slower the wine is warmed the better. Rapid warming can have harmful effects on any wine, white or red, but, conversely, rapid chilling does no damage. In hot climates, the wine very soon loses its chill.

CHAMPAGNE This sparkling wine is made exclusively in Champagne in France. No other sparkling wine may legally be called Champagne. The wine is nowadays made from a blend of grapes from different vineyards and the two most common varieties are the black Pinot Noir and the white Chardonnay. Because of the poor chalky soil and the cool climate in Champagne, the still wines are somewhat thin and delicate in flavour. Furthermore, because of the need to leave the grapes on the vines as long as possible, in the hope that they will all ripen, the fermentation of the must is often inhibited by the onset of cold weather. A secondary fermentation starts with the coming of warmer weather in the spring.

Dom Perignon, the cellar master of the Haut Villiers monastery in 1668, was the first to turn this phenomenon to advantage. He bottled his wine during the winter in the strongest bottles he could obtain, stoppered them with pieces of cork which he tied on to the bottles and allowed the secondary fermentation to take place in the bottle. When the wine was subsequently poured, it possessed a new and fascinating flavour and was accompanied by an exciting effervescence. The one problem was the clarity, for the sediment from the secondary fermentation was lifted up by the surge of the gas when the bottle was opened. More than 100 years passed before Mme Cliquot, the widow of a Champagne wine merchant, discovered how to remove the sediment. She up-ended the bottles until the sediment had settled firmly on the cork, then removed the cork and sediment whilst the bottle was still at an angle, and replaced the cork with a new one after topping up with a little sweetened wine and brandy.

Fundamentally the process remains unchanged and is known as the *méthode champenoise*. Most wineries nowadays freeze the neck of the bottle so that the sediment is encased in a small plug of ice. Sugar, too, is added since very few people care for a wine totally devoid of sweetness. The quantity varies from firm to firm and even from time to time, reflecting the public palate. Brut Champagne, the very dryest, contains from $\frac{3}{4}$ to $1\frac{1}{2}$% by volume of added sugar; Extra dry from $1\frac{1}{2}$ to 3%; Dry from 2 to 4%; Medium dry contains up to 8% and Sweet up to 10%.

The basic wine is often blended before the secondary fermentation with other wines from the area and/or wines from other years, although occasionally a wine from a single harvesting will be made and called a vintage champagne. The alcohol content is between $11\frac{1}{2}$ and 12% by volume. It is important that the flavour of the wines be not too pronounced so that the Champagne flavour may predominate. To this end, winemakers in other countries often use for their sparkling wine a blend of white wines that are nondescript in flavour and quality.

In modern wineries the fermentation is completed in the autumn, the wine racked, cleared and matured during the winter. It is then bottled in the spring with the addition of *liqueur de tirage*, to increase the sugar content to 24 g sucrose per litre, and an active champagne yeast. Crown caps are now often used in place of corks during the secondary fermentation and Champagne maturation. The wine is left on its lees for at least six months and often several years before *remuage*, *dégorgement* and *dosage*. When this takes place the wine is ready for drinking without further storage.

CHAPTALIZATION The practice of adding sugar to a grape must which is deficient in sugar and could not otherwise be fermented into a wine containing sufficient alcohol for normal purposes. Not only does chaptalization increase the alcohol content but also the glycerine and other secondary products that influence the aroma. It is named after Jean Antoine Chaptal (1756–1832) who introduced the practice of adding sugar to wines in a poor vintage. It is also known as *le sucrage*.

The practice is banned in Spain and Portugal where the normal sunshine is sufficient to produce in the grapes all the sugar that is required. It is also banned in the Bordeaux area. In other parts of France, however, the addition of sugar is permitted, but it is strictly governed by the Code du Vin. The only sugar permitted is crystalline sucrose (white granulated sugar), all others being forbidden. Generally the more northerly the vineyards the more common the practice, because the sunshine is insufficient to produce the required sugar in the grapes. Germans used to label their wines *Naturwein* when no sugar had been added, but this is

48

now forbidden. They mostly add concentrated grape juice as well as crystalline sugar to their musts.

CHARCOAL   One of the purest forms of carbon, charcoal is sometimes used for fining, but it readily absorbs the colouring and the esters of wine. It therefore has to be very carefully used, as too much will result in an almost colourless and flavourless liquid. As amorphous or powdered charcoal, it is used for fining wine. For use *see* FINING.

CHARMAT SYSTEM   *See* SPARKLING WINE.

CIDER   Fermented apple juice. Experience has shown that some varieties of apples are more suitable than others for making cider, and certain farmers grow a number of different varieties thought to be the best for the purpose, mainly because they have a high tannin content. Some of the apples are sweet, some sharp, some bitter, some of good flavour and so on. They are mellowed for a while after being picked, then they are washed, crushed, sulphited, pressed and juice fermented in the usual way. About 7% alcohol is formed. The cider is stored in casks for a few months if it is to be served sparkling. Cider has a relatively short life due to its low alcohol content and begins to deteriorate after some months' storage. Cider can be made only if a good press is available. The pulp must be sulphited as soon as possible to prevent oxidation and a suitable active yeast added twenty-four hours later, with added tannin if the normal content was low. Suggested for further reading is *Cider Making* by Beech and Pollard (*see* BIBLIOGRAPHY).

Cider has been made in England for many hundreds of years and, indeed, some of the so-called vineyards were possibly cider orchards, since they produced a fermented liquor which may have been called 'wine' by uneducated people. The quality cider from Herefordshire has always been of an extremely high standard and was at some time thought by connoisseurs to be superior to the wine imported from the Continent in the sixteenth and seventeenth centuries. It lost popularity during the Industrial Revolution but modern methods of bulk production have brought back its popularity in more recent years. So also has the production of higher alcohol and vintage ciders. But cider is made wherever apples are grown. Cider can be sparkled in the same manner as wine.

CITRIC ACID   *See* ACIDS.

CLADO-SPORIUM CELLERAE   A microscopic blackish-brown mould which grows on walls and fittings in wine cellars. It assimilates and lives on vapours from alcohol (esters and volatile acids) which explains its fondness for wine cellars where such food is always available. It is not dangerous to maturing wine, but a must left in a cellar where this mould is present might possibly become turbid.

CLARET   A dry, translucent red table wine of variable colour from dark to light red. It has a light to medium body with acidity to match. Traditionally it has a high tannin content that necessitates long maturation. The alcohol content is around 11%. It is made from a blend of grapes including the Cabernet Sauvignon, Cabernet Franc, Merlot and Malbec. Chaptalization is forbidden.

CLARIFICANTS   Substances used in winemaking to make cloudy or hazy wines clear and bright, for example amylozyme 100, pectozyme, bentonite, isinglass, white of egg, gelatine and tannin etc. (*See also* FINING and FILTERING.)

CLARIFY and CLARIFICATION   The process of rendering a wine clear and brilliant. Mayer-Oberplan (1956) summarized the objectives as (i) removal of suspended materials,, (ii) removal of off-tastes and odours, (iii) removal of off-colour, (iv) removal of substances which would later cloud the wine, (v) removal of foreign or toxic materials, (vi) removal of residual fining agents, (vii) to hydrolyse pectins and proteins and (viii) to make wines and musts filterable. Commercial clarification involves storage in various containers, racking, filtration, fining, centrifugation, pasteurization (or heat treatment), refrigeration and other processes. Domestic clarification involves the same processes excepting centrifugation, pasteurization and 'other processes' such as passing the wine through ion exchange resins.

CLASSIC WINES   These are the traditional wine types, including red, white and rosé dry table wines, sweet table wines, red and white dessert wines, sparkling wines, Sherries and Madeiras.
   The red table wines can be full and fruity like Burgundies or lighter and more individualistic like Clarets, or stronger, softer and rich in aroma like Hermitage. The dry whites can be light, fresh and delicate like Moselles, firm and full of character like Chablis or softer and fuller flavoured like Vouvray. The sweet whites come in two versions, medium sweet like the soft round well-flavoured Hocks and the slightly sweeter Dordogne wines and the very sweet, luscious dessert wines like the great Sauternes, Tokay and Trockenbeerenauslese wines. Rosé wines are a pretty pink, well flavoured, medium weight and just off dry.
   Vermouths are fortified, dull wines, flavoured with wormwood and other herbs, spices and fruits. The whites are usually medium dry/sweet whilst the reds are sweet. Sherries are fortified white wines that have been heavily oxidized. Red dessert wines are well bodied, full-flavoured and fortified, like Port wines. Madeira wines are mostly sweet, caramelized and long matured. (See under individual headings for further details.)

CLEARING WINES   Hazy or cloudy wines have no eye appeal and should be treated to make them brilliant. There are two methods of achieving this which are described under the headings FILTERING and FINING. Reference should also be made to HAZES.

CLIMAT/CLOS Different names for a vineyard, sometimes used on labels of bottles of wine from Burgundy and elsewhere. Positions and exposure to the sun, and proximity to hills and trees, vary almost enough to produce individual micro-climates for the vineyards. Those surrounded by a wall are usually called 'clos'.

CLONE Clones are vegetatively reproduced plants from one superior parent plant. The new plant being part of the parent accordingly has all its characteristics. A single specimen of vine or other fruit is selected for its individual abundant crop, quality of crop, resistance to disease and to drought or to wet conditions, its tolerance to other growing conditions, earlier or later flowering/fruit ripening or for any other desirable characteristic. It is then vegetatively reproduced and the new plants are known as such and such a clone or clone number –. Such clones although of the same variety are superior to the original cultivar and can produce better quality and/or bigger crops resulting in finer quality and/or greater quantity of wine, even up to 30%.

CLOSURE A closure is any means or device for covering and closing the opening into any fermentation or storage vessel. It can equally well be a bung, cap, cork, cover, lid, plug, screw cap, seal, or stopper etc., irrespective of the material. As the wine should not be in contact with the closure during fermentation it is of little consequence of what material it is made, though it is advisable to avoid plain metals. This normally applies to bulk storage also.

Plastics are now being used for bottle closures, even for sparkling wines, but for this purpose bottle necks have to be made to the same closure tolerance as the closures. Unless the bottles and closures are matched, natural corks are still the best bottle closures for ageing and maturing.

CLOUDY A term used to refer to wine which is not clear and appears to be muddy or murky. Wines which are less thick are said to be hazy. For causes of these conditions refer to HAZES.

COLLAGE Another name for fining. *See* FINING.

COLLOIDAL HAZES Hazes caused by colloids. *See* HAZES and FINING.

COLLOIDS Substances of a non-crystalline, semi-solid nature, suspended or dispersed in a medium. In wine the colloids consist of gums, pectic substances and proteins that, as hydro-colloids, cause hazing. (*See also* FINING.)

COLOUR The colours of wine are divided into three groups; white, rosé and red. All grape juices are white whether pressed from white or black grapes. The teinturiers are the exception, having pink juice, but are not favoured for winemaking. The rosé and red colours are obtained by maceration or fermentation of the black grape skins and pips. The depth of colour varies from the grape variety and soil and weather during growth and quantity of skins and length of maceration/fermentation. Not only is colour extracted, but also tannins are leached out as well. These tannins alter the wine and cause the difference in drinking characteristics between white, rosé and red. The basic differences being that white wine has little or no tannin content, rosé has only a modest amount, whilst red wine has a high tannin content.

Black grapes grown in cooler areas usually make poor red wine and are mainly used for making white wine. They lack the tannin content of grapes grown in sunny areas as do black but unripe berries. The same comments apply to all other fruits apart from a few exceptions such as under-ripe pears and some apples that produce white wine with considerable tannin content. Some red fruits are very low in tannin. The colours of the groups react in different ways with ageing, but their colours at any age, except during youth, do not indicate actual age. The method of maturing affects the rate of change so that colour can be some reflection of maturity.

White No wine should be truly colourless and if it is, it is a poor wine. Green tinting may be apparent in young wine due to the presence of chlorophyll which does not affect the wine. Dry white wines start a very pale yellow or a pale straw with some hint of green. As they age the colour deepens through yellow, to golden, then maderized and brown. Sweet white wines start their life much more yellow than dry wines, then follow the same deepening until they finish a tawny-brown. In other words, white wines gain colour with ageing and when they have naturally turned brown with age are over the hill and usually not worth drinking. A white wine can brown by enzymatic oxidation but the flavour will not be affected. The colour of other brown wines such as Sherries is the result of processing or the addition of 'colour wine'.

Rosé These wines range in colour from the palest pink to light red: a brightish colour that lacks the full robe of the red wine. The amount of colour and the character of the wine depends on the method of production. Orange tinting may be present from some varieties of aging poor red wine called Pelure d'Oignon. Some varieties of fruit can give an orange tint to wine. Any blue or purple tint in a rosé will denote a disorder. Age also affects colour, the palest pink deepening to orange and the bright red lightening to orange. All would eventually become brown if left long enough, but most are usually drunk before they are old enough for the colour to begin to change.

Red All red wines start a deep red or a deep red/purple. The purple in the red is present only in some young wines, seen particularly in the rim of the wine in a tilted glass; it later disappears.

During ageing, tannin causes the red pigment to precipitate and the colour to change from red/purple or deep red to ruby, red-brown, mahogany, tan (tawny) amber-brown, brown. Brown wines from ageing are well over the hill. Brown wines can also be caused by very bad over-oxidation, or as a result of processing. A wine can be tawny from long bottle age, from long maturation in cask or from badly blending white and red wines.

Unlike white wines, red wines lose colour with age, but all wines eventually finish brown if left long enough.

COOKING WITH WINE A wide range of food recipes have now been prepared which include wine. The main purposes are to add a piquancy and to enrich the dish. Since the alcohol is driven off by the heat during the cooking, wine is sometimes added only just before serving when retention of the alcohol is required. Other recipes use wine as a liquid in which to cook the ingredients and so enrich and enhance their flavour. Some fish and meats are marinaded or soaked in wine for twelve hours before cooking not only to improve the flavour, but also to tenderize them. Any wine is usually suitable, including the dregs of a bottle; indeed it is unnecessary to use good quality wine and any sound wine of good flavour will do. Wines made at home can be substituted with complete success for commercial wines. (*See also* MARINADE.)

COOPER, COUPERAGE The making of casks and barrels is an ancient and honourable craft, now, alas, dying out. Oak is mainly used, although sometimes chestnut is accepted as an alternative, and in America, redwood. The staves are carefully seasoned and selected for their quality and are scorched on the inside by finishing the casks over an open fire of the wood chippings. This sterilizes and seals the wood. Casks made from inferior wood are usually sealed inside with a thick coating of wax. Different casks produce varying qualities of wine, depending on the quality and type of oak or the wood used for their manufacture. (*See also* CASKS.)

CO-OPERATIVES A group of vine growers who have joined together to form an organization to make and market their wines. Individual growers are sometimes too small or too undercapitalized to be able to purchase modern equipment and employ qualified winemakers and marketing staff. By joining a co-operative they are assured of a sale for their grapes at a reasonable price. The co-operative will be large enough to make better wines than its individual members and use modern machinery, technology and marketing methods. A wine from a co-operative is usually of better value than from a small estate. Bottles are usually labelled with the name of the co-operative. In France they are called *caves co-opératives*, in Italy *cantine sociale* and in Germany *Winzergenossenschaft*.

COPITA   A tulip-shaped glass, the bowl of which is some 7 to 10 cm or so long and tapering from 5 cm at the widest point of the bowl to 3 cm at the rim. It is the true Sherry glass and is commonly used in Spain for tasting and sampling this wine. It is ideal for the appreciation of wine because its shape entraps the bouquet and aroma better than any other glass.

CORKAGE   A charge made by hotel proprietors for permitting wine to be drunk on their premises which they have not themselves sold to the consumer. It is supposed to offset the loss of profit that would have been made if the proprietor had sold his wines and to discourage others from wishing to do the same.

CORK BORER   A metal instrument used for boring holes in bungs, corks or stoppers made from cork or plastic. It is a very simple implement consisting of a tube, normally brass, which is chamfered at one end so as to give a knife edge around the outer circumference, and fitted with a 'T' piece at the other, the 'T' piece being so fitted as not to block the tube. The item to be bored is placed on a firm surface and the borer pushed through with a screwing action.

The borer is easy to use and quick in action and can be obtained in different sizes, which makes it possible to bore bungs, corks etc., to take any size or type of air lock or spile as required, and be sure of a correct fit.

CORKED WINE, CORKY WINE and CORKINESS   These are terms used to mean the same thing—a condition of wine that is disagreeable. Very occasionally, when a cork is drawn from a bottle a fusty odour is given off, and the wine tastes mouldy and unpleasant. It has long been assumed that the wine extracted the flavour from the cork, but the reason was unknown. It is now considered almost certain that the cause is *Penicillium* in the cork.

The condition is relatively rare now and the reason lies in the better cleaning of the natural cork and the sterilization of corks by immersing them in a sulphite solution before use.

The term 'corked wine' also has the second meaning of wine being sealed in a bottle by a cork.

CORKER   An instrument for fitting cylindrical corks into bottles that are to be laid down. There are several reputable varieties on the market, ranging in suitability for corking a small number of bottles to a large number. One that compresses the diameter of the cork is well worth having to ensure a good airtight fit. The corks have first to be softened by soaking them in a sulphite solution.

CORK FLOGGER   A flat piece of hard wood, some 2 cm thick and 20 to 25 cm long. One end is shaped for holding, the other is about 8 cm broad for flogging. The cork is softened and placed in the neck of the bottle and hit with the flogger to ram it home flush. With experience this can be done with one stroke of the flogger.

CORKS   Cork is the bark of a tree grown mostly in Spain and Portugal. When the tree is twenty years old, the bark is cut off in sheets, which are soaked in water to soften them so that they can be pressed flat. The sheets are then lightly charred to kill bacteria and to improve the appearance. The corks are cut out by machine and finished off by hand to ensure a smooth surface at the end to be in contact with the wine.

Wine corks are cylindrical in shape and these are undoubtedly the most suitable for bottles that are to be laid down. Cork stoppers, i.e. short cylindrical corks with a flange at one end, have been produced in the past for industries other than wine. These other industries are tending to replace the cork flange with a plastic top, which can be coloured and/or printed. Composite stoppers from small pieces of cork glued together in the manner of Champagne corks, are also available as well as plastic stoppers. Cork is becoming increasingly expensive and in short supply.

Good-quality corks must always be used in bottles that contain wine to be kept for a number of years. The cellar masters of the famous wine firms of France, supported by a nation notoriously thrifty in so many ways, pay at least three times, and occasionally ten times, as much for their corks as do most amateurs.

Before using corks they should always be softened and sterilized. This can be done by soaking them in a solution of sodium metabisulphite for half an hour or so. They can then be compressed the more easily to enter the neck of the bottle. Never sterilize corks by boiling them, since this destroys the very virtues of which you want to take advantage, and frequently causes them to be so porous that wine can seep through the holes.

Corks are being replaced by plastic stoppers wherever possible, but it should be noted that stoppers of an exact size are used in bottles with close tolerance diameters inside the neck, to make a perfect fit between stopper and bottle. Standard plastic stoppers, as commonly sold, if used in ordinary wine bottles do not fit correctly and do not effect a perfect seal. Crown caps are frequently superseding corks as closures for everyday wine.

CORKSCREWS   These essential instruments of the wine drinker have been in use as long as cylindrical corks have been used, that is since the early eighteenth century. They should possess a broad rather than a narrow screw, so as to grip the cork firmly and yet in such a manner as not to cause disintegration and so precipitate portions into the wine. They are best used for withdrawing firm corks.

Another variety possesses two, flat, spring-steel blades, which are pressed down between the cork and the neck of the bottle, the cork then being removed with a twisting motion without causing any particle of cork to enter the wine or the cork to disintegrate. It is the best method of withdrawing corks which are soft from long storage during bottle ageing.

The latest variety is a hypodermic type needle which is plunged right through the cork, a charge of carbon dioxide or compressed air is passed through the needle and the pressure pushes the cork out instantly in one piece.

CORRECTION OF WINE   The grapes from the same vines vary from year to year. In France local oenological stations specify must corrections to improve the wine. Though these are limited by French law, it clearly indicates the necessity to test and adjust all musts. The adjustments recommended by the stations include de-acidification or the addition of acid, the addition of sugar, the removal of excess tannin or the addition of tannin; colour improvement by heating part of the vendange or harvest; blending the finished wine with one from an earlier vintage to maintain a uniformity and so on.

COTTON WOOL   A wad of cotton wool makes a very efficient closure for fermentation vessels with a smallish opening. A bored bung plugged with cotton wool is just as effective. The cotton wool whilst preventing bacteria from entering, readily permits carbon dioxide to escape. The carbon dioxide prevents air from getting to the wine. After fermentation, a wad of cotton wool can be used as a closure for non-porous (glass etc.) storage vessels, provided the vessels are kept full. The cotton wool enables a small amount of air to enter the container for the initial oxidation of maturation, in the same way as a cask enables a small amount of air to pass through its pores to the wine inside. Care has to be taken in the same way as with a cask, i.e. that the wine is not left too long under the cotton wool and so becomes over-oxidized.

COUPAGE   The blending of a thin, acid, low-alcohol wine, made in a poor year, with a high-alcohol, more robust wine. The blended wine is not more than a *vin ordinaire*, but at least it is drinkable and the wines which formed its basis certainly were not. This practice is not unreasonably carried on commercially, and France, for example, imports substantial quantities of Algerian red wine to blend with poorer wines and so improve them. (*See also* CUT.)

CRADLE   When a bottle of superb wine has been laid down for years it is important to carry the wine carefully, so as not to disturb the crust, the crust being the sediment that has collected on the side of the bottle. It is usual to carry such a bottle of wine in a cradle, shaped rather like a miniature baby's cot with a niche cut out of one end or provided with a ring for the neck of the bottle. There is a handle for carrying which is also used for pouring the wine slowly after the cork has been carefully withdrawn with the bottle lying in the cradle.

In practice some cradles are not as effective as one would wish them to be. When using certain types of simple, elementary cradles made from bent iron rods or from cane, the wine bottle is almost invariably jolted as it is fitted into the cradle. With the more sophisticated cradle, the bottle sometimes slips during the pouring process, thus jolting the wine.

Wines which have thrown such a deposit as to need a cradle can be poured carefully from the bottle to the glass, but preferably should be decanted, not only to remove the wine from the crust, but also to enable it to breathe for even a short while before serving it. The cradle may still be used for the decanting. Wines which have been stood upright for a sufficient period to form a crust on the bottom are not carried in a cradle but carried upright. From such bottles it is more difficult to pour without disturbing the crust. (For cask cradle *see* STILLAGE.)

CREAM OF TARTAR *See* POTASSIUM HYDROGEN TARTRATE.

CRITICAL CONCENTRATION A critical concentration exists when one part of a mixture reaches a specific ratio, enabling it to start or stop a given reaction. For example, after an active culture of yeast is added to a must, there are no visible signs of fermentation for a varied length of time whilst the yeast multiplies. When there are sufficient yeast cells present, fermentation can be seen. The number of yeast cells required to produce the visible fermentation is the 'critical concentration'.

Likewise, when a wine contains some residual sugar, adequate acid and nutrient, yet stops fermenting, it is probably because a sufficient quantity of alcohol has been formed to inhibit further yeast activity. When the yeast can tolerate no more alcohol its 'critical concentration' has been reached.

CRU From the verb *croître*, to grow. Used in reference to wine it designates a particular area and the wine product of that area. By French law the terms *grand cru*, *premier cru* and *cru classé* can each only be applied to certain wines.

CRUSHER A mechanical means of crushing or bursting fruit to allow the juice to run more freely when pressed. It replaces the treading of grapes.

CRUST All wines throw lees and deposits as they clarify and mature. The contents will include tartrates, tannin, cellulose tissue and dead yeast cells (and some live ones and spores too). Some wines, especially white wines, throw their deposits of unwanted matter quite quickly and then remain star-bright and stable. Others, notably the reds, continue to throw deposits throughout their life. So, although they have been racked in the usual way to remove the sediment formed, further sediment forms during maturation in bottle. This collects in a firm crust down the side of the bottle, assuming that the bottle has been laid down on its side, and is only called a crust when it occurs in a bottle from long storage. Knowing this will happen, the wise cellarman drops a blob of whitening on the top side of the bottle as it is laid down. When the time comes to move the bottle it is easy to keep the white blob uppermost and so avoid disturbing the crust.

If the wine has not been too long laid down, the bottle may be stood upright for twenty-four hours so that the crust can slowly slide down to the punt. Having carefully got rid of this unwanted matter during maturation it would be a great pity to stir it into the wine again and in a few seconds undo the work of the years in bottle.

CRYTOCOCCUS   One of the species of slime yeasts which can attack and spoil a wine. Use of sulphite is the prevention.

CUSTOMS AND EXCISE   Every country controlling the taxes on wines and spirits has different regulations, and these change from time to time. Most countries permit wine to be made in modest quantities for family use but charge duty on any wines offered for sale. In the U.K. this often amounts to more than half the cost of a bottle of wine. In the U.S.A. a licence to make wine is normally only granted to the head of the household and is restricted to 200 gallons per year. In Australia the limit is 400 gallons after which a licence must be purchased and duty paid. Winemakers are advised to consult their nearest Customs and Excise office to ascertain the local regulations. Larger duties are usually imposed on spirits and all regulations prohibit the making of spirits without a licence.

CUT   The term used to describe the adulteration of a better wine with a poorer one or even with water. The wine has been cut, i.e. reduced in quality.

CUVE CLOSE   A method of making sparkling wine in large quantities and avoiding the disgorgement process essential to the méthode champenoise. The wine to be sparkled is refermented in a large closed tank, matured, filtered, bottled under pressure, then sealed. The method makes a pleasant sparkling wine, but one that lacks the fine character of one made by the méthode champenoise. The cuve close method is widely used everywhere other than in Champagne.

DARKENING   *See* BROWNING and METAL CONTAMINATION.

DE-ACIDIFICATION   When grapes and other fruits do not ripen normally the must from them can be too acidic and should be corrected by de-acidification. Pure calcium carbonate is added to the must at the rate of 7·5 g per 5 litres for each 1·5 ppt acid, expressed as sulphuric, required to be reduced. Allowance must be made for the foaming which will occur.

DE-AMINATION When protein is broken down to amino acids and the nitrogen containing group of atoms is removed, it is called de-amination. Wine yeasts require nitrogen for building protein and if there is a lack of it during fermentation they will de-aminate dead yeast cells to obtain some. The poisonous amyl alcohol is produced in the process which is potentially dangerous.

DECANTER The forerunners of the glass decanters and the glass bottles of today were first made in the seventeenth century. These were called 'bottles', 'serving bottles', 'bottle-decanters' or 'decanter-bottles' and were rather crude productions in soda or potash glass for serving wine at the table. Even George Ravenscroft who first produced glass-of-lead (leadglass) about 1675, referred to his products as 'bottles'. These were made of colourless fine glass, provided with glass stoppers, were with or without handles and were decorated. They were far nearer the decanters as we know them, than the crude serving bottles. Nevertheless, the term decanter probably did not come into use until the last decade of the seventeenth century. It was first recorded in 1690 and used in reference to a pottery jug.

In shape, Ravenscroft's 'bottles' and the early decanters resembled narrow-necked jugs with stoppers, or were shaft-and-globe shape with or without handles. Then between 1715 and 1730 there were first produced the mallet decanters, so called because they resembled a mason's mallet, of which there were three shapes, the circular, the polygonal and the cruciform. In those days all wines were served cool, after the decanter had been stood in a wine-cooler, and the cruciform shape was evolved to expose the maximum surface area of glass, and thereby the wine, to the cold water in the cooler.

All serving bottles and decanters made up to this time had a kick in the bottom. (*See* PUNT.)

As the century passed, changes in design appeared. There was the modified shaft-and-globe that was almost a cross between the shaft-and-globe and the mallet, and there was the shouldered-mallet. Decorations were added and about 1745 to 1750, the lip at the top of the neck to facilitate pouring without dripping was introduced. It did not, however, become common until about 1770. Between these times, 1745–1770, shallow diamond-faceting was introduced and was later developed so that the shallow concave facets introduced a varied play of internal light and shade, greatly enhancing the rich appearance of the wine in the decanter. By 1780 the decanters were becoming more cylindrical, and the

59

upright ones became the most fashionable. Production of the shaft-and-globe decanters then ceased and were not made again until the Victorian era. During the Victorian age, decanters reached their eminence and were used both for spirits, usually square shaped, and for wine, in all shapes and decoration. The broad-based 'ship's decanter' was particularly popular for Port and Madeira wines.

With the application of science to winemaking and the wine trade and with improved methods of bottling and distribution, fewer and fewer wines threw a sediment in the bottle, and it was thought that there was now no need to decant. The decanter became unfashionable and almost fell into disuse. Wines were served either direct from the bottle, or from the bottle in a cradle.

Since the end of the war in 1945 there has been a great resurgence of winemaking and an increased consumption of wines. With this has come a sorting out, a cleaning and a polishing, and the return into use of the old decanters. Newly made ones have appeared on the market, ranging from copies of old designs to modern cut glass and ultra-modern designs of unusual shapes. Unfortunately, designers are not always lovers of wine and they sometimes forget that the main purpose of a decanter is to display the wine to its best advantage. Fussy shapes and tinted glass unquestionably spoil the effect.

The first requirement of a decanter is that it should be a suitable vessel into which a wine can be decanted from its sediment and from which the wine can be served. The second and equally important requirement is that it should display the wine to its best advantage. The appearance of wine before drinking can greatly improve its appreciation. It is an advantage for the decanter to have a longish neck, so that despite the varying quantities decanted from a bottle, the wine when in the decanter presents the smallest surface area to the air. The most suitable decanters, and the best, can be summarized as follows. They should themselves be pleasing to the eye, yet of simple design to facilitate ease of filling and cleanliness in pouring. They should have a longish narrow neck and may be cut with shallow facets, that, by causing interplay of light and shade through the wine, add to its brilliance and enhance its colour. Above all they should be made of clear, colourless glass and free from coloured decoration.

DECANTING Wines were decanted long before the first decanters were thought of or made, for the original meaning of 'decant' was to pour a liquid into any vessel by canting (tilting) the container. With wine 'decanting' would have meant pouring it into a jug or even direct into a drinking vessel from the container, usually a cask. Not until the end of the seventeenth century was 'decanting' specifically used to mean pouring wine, still normally from the cask, into a 'bottle' ('serving bottle', 'bottle-decanter', 'decanter-bottle') and not until later into a decanter for serving at table. Swift in his satirical work *Directions to Servants* says, 'Take special care that your Bottles be not musty before you fill them.' A very pertinent direction, unlike his ironical statement in the same book, 'Some Butlers have a way of decanting (as they call it) bottled Ale by which they lose a good part of the Bottom: Let your Method be to turn the bottle directly upside down, which will make the Liquor appear double the Quantity: by this means you will be sure not to lose one Drop, and the Froth will conceal the Muddiness.' The 'bottom' was of course the lees or heavy sludge which sank to the bottom of the bottle if it had stood sufficiently long.

Today, decanting is the art of pouring wine from the bottle in which it has aged, into a decanter, without disturbing the sediment or allowing any to go over.

It was once thought that only red wine which had thrown a deposit, such as Burgundy or a crusted Port, need be decanted. The view has now changed and writers on wine are recommending decanting generally, including white wines. One advantage is that the wine looks superior in a polished glass decanter of delicate design, than it does in a bottle, which may not be too clean or may have a ragged label and the general appearance of which may be dirty and untidy. A much more important advantage, however, is that the act of decanting enables the wine to breathe or absorb oxygen and so develop its bouquet to please both the nose and the palate, whilst standing in the decanter. This is especially true of the richer and heavier wines that have been in the bottle for some years. It is also true of younger robust wines which mellow quite incredibly with some time in a decanter. The length of time which a wine should be left in the decanter before it is served depends entirely upon the individual wine. In general, the older and finer wines as well as the lighter wines need no longer than half an hour, whilst robust and heavier wines may safely be left in a decanter for an hour or more. Red wines generally require longer than white.

Before attempting to decant a wine, the decanter should be thoroughly washed and polished on the outside, rinsed and thoroughly drained on the inside. Any stains should have been previously removed with the aid of a bleach, hot shot, chain or sand. But when bleach has been used, thorough rinsing with several lots of water should follow to ensure the removal of any taint.

The first step in decanting is very carefully to remove the bottle from its storage and place it in a cradle. This will ensure keeping the bottle lying at an angle of 35 degrees which is most essential with bottles containing sediment, as it minimizes the risk of disturbing the deposit. Bottles of red wine and those high in tannin content, should be stood in their cradles for twenty-four hours in the room where they will be served. The decanter should also be stood with the bottle to acquire the same temperature. White wines free of sediment can be decanted without the standing period. All handling should, of course, be done with extreme care so that the sediment is not disturbed.

Remove the capsule, if any, and gently wipe the neck of the bottle with a clean napkin. All this time, the bottle should remain firm and tilted at 35 degrees. The cradle is then raised with the bottle in it and held against a light or a white surface so that the sediment can be clearly seen even in a dark bottle. The decanter is raised to the bottle and, neck to neck, so as to form an inverted 'V', the wine is gently poured, so as to run down the side of the decanter. If the sediment is hard it will not rise until almost all the wine has been decanted, but a loose sediment will start to flow towards the neck as soon as the base starts to rise above the neck of the bottle. The pouring is stopped immediately any sediment reaches the bottle shoulder and starts to rise towards the neck. No sediment should be allowed to flow over into the decanter. The stopper is placed in the decanter which is then stood on the table to remain at room temperature for red wine, or placed in a refrigerator or in an ice-bucket for white wine, until served.

For white wines with no deposit in the bottle it is not necessary to use a bottle cradle. The bottle can obviously be carried and stood upright without any danger to the wine. Red wines if they have been in the bottle for any length of time have probably thrown some deposit, even if it is not noticeable through the bottle, and it is, therefore, a wise precaution always to use a bottle cradle.

DÉGORGEMENT *See* DISGORGEMENT.

DEMERARA SUGAR A brown sugar which is used in cooking and known in the trade as a caramel. It contains in addition to pure sugar crystals a certain quantity of other matter which gives a subtly different flavour. This sugar has of course been so refined that it is free from any harmful or injurious ingredients. It is perfectly suitable for use in winemaking as long as it is realized that the flavour is positive and different. It is unwise to use it in white wines or with ingredients of delicate flavour, but it can be used when making wines of pronounced flavour, such as Madeira.

DEPOSIT In its general sense deposit means to put or set down, as well as that which is put down. Used in connection with wine it has the same, although narrower, meaning. Strictly, any sediment in wine is a deposit, but by general usage the sediments formed during alcoholic fermentation are referred to as lees, and it is the sediments formed after fermentation which are referred to as deposits. The action of forming the deposit is described as 'the wine throwing a deposit'. When a wine is aged in bottle the deposit thrown sometimes forms into a hard layer and is then referred to as a crust.

DESSERT WINES Traditionally drunk at the end of a meal with the dessert and/or subsequently. When drunk with the dessert course itself, a sweet, moderately alcoholic wine such as a Sauternes type is suitable. When taken subsequently, a much heavier and often fortified wine is drunk, such as a Port wine or a cream Sherry. They are normally also full-bodied. The sweetness cloys the palate and reduces the appetite were that then necessary, closing the meal as it were.

DETERGENTS   Chemicals which increase the cleaning quality of water by lowering its surface tension. Despite manufacturers' claims that it is unnecessary to rinse the articles washed in detergent, it is advisable to do so. Residual detergents in bottles to be used for sparkling wine will cause premature release of the carbon dioxide because the wine cannot hold the gas due to the lowered surface tension.

DEXTROCHECK   A reagent in tablet form for testing the residual sugar in a still wine before dosage to produce a sparkling wine. Ten drops of wine must be placed in a test tube and one tablet dropped into the wine. When fizzing ceases, the colour of the solution is compared with a chart supplied on which is overprinted the sugar quantities appropriate to each colour. (*See also* SPARKLING WINE.)

DEXTROSE   Another name for GLUCOSE under which details are given.

DIACTYL   A substance produced by lactobacilli that gives a wine a bitter taste that cannot be removed. It can be prevented by the use of sulphite. (*See also* MANNITE INFECTION.)

DIAMMONIUM PHOSPHATE   The correct name for what is commonly called AMMONIUM PHOSPHATE, under which details are given.

DIASTASE   The enzyme that hydrolyses starch to sugars. It is naturally present in unmalted cereals but it is not secreted by yeast. It splits starch into dextrin and maltose.

DILUTION   The weakening or making thinner of a solution. Dilution is practised in the making of fruit wines by the adding of water to fruit juices or extracts in order to reduce strong flavours, to reduce excess acidity from some fruits, to lessen tannin content, and/or to thin thick juices. In reducing one factor, other factors may be over-reduced and will then require making up. For example, when diluting to reduce a strong flavour, the acid and tannin content may be lowered too far and these have then to be added in some form to obtain the required level. One factor that is almost always reduced too much by dilution is the nutrient available as 'yeast food'. It is, therefore, always a good practice to add yeast nutrient to musts which have been diluted by water.

During fermentation the alcohol produced dilutes the water because the alcohol is thinner than water.

DIONYSUS Bacchus is most frequently referred to as the God of Wine, Bromius 'the boisterous' was another name, but both are only other names for Dionysus. In Homer's time, Dionysus was not one of the aristocratic Olympian deities but a god worshipped by humble folk, who had been brought into Greece from Thrace about the eighth century B.C. by wandering bands of ecstatic worshippers. The cult was characterized by mystic frenzy when worshippers, intoxicated with wine, believed themselves to be one with Dionysus. Male followers were known as Bacchoi and female as Bacchae, Bacchantes, Maenads or Thyiads. The cult became immensely popular, especially with women, indicating their deep longing for a more instinctive and impulsive life, valuing enthusiasm rather than prudence.

In the sixth century B.C. it was introduced among the state religions, and Dionysiac festivals were established. The Temple of Bacchus in the form of a theatre was built at the highest point of the sacred precinct in Delphi. In Athens the Dionysian Games were founded and a theatre set up where the worshippers of Bacchus enacted the first primitive drama. When the Parthenon was finished in the fifth century B.C., the new god had been fully accepted and was accorded among the twelve Olympians, taking the place of Hestia.

Legend has it that Dionysus was the son of a mortal woman, Semele, by Zeus the omnipotent King of the Gods, who visited his love disguised as a mortal. When Semele was six months with child, jealous Hera, disguised as an old woman, persuaded Semele to ask her lover to appear in all his divinity. Unwillingly Zeus consented and Semele was consumed by the fire that emanated from him. Zeus snatched from her womb his unborn child, enclosed him in his own thigh to be delivered three months later as Dionysus. Entrusted to Athamas and Ino of Boeotia, the child lived in the women's quarters, disguised as a girl, until Hera punished Athamas with madness. Hermes then took Dionysus to Mount Nysa where nymphs cared for him, feeding him with honey, and where he first invented wine.

When he reached manhood, Dionysus was driven mad by Hera and wandered with a wild rout of Satyrs and Maenads through Egypt, Syria and Asia to India, overcoming military opposition and teaching the culture of the vine, founding cities and establishing laws. He returned through Phyrgia to Thrace, thence to Boeotia and Thebes, where he was resisted by King Pentheus. But Pentheus was driven mad and torn to pieces by Maenads and Bacchae, among whom were his own mother and two sisters, who in their frenzy believed him to be a wild beast. Dionysus then visited the islands of the Adriatic, and at Argos the people repulsed and refused to accept him, but when the women had been maddened by him, they admitted he was a god. His worship established throughout the world, Dionysus was received into Olympus as one of the twelve great divinities. He brought Semele from the underworld and she henceforth was known as Thyone.

Dionysus was worshipped not only as the god of the vital and intoxicating powers of nature, but also as a law giver and the god of tragic art. In art he is depicted in company with wild crowds of Satyrs and Maenads, the latter frenzied with wine and mystic exaltation, and carrying cymbals, swords, serpents, or the Thyrsus (a wand wreathed with ivy and crowned with a fir cone).

The wanderings of Dionysus would appear to portray the spread of the vine and winemaking, since wine from the grapes was not invented by the Greeks. Wine was probably first imported from Crete where the vine culture had spread from Nysa. Nysa has sometimes been said to be Mount Nysa in Libya, amongst other places, but it is a singularly wandering place. Most probably it was somewhere in 'Arabia'.

DI-SACCHARIDES *See* SUGAR.

DISEASES and DISORDERS Fortunately there are not many diseases from which wines suffer and these can readily be prevented by cleanliness and sound hygiene. Details are given under the different headings as follows: (1) ACETIFICATION, (2) BITTER DISEASE, (3) CASSE, (4) FLOWERS OF WINE, (5) LACTIC ACID BACTERIA, (6) METAL CONTAMINATION, (7) ROPINESS, (8) TOURNE.

DISGORGEMENT From the French *dégorgement*, meaning 'throat clearing'. The removal of sediment from the neck of bottles of sparkling wine. After *remuage* and when the bottle is *sur point*, the sediment has settled on the cork. That sediment has to be removed—*dégorgement*. If it is not, the wine, like Champagne in the eighteenth century, will be cloudy. Indeed, at that time Champagne glasses were made with a frosted appearance to hide the cloudiness of the wine!

Before disgorgement the temperature of the wine should be lowered, but to no less than 5 °C (41 °F). The chilling reduces the pressure in the bottle but below 5 °C (41 °F) the water in the wine starts to freeze and as it expands increases the pressure.

The old method of disgorging was to hold the bottle in a cloth, keeping the neck downwards, but pointing away from the body. The 'agrafe' or 'muselet' was removed and the cork eased out taking the sediment with it. At the same time a finger or thumb was placed in or over the mouth of the bottle and the bottle was brought quickly to an upright position. It takes longer to describe the process than to perform it and, with some practice, very little of the wine is lost. Nowadays, the neck of the upside-down bottle is placed in a freezing solution for a few minutes until ice forms on the cork when the bottle is then stood upright. The cork is removed and with it the sediment held by the tiny block of ice. There is a little foaming and the neck is wiped clean with a cloth. *Liqueur d'expédition*, some sweetened wine, is added according to the degree of sweetness required. If a dry wine is required the bottle is simply topped up with similar wine from another bottle. New corks or stoppers are then pushed home and muselets fitted. (*See* SPARKLING WINE and FREEZING SOLUTIONS.)

It is an advantage to use crown caps or hollow-domed plastic stoppers during the bottle fermentation, since these collect and retain the sediment more effectively than the end of the cork.

DISTILLING When a wine is heated to the correct temperature the alcohol vaporizes with little or no vaporization of the water. In distilling, this vapour is collected and cooled to form a colourless almost odourless spirit depending on the type and efficiency of the still. There are, however, several varieties of alcohol, some of which, such as amyl and butyl, can be dangerous, even if consumed in relatively small quantities. The alcohol comes off in three stages during distillation. The French refer to the head, the heart and the tail, when describing the various alcohols that are produced, and they use only the heart. British distillers refer to fore-shots and feints to describe the undrinkable portions. Because it is illegal to distil without a licence and still more because it can be extremely dangerous, no further information on distilling will be given here.

DOSAGE During disgorgement a small amount of space is created by the removal of the sediment and loss of wine. This has to be filled by wine for a finished dry wine, or syrup for a sweet wine, plus grape spirit so that the balance of alcohol is maintained. This operation is called dosage. It is customary always to add just a little sugar, even for a dry sparkling wine. One that has absolutely no sugar is barely palatable. The amount of sugar to use depends on the sweetness required, but is unlikely to be less than 6 g per litre (1 oz per gallon) and could be much more. (*See also* DRY.)

Dosage is also used in the context of adding additional sugar during the process of fermentation of high-alcohol wines. A really active ferment is best obtained by starting with a somewhat lower specific gravity than that actually required, then adding two or three dosages of sugar syrup from time to time as the specific gravity falls. (*See also* PROLONGED FERMENTATION.)

DROSOPHILA MELANOGASTER *See* VINEGAR FLY.

DRY Means 'lack of' and in reference to wine is 'lack of sweetness' on the palate, not 'without sweetness'. The degree of sweetness that is lacking is relative to the norm for the type of wine, since no wines are completely without any sweetness. For instance a table wine with no detectable sweetness would be a dry table wine but a dessert wine with medium sweetness would be a dry dessert. Two very considerably different degrees of sweetness, but both dry. The actual degree of sweetness can also be masked by other factors, so that two wines with different sugar content, but having the same lack of sweetness on the palate, would both be called dry. In addition, as with degrees of sweetness, there are degrees of dryness relative to the norm of the wine type as indicated below. The first, Champagne, is a classic example, because the sugar content is measured and controlled by dosage with *liqueur d'expédition* (old wine and sugar).

CHAMPAGNE

Brut	0 to 1·5%	sugar by volume
Extra dry	1½ to 3%	sugar by volume
Sec (dry)	2 to 4%	sugar by volume
Demi-sec (semi-dry)	6 to 8%	sugar by volume
Doux (sweet)	8 to 10%	sugar by volume

APERITIF and OXIDISED SHERRY-TYPE WINES Drunk before or separate from a meal and dry, these wines are usually preferred slightly sweeter (less dry) than a table wine.

Sweet	–	Sweet
Dry	–	Slight sweetness
Extra dry	–	Lacking the sweetness of dry

TABLE WINES Usually drunk with the meat course of a meal they have a minimal sweetness.

Table	–	Minimal sweetness
Dry table	–	Lacking the sweetness of 'table'

DESSERT WINES These have to have considerable sweetness.

Dessert	–	Very sweet
Dry dessert	–	Sweet (less sweet than a dessert. Frequently a dessert that has been aged and has 'fed on the sugar' e.g. vintage Port)

EARTHENWARE Sometimes called stoneware, this is a term used to describe a vessel made of baked clay. In its basic state it is porous but when coated with a thin slip of salt glaze and baked again, the surface becomes impervious. Stoneware vessels are sometimes used as storage jars, because although they are heavy, they are easy to clean and fairly resistant to breakage. They keep out the light, act as good insulators for keeping the wine at an even temperature, and no loss occurs through evaporation, so that many winemakers prefer them to small casks. Wine stored in such jars however, can take longer to mature than wine stored in a cask. Stoneware jars are traditionally made with fawn- or stone-coloured bodies and brown shoulders.

The kind of slip used in coating pottery is important however, for in foreign countries and in this country until the turn of the century, lead was frequently used as a glaze. As a result of the action of the acids in the wine on the lead, poisonous salts are released into the wine. The salts are accumulative and the regular drinker of wine made in such crocks can suffer from lead-poisoning. Lead-coated vessels are not usually called stoneware but simply known as pottery jars. Usually they are also a brown or darker colour all over the jars.

EBULLISCOPE   An instrument for measuring the quantity of alcohol present in a liquid by observing the boiling point of the molecular weight of the alcohol.

EGG WHITE   An albuminous protein that combines with tannin to form an insoluble complex that precipitates and removes colloidal hazes from wine. For use *see* FINING.

ÉGRAPPAGE   The separation of the grapes from their stalks before pressing or being put into the fermentation vessel. Though first practised in the eighteenth century it is only during the last forty years that it has come into general use with grapes of high tannin content so as to reduce the astringency. The practice can vary. In Bordeaux it is widely used for high tannin grapes, but in some instances only part of the harvest is so treated. It depends on soil, variety of grape, maturity and the weather. Egrappage gives the wine more body, finesse and colour and there can be an increase of $\frac{1}{2}°$ of alcohol.

The stalks are not removed from grapes which otherwise make a flat, flabby wine, but left in so that their tannin will make the wine firm.

ÉGRAPPOIR   A machine for removing stalks and crushing grapes.

ELLAGIC ACID   A simple tannin, or polyphenol, that is one of the causes of astringency in wine. It readily combines with gelatine so that gelatine-fined wines are often less astringent after fining.

ENERGIZER   Compounds originally sold under various trade names to be added to slow, reluctant, or sticking fermentations to reactivate the yeast. They are more or less the same composition as the compounds sold as yeast nutrients but with the addition of vitamin B_1. Yeast nutrients plus vitamin B_1 can be successfully used as an energizer.

ENZYMES   It is believed that all forms of life exist by enzymes of one kind or another. Certainly man's body is known to produce many types, and there are probably many more as yet unknown. Yeast cells, too, live by the enzymes they secrete. Enzymes are catalysts produced by living organisms and each acts upon one specific substrate. As far as winemaking is concerned, these are protein (apo-enzyme) joined to an organic compound (co-enzyme) which effect a chemical change in a substance. Though the enzymes cause the chemical activity, they undergo no change themselves. They are specific in their action and only have to be present for the chemical change to occur. For example, when secreted by wine yeasts, the enzyme sucrase (invertase) causes sucrose to split into fructose and glucose. The enzymes of the zymase complex then cause the reduction of the sugar's fructose and glucose to alcohol and carbon dioxide. Each enzyme acts as a catalyst for one activity only and is specific for that purpose and no other. The amazing thing about enzymes is the stupendous amount of chemical reaction they can cause before becoming exhausted; and they are not dependent on the parent body. Enzymes of the zymase complex cause fermentation, long after the yeast cell that secreted them is dead.

Enzymes can be destroyed by heat and inactivated by freezing to 0 °C (32 °F) or below. Between the extremes, the rate of reaction increases with the rise in temperature but denaturing of protein also increases. Optimum fermentation temperatures are therefore determined by a balance between the two and these are around 15 °C (59 °F) for white wines and 22 °C (71·6 °F) for reds.

EPOXY RESIN   Used by winemakers as an adhesive cement for joints in wine containers made from asbestos, concrete or wood. It is inert to the acids and alcohols of the wine and imparts no flavour. It is also occasionally used partially to seal the exterior surface of a cask to slow down oxidation of the wine.

ESTERIFICATION   This is the production of esters in a wine. One reason for the softening of old wine is the acidity being reduced in the process of esterification.

ESTERS   These are compounds which are formed when the hydrogen of an acid is replaced by a hydro-carbon radical of the ethyl type. They are sweet-smelling compounds which come from the fruit and from redox reactions between acids and ethyl alcohol during maturation. They are responsible for the aroma/bouquet and flavour of wine. The fruit esters are volatile and can be driven off by heat both by heating the must or too high a fermentation temperature. The esters from maturation develop most from malic and succinic acids.

Spoilage yeast and bacteria can cause the formation of esters, such as excess ethyl acetate, which ruins wine.

ETHANOL   The chemical name of ethyl alcohol. It is normally used to refer to the synthesized spirit rather than to the alcohol of wine derived from yeast fermentation.

ETHEREAL   As the *Concise Oxford Dictionary* states, the word is generally used to mean 'heavenly; of unearthly delicacy of substance, character or appearance'. In physics and chemistry it means 'of or like ether'. When applied to wine it has a combination of these definitions. 'It is a wine of heavenly bouquet and character.' Naturally the term is only applied to a superb wine.

ETHYL ACETATE   This is the ester of ethyl alcohol and acetaldehyde and it has a smell akin to the 'pear drops' smell of nail varnish (amyl acetate). In very low concentrations it is pleasing and adds to the bouquet. In stronger concentrations it becomes unpleasant, as it does when a wine acetifies. The smell of excess ethyl acetate is an indication that the wine is being converted to vinegar. If the wine is sulphited at the rate of 100 ppm before the vinegar taint occurs, it can be saved. The dominance of the ethyl acetate will decrease with storage. Some wild yeasts capable of low ethyl alcohol fermentation produce an excess of ethyl acetate and for this reason are regarded as spoilage organisms.

ETHYL ALCOHOL   *See* ALCOHOL.

ETHYL PYROCARBONATE   Formed by the combination of carbon dioxide with ethyl alcohol during the bottle fermentation and storage of sparkling wine. Thus the size and rate of the bead formation in a glass is proportionate to the decomposition of the pyrocarbonate. The more pyrocarbonate formed in the wine, the longer the beads will rise.

EUPHORIA   A relaxed and general feeling of contentment induced by a glass or two of good wine. The mind is often very lively and the tongue even loquacious, but the emotions lose their inhibitions and the nerves their tensions, whilst the body attains a calmness and a satisfied feeling.

EVAPORATION   During maturation of a wine in cask, there is always a certain amount of evaporation. Much of it is no doubt due to simple water vapour, but undoubtedly in a humid climate at least, there is also some evaporation of alcohol as well. This space so formed in the cask, called ullage, must be filled frequently, every two weeks or so, either with wine of the same sort or with some grape spirit. Failure to do this, especially with light wine of 9 or 10% alcohol, will cause excess oxidation and flatness. In view of the problem of evaporation, it is best to mature only strong wine in cask and to store the casks in as cool and dry a place as possible.

EXHIBITING WINE   When you wish to enter wine in a Show, first obtain a copy of the schedule as early as possible. Carefully study the conditions of entry and decide in which classes you will enter wines. Send off your entry early, the earlier the better, and then begin to prepare your wines. Bear in mind that immediately after racking, the bouquet and flavour of a wine suffer some setback and need a while to recover—four weeks is often necessary. If the wine has to be filtered to give brilliance, the recovery period will be at least six to eight weeks. It is therefore necessary to bottle the wines in their show bottles early, with temporary tie-on labels for identification. The wines should be star-bright and free from any bits and pieces of cork and debris. The bouquet, aroma and flavour should be clean, vinous, subtly fruity or characteristic and, of course, without taint. The wine should be of good body and balance and according to type. It is pointless to enter a poor or a bad wine.

The next most important consideration to bear in mind, is the schedule regulations governing the Show. Make sure that the wine or wines that you wish to enter comply precisely with the regulations as to colour, sweetness, and type or ingredient. If there is any doubt consult the Show Secretary. Wines entered in the wrong class will not be adjudicated but marked N.A.S.—(Not according to schedule). The most common fault is the entry of sweetish wines in dry classes and *vice versa*. A dry wine will have a specific gravity relative to its acids and other contents and will lack sweetness. The sweetness of 'sweet' varies from palate to palate, the quantity of residual sugar and the acid content of the wine. The specific gravity reading is no certain indication. The wine should taste sweet.

Colour causes difficulty too, and there is sometimes doubt as to the placing of tawny and rosé wines. Unless specified to the contrary, tawny should be entered in white classes and rosé in red. Use only the type of bottles prescribed by the regulations and ensure that the corks are in perfect condition. Labels should be affixed as specified in the regulations and care should be taken to ensure that the gum is not smeared on the surrounding glass and that the label is stuck centrally between the two seams. Finally the bottles should be polished free from finger-prints and wrapped in tissue paper, ready for delivery at the proper time and place.

EXTRACTORS *See* JUICER and PRESSES.

EXTRACTS An extract is a preparation containing the active principle of a substance in concentrated form, which has been obtained by use of solvents that are then evaporated. Such are the concentrates which are sold for flavouring wines and liqueurs and supposedly producing imitations of particular commercial types; for example Vermouth extract for producing imitation Vermouth. They should be used according to the individual manufacturer's specific instructions.

The second meaning of extract is to draw forth or obtain by pressure, suction, leaching or other means. Such are the musts resulting from steeping, then straining and finally squeezing the pulp. Extracts are also made by fermentation of raw materials. Juices or saps obtained by pressing, heating or centrifuging are often referred to as extracts, but for these reference should be made to JUICES and JUICER.

FAREWELL *See* AFTERTASTE.

FAT A wine that has lots of body and is usually high in glycerol.

FERMENTATION The world, as we know it, continues by creation and decay. Without decay the accumulation of debris, dead plants, dead animals, in fact dead organic matter of all kinds, would so clutter the earth that life itself would be stifled. The decay is caused by bacteria, fungi and moulds; micro-organisms that break down the debris to elements and chemicals that will sustain further life as it is created. One stage of decay, a stage that is only one of a cycle in the overall process, is fermentation which causes effervescence, heat and a change of properties. Any chemical change which releases gas is, in fact, a fermentation. The decay of a pile of plants—a compost heap—is one form of fermentation, in which the plants are attacked by bacteria, gas released, heat generated and the plants converted to compost.

The production of wines and beers is also fermentation, although of another kind. This time it is the action of sugar fungi, a yeast of the type called *Saccharomyces*, which decays, or breaks down, the sugars of vegetable matter. This fermentation of sugar is but one stage in converting vegetable matter which contains sugar (e.g. fruit) from its complete form to chemicals and compost. After the *Saccharomyces* has fermented the juice, sap or extract, to wine, other yeasts and bacteria produce further fermentations that ultimately reduce the wine to carbon dioxide and water. This full process has only been understood in recent years, and with the knowledge has come better control of the production of wine and the prevention of spoilage during and after its production.

There was published in 1814 *A Treatise on Family Winemaking*, written by a somewhat pompous fellow of the name of Cushing. In it he wrote of vinous fermentation, 'This may be said to be a Divine Operation which the Omniscient Creator has placed in our cup of life, to transmute the fruits of the earth into wine for the benefit and comfort of His creatures.' This remark sums up how little was known about fermentation at that time. Earlier writers had referred to 'wild spirits' although the fermentation from the leavening of bread and the yeasting of ale had been known for centuries, possibly as far back as 7000 B.C. It has been considered that both civilization and beer originated in Egypt about 4000 B.C.: but there is strong evidence that the Egyptians learned the art of brewing from earlier civilizations of the Tigris and Euphrates valleys, where wild barley was converted to beer probably as early as 7000 B.C. In Babylon, as later in Egypt, the bakers were also the brewers, undoubtedly because both bread and beer have the same root—grain, water, yeast.

In 1837, Cagnard Latour in France and Schwann in Germany demonstrated that fermentation was caused by microscopic spherical bodies belonging to the vegetable world. There was an immediate reaction from chemists and biologists who believed that fermentation was caused by oxygen or by spontaneous generation. The general belief had in fact been that fermentation was the crucible of life. The great controversy was not settled until Louis Pasteur conducted his epic research work on sterilization and proved that a yeast cell that had been grown in a pure and sterile medium caused fermentation when introduced into a pasteurized beer wort. This proved beyond doubt that yeast was the cause.

Subsequent research workers, especially in France and Denmark, later proved that the actual cause of productive wine and beer fermentations were enzymes secreted by yeast that, acting as catalysts, reduced single sugars or mono-saccharides, to ethyl alcohol and carbon dioxide. Sucrose, the correct name for white sugar and a natural sugar found in fruits and plants, and maltose from grain are also involved. These, however, are di-saccharides, and cannot be directly fermented by the zymase complex of enzymes.

The sucrose which is present in a must, either from the raw materials, or added as white sugar, is hydrolysed into simple sugars by the enzyme sucrase, often called invertase. This enzyme, which is secreted by the *Saccharomyces* yeasts, invert the sucrose (white sugar) to glucose (grape sugar) and fructose (fruit sugar) which are simple sugars or mono-saccharides.

$$C_{12}H_{22}O_{11} + H_2O \qquad\qquad C_6H_{12}O_6 + C_6H_{12}O_6$$

sucrose + water $\diagup$ sucrase   glucose + fructose
(invertase)

The yeast also secretes other enzymes, called the zymase complex, which ferment the glucose and fructose to carbon dioxide and ethyl alcohol whilst releasing energy.

$$C_6H_{12}O_6 \longrightarrow 2\ CO_2 + 2C_2H_5OH + \ 15\cdot4\ kg\ cal$$

Glucose	zymase	carbon +	ethyl	+ large calories
or fructose	complex	dioxide	alcohol	of energy

The escaping carbon dioxide gas is the effervescence or bubbling which is called the visible signs of fermentation, the ethyl alcohol is the basic part of wine, and the large calories of energy are utilized by the yeast.

Maltose used in the brewing of beers is hydrolysed and fermented in exactly the same manner. The only difference is that it is the enzyme called maltase which hydrolyses the maltose to glucose only. The glucose is then fermented by the zymase complex as described above.

$$C_{12}H_{33}O_{11} + H_2O \longrightarrow C_6H_{12}O_6 + C_6H_{12}O_6$$

maltose + water   maltase   glucose + glucose

It was generally believed at one time, that all forms of life required oxygen as an energy source to exist. It was therefore argued that in a covered must the yeast obtained oxygen from sugar as a result of fermentation. This belief has persisted for a very long time and is still frequently stated. It is definite, however, that wine yeasts do not require oxygen as an energy source to exist. The energy they require is that released by the fermentation and they take no oxygen. It can be clearly seen from the fermentation formula given above that there is no free oxygen for the yeast to take.

Otto Myerhof conclusively proved in 1948 that yeast required oxygen only for reproduction; it can live without oxygen but will not reproduce itself. This oxygen is obtained from the air or from the oxygen dissolved in a solution. Thus the sole purpose of fermentation, as far as the yeast is concerned, is to provide itself with energy not oxygen.

It is interesting to note that in 1919 Otto Myerhof also showed that although complex organisms like human beings made efficient use of oxygen, they were capable of anaerobic glycolysis, i.e. the breaking down of sugars without air. He further showed that yeast and muscle possessed the same co-enzymes. This suggested, and the view has been strengthened by all research since, that the metabolic pathways of all organisms are essentially similar, having only minor differences. Under peaceful conditions human muscle obtains energy by complete conversion of glucose ending in water by utilizing oxygen. With exertion, sufficient oxygen is not available and extra energy is provided by the conversion of glucose to lactic acid without oxygen (anaerobic glycolysis), in exactly the same process as yeast obtains energy by converting glucose to alcohol. The only difference is that whilst yeast continues to alcohol, muscle stops one step short at lactic acid. This is fortunate for us otherwise we would become drunk every time we ran! The last conversion by yeast is a simple one producing little extra energy.

$$C_3H_6O_3 \longrightarrow C_2H_5OH + CO_2$$
lactic acid $\longrightarrow$ alcohol + carbon dioxide

The optimum conditions for maximum fermentation and the production of the best wines are: (1) the use of selected yeast; (2) the appropriate temperatures; (3) the correct balance of acids, nutrients and sugars, and (4) the control of air. (*See also* ACIDS, AIR CONTROL, NUTRIENTS, pH, SUGARS, TEMPERATURES, and YEAST for full details of each.)

The duration of a fermentation of wine under optimum conditions is approximately three weeks, but for no apparent reason it may continue for many weeks longer. Unfavourable conditions in one form or another can protract the time to six or nine months, or even longer.

If the conditions are favourable for them, the wine, either during fermentation, or when stable, can be attacked by various micro-organisms. These continue the process of decay, either by oxidation or fermentation. All, from the winemaker's point of view, are spoilage actions which cause the wine to have off-flavours, develop hazes, become vinegar or, finally, to be reduced to carbon dioxide and water. The one exception is the malo-lactic fermentation which is permitted to occur in wines of high acidity in order that the acidity may be reduced, but even so, the wines can be spoilt by a mousy taste. Prevention of spoilage fermentations is achieved simply by the exclusion of air and the use of sulphite.

FERMENTATION OF SUGAR TO ALCOHOL

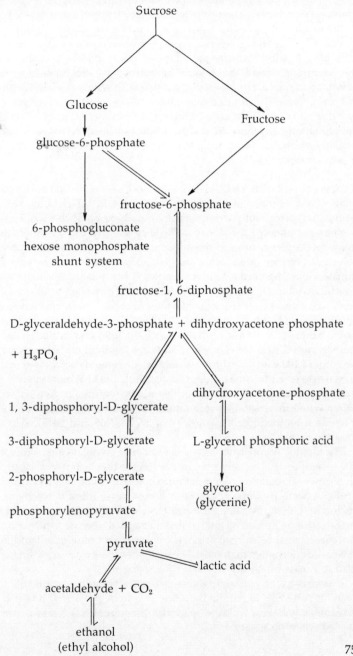

Sucrose

Glucose

Fructose

glucose-6-phosphate

fructose-6-phosphate

6-phosphogluconate
hexose monophosphate
shunt system

fructose-1, 6-diphosphate

D-glyceraldehyde-3-phosphate + dihydroxyacetone phosphate

+ H_3PO_4

1, 3-diphosphoryl-D-glycerate

dihydroxyacetone-phosphate

3-diphosphoryl-D-glycerate

L-glycerol phosphoric acid

2-phosphoryl-D-glycerate

glycerol
(glycerine)

phosphorylenopyruvate

pyruvate

lactic acid

acetaldehyde + CO_2

ethanol
(ethyl alcohol)

Fermentation of sugars in a solution often produces frothing and bubbling. At the higher temperatures the bubbling can be so vigorous that the must appears to boil. Hence the word fermentation from *ferver*—to boil.

Some wines have visible signs of fermentation in the spring after their production. This has given rise to the pretty and romantic idea that wine acts in sympathy with its parent plant, e.g. gooseberry wine starts fermenting again with the blossoming of the gooseberry bush. However, it is not that they act in sympathy, but that both activities are the result of the same factor—a rise in temperature. Wines kept in a constant temperature do not develop the 'sympathetic' fermentation. These spring fermentations are more frequently produced by enzymes and micro-organisms, such as lactobacilli, than by yeast fermentation of sugar. (*See also* TEMPERATURE.)

FERMENTATION CHAMBER   In most residences in cool climates there are a number of suitably warm places in which wine can be fermented successfully. In others there may be no such place, or the winemaker may for the sake of efficiency wish to use a fermentation chamber. A glance around the house may reveal an existing cupboard which can be converted for the purpose, or a cupboard can be specially constructed. The needs are quite simple. There must be adequate room in which to stand the vessel of fermenting wine on a shelf or false bottom with space underneath for a small heater or electric bulb, which is wired to a thermostat. If bulbs are used, those sold as Rough Duty are preferable for one will outlast several ordinary light bulbs and, although dearer initially, are cheaper over a period and save frequent replacing. Heaters or bulbs of 100 watts are the most suitable for general use but two, wired in series to give the same rating, will distribute the heat more evenly. For such purpose two of 200 watts each would be required to give 100 watts when wired in series. It is recommended that the thermostat be set to provide a temperature between 19 and 21 °C (65 and 70 °F). (*See also* TEMPERATURE.)

The method of construction of a new chamber is not of importance, but the insulation is. The better the insulation the less heat is lost, resulting in a slower fluctuation of temperature and considerably lower running costs. A well-insulated chamber will cost very little for electricity to maintain the required temperature. The cleanest, easiest to use and the most efficient insulating material is expanded styrene which can be purchased in sheets or squares (ceiling tiles). Aluminium foil and fibre board are alternative materials. The door should be a closely fitting one, also to prevent heat loss.

If there is any choice, a situation that does not require reaching high, or standing on steps to handle the vessels, is to be preferred. It is also an advantage to have a working space nearby on which the vessels can be placed when necessary.

FERMENTATION LOCK *See* AIRLOCK.

FERMENTING ON THE PULP *See* PULP FERMENTATION.

FILTERING There are several methods of filtering but they all follow the same principle, that of passing wine through a medium with pores small enough to remove suspended matter but not fine enough to remove the molecules of bouquet, colour or flavour.

Commercial filtration is widely practised especially at the bottling stage. Here, large volumes of wine are processed by special techniques, not practical with small volumes, and the wine suffers little or no ill effect. The practical methods for small volumes of wine can cause some loss of bouquet or flavour highlights, or cause over-oxidation. However, such wines if allowed to stand for a while usually recover considerably, but not always completely, by the normal chemical reactions of maturing. Tainting can occur from the filter medium, whatever is used, and the taint is difficult to remove. Furthermore, infection can occur in some wines in which sulphite and/or inert gas have not been used, although these can also prevent or minimize over-oxidation.

Loss of bouquet and flavour highlights are due to dispersal of volatile esters but some loss of flavour can result from the use of asbestos pulp due to its absorptive action. Over-oxidation results from slow filtration because the wine is for so long in contact with air that it consequently forms aldehydes. Against this, a single filtration that is too rapid, although minimizing oxidation, may not clear a wine, and the filtration may have to be repeated two or three times with increasing liability to over-oxidation.

Tainting results from the use of a filter medium that has not been cleaned properly. All mediums carry some taint and it is necessary to remove this before they are used with wines. Hot or cold water should be passed through the medium, in the filter or out of it, until no taint can be detected upon tasting the filtered water.

There are different methods and types of filters as shown by the following:

Gravity filtering This is the passing of wine through a filter solely by the pull of gravity. This method is generally slow and causes the higher risk of over-oxidation and infection. The risk can be reduced by first filling the receiving vessel with carbon dioxide from an active fermentation and by adding sulphite to the filtered wine.

(a) FILTER BAGS These are conical-shaped and usually made of felt, nylon, or strong, close-woven cloth. Filter bags are used only for small volumes of wine. They are much faster than other gravity filters because their pores are larger. Although they produce a clearer wine, they rarely produce a bright wine. Nevertheless they can be very useful for reducing the haze in a 'muddy wine' and for removing the larger particles before the use of a fine filter. Without this assistance fine filters can be rapidly clogged. They are also useful for removing pulp from a fermentation.

In use, the bag is suspended from a ring or from a stand with the receiving vessel below. If the vessel has a small neck a large funnel is inserted into it. The wine is simply poured into the bag and allowed to run through.

(b) FUNNEL and FILTER MEDIUM This is the simplest form of fine filtering and used only for very small volumes of wine. A large funnel is inserted into a jar and into the funnel neck is placed a wad of cotton wool. An asbestos or cellulose slurry is then poured into the funnel. When the water has drained away and a mat is formed, it is ready for the wine. Frequently, something is placed over the mat to prevent its being disturbed when the wine is poured in. In place of the cotton wool and slurry a folded filter paper may be used.

(c) FILTER TUBES These are used by amateurs for polishing a wine when bottling it, especially when bottling for an exhibition. They are fibre tubes, either fine, medium or coarse, which are fitted at one end with a plastic cap to prevent the wine from by-passing the filter medium and at the other end with a plastic tube. The fibre tube is placed in the wine and the wine is caused to flow through it in the same way as through a siphon. The open end of the plastic tube is inserted into an empty bottle which is placed at a lower level than the wine being filtered. These filter tubes polish a bottle of wine surprisingly quickly.

(d) CONTINUOUS FILTERING This is manufactured for the amateur but it can easily be made by a handyman. It consists of a sealable chamber filled at the top with one long inlet tube and one short tube that can be sealed. From the bottom is one long delivery tube. The filter medium consists of asbestos or cellulose pulp/powder, or filter pads or discs. The medium is placed inside the chamber before it is sealed.

The filter works as follows. The long inlet tube is placed in the wine and the delivery tube is placed in an empty vessel at a lower level. Air is drawn out of the chamber via the short tube and causes the wine to be siphoned. When the chamber is almost full of wine the short tube is closed. The wine then passes through the filter and runs into the empty vessel. The wine continues to run until it has all passed through the filter.

Vacuum filtering This is a rapid method of filtering small volumes of wine. Basically it is a Buckner funnel with a sinter which is fitted into a vacuum flask with a rubber bung. The flask is connected to a vacuum water pump with polythene tubing. A filter paper (a slurry is sometimes used) is fitted over the sinter and the funnel is filled with wine. The water pump is then fitted to a tap which is turned on. The running water draws air from the flask causing a vacuum which sucks the wine through the filter paper.

Pressure filtering   This is the method used for large volumes of wine and the equipment used is sometimes called a filter press. It consists of a tank that can be pressurized, connected to a filter bed, usually consisting of several divided layers or plates; in turn this is connected to a receiving vessel or to a bottling machine. The wine is poured into the tank and put under pressure by the injection of carbon dioxide, nitrogen or a similar inert gas. If the receiving vessel or bottles are flushed with the same gas, infection or over-oxidation very rarely occurs and there is minimal loss of volatiles.

FILTERING and FINING   A wine must have clarity and brilliance to have eye appeal and be attractive. Properly racked wines nearly always fall bright naturally after standing for a while in a cool place, and there is considerable advantage in allowing them to do so. Some wines, however, persistently remain hazy even after several rackings, and it is these wines that have to be subjected to other means of clarification. They should first be tested for pectin or starch hazes (details given under those words), and if they show positive they must be treated with the appropriate enzymes. If the cause of the haze is neither pectin nor starch the wines are subjected to fining or filtering which are two very different methods of achieving the same object—clarification.

Neither fining nor filtering adds anything to a wine but if the processes are not properly carried out they may detract from the flavour, bouquet or quality, remove colour or even cause further hazes. Care must therefore be exercised to ensure that the most appropriate method is used, and that it is used correctly, although the choice may depend on the facilities available. Filtering is the most suitable method for removing suspended particles of matter but is not so suitable for removing colloidal hazes, whilst fining is excellent for causing the precipitation of colloids. A hazy wine is therefore tested to decide whether it should be filtered or fined. A small amount (a glassful is sufficient) is passed through a No. 1 Whatman filter paper. If the filtered sample is star-bright, filtering is the answer. If it remains hazy the cause is colloidal and fining is the recommended remedy. Colloidal hazes can be removed by filtering but only in conjunction with heating or chilling. Heating the wine to about 60 °C (140 °F) for two minutes causes coagulation of the colloidal particles. Clarification is then mainly by absorption of the colloids on the surface of the filter fibres. This method results in loss of body and character in the wine. Lowering of the temperature to near 0 °C (32 °F) denatures the colloids, and filtering through horizontal filter presses with pressure-plate filters removes them. There is no loss of body or character with this process.

Wines which haze after falling bright invariably do so from microbial

79

activity. The answer to this hazing is not filtering or fining but the immediate use of sulphite. If the wine remains hazy after sulphiting then filtering or fining can be considered. (*See also* FILTERING, FINING.)

FINESSE   A word used to describe the subtlety of flavour in a finished wine. A wine totally lacking in finesse might be described as coarse. Experienced wine tasters use an extensive vocabulary in their description of wines. A wine with great finesse, for example, might also be described as having personality or individuality or breed or distinction.

FINING   Fining has been practised since Roman times but it is only within very recent years that its working has been understood. There are two forms of fining and the most common is the clarification of wine by the addition of an agent that causes precipitation, or physical fining. The other is purification by use of an agent, or chemical fining.

Clarification   The sub-microscopic particles that make up colloidal hazes have a minute electrical charge which is either negative or positive depending on the particular colloid. All the particles causing a haze have the same charge and repel each other in the same way as poles of a magnet repel each other. By this action they remain in suspension. When a fining agent with an opposite charge is added there is mutual attraction. The particles agglomerate and their combined weight is sufficient for them to fall by gravitation to the bottom and the wine is cleared.

If an excess of a fining agent is added, the colloidal particles will be neutralized, but the electrical charge of the fining agent in excess will increase the haze instead of removing it. Herein lies the reason for TRIAL FININGS, to ascertain the best agent for good clarification and the minimum quantity that will clear the wine to prevent over-fining.

Clarification also results from the use of albuminous substances that having amino or imino groups establish hydrogen bonds with tannin. A protein–tannin complex is formed which coagulates and precipitates, taking with it the suspended particles. Tannin in the wines is essential and is the reason for red wines having been more successfully fined than white wines in the past.

There are many different fining agents and the following are only those in most common use.

(a) ALBUMEN (ALBUMINOUS PROTEINS)   Used in the form of blood or egg white the use of which are detailed separately below.

(b) BENTONITE   Negative charged and most suitable for fining wine with hazes due to protein and colouring matter. One difficulty with its use is lumping when added direct to wine. This is overcome by using a 5% suspension. Into each 100 ml of wine or water 5 g of bentonite is slowly added whilst being vigorously stirred or whisked. The slurry is then rubbed through a fine sieve and left standing for 24 hours when it is again vigorously stirred or whisked. The required amount of the 5% suspension to clear 5 litres of wine is generally between 20 ml and 100 ml.

A bentonite gel is now available which is much easier to use.

(c) BLOOD   Positive charged. Best results are obtained with red wines, particularly those that are harsh from an excess of tannin, because of the interaction of blood with tannin. It does not react so well in white wines even in those to which tannin has been added for the purpose of fining. There is also the disadvantage of very easily over-fining and the use of blood is now declining.

Fresh blood is used at the rate of between 2 and 4 ml per 5 litres of wine. The rate of dried blood, which can be readily stored, is between 0·25 g and 1 g per litre.

(d) CASEIN   Pure casein is for practical purposes insoluble in water and wine and has to be dissolved in an alkali. Two methods are in general use for doing this:

(i) 5 ml of strong ammonia is added to 100 ml of water and 6 g casein is then dissolved in it. The solution is afterwards boiled until no odour of ammonia is detected in the steam. The volume is then increased to 300 ml by the addition of water and results in a near pure 2% casein solution.

(ii) 0·5 g of sodium bicarbonate is dissolved in 100 ml water, 2 g of casein is stirred in and produces a 2% casein solution.

The salt, sodium or potassium caseinate, will dissolve in water and 2 g dissolved in 100 ml water makes a 2% solution.

Casein is best used for white wines as it will remove colour from reds. The dosage is between 12·5 and 50 ml of 2% solution per 5 litres of wine. Milk can be used instead of casein as detailed below.

Reaction of casein is with tannin and it is normal to add the same amount of tannin with the casein, i.e. 1 g tannic acid or grape tannin with 50 ml of 2% casein solution. (*See also* FINING, (2) Purification.)

(e) EGG-WHITE   Positive charged. Reacts with tannin and is therefore used in high-tannin wines or ones to which tannin is added for fining. Over-fining can easily occur as between 5 and 10 fresh egg-whites will fine 500 litres of wine. Thus one egg-white is not suitable for use in less than 50 litres. It is first beaten into a froth or whisked in 1 to 2 litres of wine before being thoroughly stirred into the bulk.

Dried egg-white, crystalline albumen, is preferable for use in less than 50 litres of wine. A 1% solution is made by dissolving 1 g in 100 ml water and a trial fining made to ascertain the minimum amount required to clear the wine. The correct dry weight is then calculated and accurately weighed for the bulk. This quantity is dissolved in a little wine before being thoroughly stirred into the bulk.

(f) GELATINE Positive charged. Forms a hydrogen bond with tannin which must also be added to low-tannin wines.

Gelatine is first soaked in cold water until it swells into a glutinous mass and then dissolved in a little hot, but not boiling, water. If the water is boiling it will denature the gelatine. It is normally used as a 1% solution, i.e. 1 g gelatine soaked in a little cold water for several hours, then the total volume made up to 100 ml with hot water. Use it in conjunction with tannin in trial finings. It can be added direct to bulk wine after soaking and dissolving at the rate of 0·5 g or 50 cm² leaf per 5 litres of wine. (*See also* FINING (2) Purification.)

(g) ISINGLASS Positive charged. As 30 g could be sufficient to clear 250 litres of wine, isinglass is not used for fining less than 25 litres of wine. Up to 6 g per 25 litres can be used by first adding 3 g and if the wine does not clear, adding another 3 g. The total of 6 g per 25 litres should not be exceeded.

Isinglass is now rarely used commercially. For use in the home, isinglass is first powdered and then soaked for 12 hours in a little water. It is then rubbed through a fine sieve into the wine which is afterwards whisked to ensure a fine suspension.

(h) MILK A simple source of casein which requires no preparation and has long been used for fining. It is best used for white wines and requires the addition of tannin. (*See* Casein page 81.) Trial finings are made by adding 0·5 ml, 1 ml, 1·5 ml and 2 ml of milk to one of each of four 100 ml samples of wine. Ten times the quantity of milk giving the best clarification is the amount of milk to be added for each litre of hazy wine.

(i) PROPRIETARY FININGS There are now a considerable number marketed and are mostly compound preparations. They should be used in accordance with the details supplied by the manufacturers, but trial finings are advisable to ensure that over-fining does not occur.

(j) TANNIN This itself is not a fining agent but is necessary for reaction with many agents and is, therefore, included here. For trial finings and for additions to bulk wines it is normal to use a 1% solution. This is 1 g tannic acid BP or grape tannin, dissolved in 100 ml of water or wine.

Purification The common agents for purification fining are:

(a) BLUE FININGS Used by skilled chemists to remove copper and iron contamination and taint. It is the addition of a very carefully predetermined quantity of potassium ferrocyanide to wine. It complexes with iron to form the dye Prussian Blue which deposits and the iron is replaced by potassium. With copper the deposit is cupric ferrocyanide (chocolate brown) and the copper is again replaced by potassium. The metallic haze is removed and also the taint, as potassium does not cause taint.

This fining must be carried out by a skilled chemist as a slight excess of potassium ferrocyanide in the acid conditions of wine could produce traces of potassium cyanide which is a deadly poison. Amateurs should never attempt Blue fining.

With the same action, but simpler in use, is a patent compound called Cufex. A further fining with gelatine and tannin is usually made after fining with Blue fining or the use of Cufex.

(b) CARBON   Used for the removal of off-flavours or to reduce colour, but its use requires laboratory facilities. Very careful trial finings have to be made to ascertain the exact dose as an excess results in a colourless water-like liquid and a considerable loss of flavour. The grade which is used is that which will not contaminate with iron and is as pure as possible.

(c) CASEIN   Used under controlled conditions after trial finings as a decolourizer without the disadvantage of also removing some flavour. Used as a 2% solution, preparation details of which are given under FINING (1) Clarification (d) Casein.

(d) GELATINE   A wine that has an excess astringency from ellagic and gallic acids is fined with gelatine to remove the astringency. Can also be used to reduce other tannin content when there is an excess. Should too much tannin be removed it is replaced by the addition of tannic acid BP or grape tannin, without ill effect in the wine.

(e) MILK   Used to lighten dark wines instead of casein given on previous page.

(f) SULPHITE   Commonly regarded as an inhibitor it is also a purifier and a minor fining agent. When used in the normal manner of 50 to 150 ppm it inhibits micro-organisms and removes bacterial hazes, reduces or helps to prevent over-oxidation and assists clearing by neutralizing some of the electrical charges of colloids.

FIRM   A wine that has sufficient tannin and acid to give it vigour. The opposite to flabby.

FIXED ACIDITY and FIXED ACIDS   The total acids less the volatile. The major fixed acids are citric, malic, and tartaric, which are important constituents of wine, not only for taste, but because they can help to protect wine from spoilage and help maintain the colour. Citric acid can be attacked by various bacteria to produce acetic acid (volatile acid).

FLAT   A way of describing wines that have lost their life. Similarly, a wine that has been imperfectly corked in bottle or left in a jar or cask not quite full will have lost its life, become over-oxidized and will taste flat. It is a taste of nothingness and a lack of vitality and life.

FLAVONES *See* ANTHOXANTHINS.

FLAVOUR The combination of smell, taste and texture. The appreciation of wine is by the three senses of smell, taste and touch (*see also*
SMELL and TASTES) functioning in combination to produce the flavour.
Flavour is therefore the result of the balance in a wine by which its quality
is judged. The better the balance of the three the greater is the quality of a
wine; the greater the imbalance, the poorer the quality.

FLOATERS Odd bits of debris from fruit pulp, filtering medium,
vessels, funnels, casks, corks etc., which find their way into a finished
bottle of wine. The wine is usually brilliantly clear but when the bottle is
moved the odd piece or pieces of matter float up from the punt. Not
usually injurious to the wine but the cause of lost marks in a bottle
submitted in a competition.

FLOCCULENT Resembling flocks or tufts of wool. When a wine is
clearing the yeast cells usually congregate in visible groups, together
with portions of pulp debris and the like and slowly sink to the bottom of
the vessel. A cloudy wine that has been treated sometimes shows the
insoluble matter flocculating and precipitating. When a sediment is said
to be flocculent it means that it is loose, probably fluffy, easily disturbed.
It rises in the wine to cloud it with the least movement of the vessel.
Yeasts which produce flocculent sediments make efficient racking
extremely difficult.

FLOGGER *See* CORK FLOGGER.

FLOR A Latin word meaning flower. A journalist who obviously
never visited the town of Jerez in southern Spain once described the
Sherry flor as 'a small blue flower that grew in the vineyards and was
strewn on the grapes at the vintage'!
   A 'flor' has no connection with flowers as such and is, in fact, a yeast
film or skin formed on the surface of a wine. The word 'flor' is often used
as an abbreviation meaning the Sherry 'flor', which is a surface fermenting yeast, now named *Saccharomyces beticus*, although the 'flor' contains
pichia, acetobacter and other organisms in symbiosis. The flavour that
develops in 'flor' Sherry is mainly due to the pichia. The film quickly
forms on Sherry if the conditions are favourable, and in one month will
be approximately 3 mm thick, almost pure white and irregularly wrink-
led all over. It will remain for many years if undisturbed. In the spring
and autumn it attains its thickest and purest white, but during the
summer and winter it becomes thinner, due to dying cells dropping off
and not being replaced; their colour also changes to grey. This is the
result of near correct temperatures in spring and autumn and either too
hot or too cold in summer and winter in the above-ground bodegas. As
the alcohol content of the wine rises, the 'flor' becomes thinner and darker

and is finally killed by the alcohol. It then drops to the bottom of the wine.

A very similar 'flor' which is thought by some experts to be produced by the same organisms is the Arbois yeast.

The Sherry and Arbois 'flors' should not be confused with 'flowers of wine' caused by *Candida mycoderma*, a spoilage yeast, or with the thick leathery pellicle produced by vinegar bacteria.

The conditions of a growth for the Sherry 'flor' as stated by Fornachon, *Studies on a Sherry Flor*, are that the sugar should have all been fully fermented (i.e. the wine is dry), the tannin content less than 0·01%, pH between 3·1 and 3·4, sulphur dioxide concentration about 100 ppm and the depth of wine about 24 in, kept under cotton wool plugs at a temperature of 20°C (68°F). The wine should not be shaken or disturbed.

FLOWERS Scented petals and florets picked free from stalks are an excellent source of aroma which, when blended with a good white wine, can be delightful to the nose. In most instances they also produce an individual, attractive and pleasant flavour. The more pungent and strongly odorous flowers are used in small quantities. Elderflowers, for example, have an overpowering perfume and never more than one pint (half a litre) of loose petals should be used for one gallon (5 litres) of wine. Smaller quantities often produce an even better wine. The usual methods of extraction are by macerating in wine or by adding to a fermentation. On the other hand heavily scented rose petals are best used in large quantities as they are only 'washed' and not macerated or fermented so as to avoid a 'cabbagy' taste in the wine. The petals are placed in a sealable container, covered with water, thoroughly shaken two or three times during a half hour and then strained. The petals are discarded. More petals are washed in the liquor and treated as before. The 'washing' of petals in the liquor is repeated until the liquor contains sufficient extract. The liquor is then added to a must about to be fermented.

Flowers provide nothing more than aroma and flavour, but make excellent additions to otherwise dull sweet wines. All flowers from bulbs should be avoided.

FLOWERS OF WINE A white film appearing on wine exposed to air, possibly due to a poorly fitting cork or bung. The most common form, appearing on low-alcohol wines, is *Candida mycoderma*, commonly known as 'flowers of wine'. It has a thinnish, whitish, powdery appearance and breaks up as soon as the bottle or container is moved. The fungus (it is actually a spoilage yeast) reduces alcohol to carbon dioxide and water. Left long enough the wine becomes off-flavoured water. The use of sulphite and/or the exclusion of air will prevent an infection. Either can stop an attack after it has started.

FOAM *See* MOUSSE.

FOILS These are thin, suitably coloured, soft metal caps which fit snugly over the neck of the bottle to hide the cork and the gap between the wine and the cork. They give the bottle of wine a professional finish and help to seal out air.

FOREIGN BODIES Any unwanted pieces of debris in a bottle of wine, such as cork dust, small hairs, specks of filtering medium and the like. (*See also* FLOATERS.)

FORTIFICATION The addition of alcohol to wine. There are different ways of doing this, the most common being the addition of *eau de vie*, grape spirit or Polish spirit. The addition of commercial brandy includes the addition of the flavour of brandy and this is usually noticeable in the fortified wine. The addition of plain spirit enables the alcohol to be increased without the addition of extraneous flavours. Certain wines such as, for example, Port and Sherry, are always fortified to improve the keeping and travelling qualities of the wine as well as the flavour, but in the case of Port, the fortifying, in the first instance, is to inhibit further fermentation whilst the grape juice is only partially fermented.

When fortifying a wine it is important to maintain the balance of sweetness, acidity, tannin, flavour and body with the increased quantity of alcohol, otherwise the wine will simply have a burning taste.

When it is decided to add alcohol to a wine it is important first to know fairly accurately the alcoholic strength of the spirit being used to fortify the wine. The spirit will be marked as so many degrees proof. This can readily be transferred to percentage alcohol by volume by dividing the degrees proof by 1·75 (multiply by 4 and divide by 7). When fortifying a wine it is advantageous to use a Pearson's square as follows:

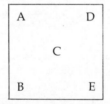

In the corner marked A enter the alcohol content of the spirit being used in fortification.
In the corner marked B write the alcohol content of the wine to be fortified.
In the centre marked C write the alcohol content that you wish to obtain.
In the corner marked D write the difference between C and B.
Finally, in the corner marked E, write the difference between C and A.
The proportion D to E is the proportion of spirit that you will need to add.

For example, assume a wine to have an alcohol content of 14% by volume and the spirit to be 100° proof, that is 57% alcohol by volume (100 divided by 1·75 = 57%). Assume also, a finished wine of 22% alcohol. Then:

$A = 57$
$B = 14$
$C = 22$
$D = C - B = 8$
$E = A - C = 35$

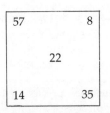

Therefore, it is necessary to use 8 parts of spirit to 35 parts of wine to achieve the desired fortification, or about 1 bottle of spirit to 4½ bottles of wine.

FRAPPÉ This means cold rather than chilled and is the accustomed temperature for serving white wines. Ice should never be added to wine as it dilutes the wine with water as it dissolves. Most white wines need crisping by cooling to a temperature of 12 °C (54 °F). It is usually preferable to stand them in a refrigerator for at least an hour, although they can be cooled more quickly by standing them in an ice bucket for ten minutes or so. Rosé wines as well as tawny wines are also better when served frappé rather than chambré (room temperature).

FREEZING SOLUTIONS Suitable freezing agents for *dégorgement* consist of intimate mixtures as given below. It is important that crushed ice is broken down into fine pieces, the finer the better. The container for the mixture should be well insulated with expanded polystyrene, fibreglass wool or the like, to prolong the freezing action.

3 parts common salt (sodium chloride)	10 parts crushed ice or snow
77 parts methylated spirit	73 parts crushed ice or snow
methylated spirit	solid carbon dioxide (dry ice)
	broken into small pieces*

* *Note*: If solid carbon dioxide comes into contact with skin it will cause 'cold burn'. Handle it with tongs and wear gloves while doing so.

FRET To undergo a secondary fermentation. A wine that has been fermented and racked and put into store occasionally starts to fret some months later; a small ring of bubbles appears and the wine ferments very slowly. This is often good wine to use when blending, since it will help to homogenize the constituent wines by refermenting them all.

FROTHING An upsurge of bubbles, cellulose tissue and debris, or fruit pulp, usually at the very beginning of fermentation. The vigorous fermentation, when there is plenty of air available to enable the yeast to reproduce itself rapidly, often causes the tiny particles of pulp in the must to be lifted up by the bubbles of carbon dioxide and to froth over. Frothing may also occur during the initial stage of fermentation even when there is no pulp included in the must. The exact cause is not certain, but the presence of excess pectins is probably one answer as frothing occurs less frequently from a must to which pectin-destroying enzymes have been added. An obvious precaution with all musts is not to fill the fermentation vessel too full initially, and then to top it up after the frothing has died down, or to use an over-size vessel for the initial fermentation.

Frothing can also occur when precipitated chalk is added to an acid must. The vigorous reaction causes a lifting up of the liquid and minute particles by the rapidly escaping gases; it dies down quickly as the chemical reaction slows down.

Another form of frothing occurs when sugar crystals are added to a ferment. The falling crystals release the imprisoned carbon dioxide which escapes with a sudden upward rush. Frothing may also occur if a sugar syrup or even a concentrated grape syrup is added too quickly to a must. Sugar in any form is best added very slowly.

Sparkling wine froths when the cork is released and the imprisoned carbon dioxide rushes out in big bubbles, carrying some wine around each bubble.

FRUCTOSE The common fruit sugar of the same atomic combination ($C_6H_{12}O_6$) as glucose, although in a different structure. It combines with glucose to form sucrose which is the familiar granulated sugar common to every household. Like glucose, it is readily fermentable into alcohol and carbon dioxide by the enzymes of the zymase complex which are secreted by wine yeast.

Fructose is also known as LAEVULOSE (*laevers*—meaning left) because it causes a plane of polaroid light to rotate to the left. (*See also* GLUCOSE.) Fructose is more readily fermented by Sauternes yeast than is glucose. The opposite of all other wine yeasts.

FRUIT Fruits, other than grapes, when used for winemaking, should, whenever possible, be of the most suitable variety and of the best quality if good results are to be obtained. They should be fully ripe, but not over-ripe, with the exception of pears which should be used while still firm just before being ripe, and gooseberries which can be used green. As yet, very little is known about the best varieties of the different fruits to use, but, in general, the varieties with high acid and sugar content and not too strong a flavour are best. This often means cooking varieties. Even so, better results are obtained by blending together different varieties of the same fruit, or even of different fruits. Some grapes may also be added, either fresh or dried or as concentrated juice to improve the vinosity, especially of table wines.

Damaged or bruised fruit should not be used, since it may have developed moulds and the oxidized parts could affect the flavour of the finished wine. Fruit should always be washed to remove the dust or grime. The stones from fruit such as peaches, apricots, plums etc. should always be removed and discarded. The kernels contain hydrocyanic acid which is released into the wine when they are broken. This imparts a bitter and almondy flavour. When crushing other fruits care should be taken not to split the pips causing bitterness or off-flavours. All fruit should be liquidized, crushed or broken up in some way, so that the juices can be more readily extracted. Strongly flavoured, acid or bitter fruits, such as blackcurrants, elderberries, figs etc. should be used in moderation, preferably in conjunction with some other fruits.

FRUIT FLY *See* VINEGAR FLY.

FRUITINESS This is the name given to the aroma or flavour of fruit noticeable in wines whether made from grapes or from other fruits. It is pleasant and even desirable in moderation, but in excess the flavour can become unpleasant and the aroma too pungent. A wine that contains too much of the original fruit flavour can be unattractive and in a dry wine this is more noticeable than in a sweet wine. In the best wines the fruitiness is subtle.

FULL-BODIED A wine that is described as full-bodied is one that contains a reasonable amount of alcohol and a high extract content. The latter is due to the condition and quality of the fruit, the weather during growth and ripening, the soil, fertilizers, other environmental growing conditions, the degree of ripeness at time of picking and the subsequent treatment. From grapes especially, and in general for other fruit, the hotter the growing conditions the more full-bodied the wine. Thus wines from the southern European grape growing areas are usually more full-bodied than those from the north.

Full-bodied commercial wines are often also high in alcohol (then correctly referred to as 'full-bodied and heavy' or 'fat') because of the higher sugar content of the grapes. It is, however, possible to have a wine which has a high extract content (full-body) but low-alcohol content which would be described as 'full-bodied but light'. The alcohol content in relation to full-body in country wines in the British Isles is dependent on the added sugar. (*See also* HEAVY and LIGHT.)

FUMOSITY The state of giving off fumes. Applied to wines it means the heady vapours that come off some wines when poured out. Notably a Port wine, for example. A hot punch usually has great fumosity too, and the vapours and esters need to be inhaled with caution since they can make one dizzy.

FUNGI One of the main groups of the phallophyta which is in turn a major division of the plant kingdom. The fungus plant is not differentiated into root and shoot and it may be a single cell, a filament of cells or even a complicated branching multi-cellular structure. There are thought to be at least 100,000 different species of fungi, among which are the moulds and yeasts.

All are without chlorophyll and are unable to photosynthesize (produce sugar from carbon dioxide and sunlight). Amongst the fungi are Ascomycetes which includes wine as well as spoilage yeasts, *Botrytis Cinerea* which causes 'grey' and 'noble rot' on grapes; *Oidium* (powder mildew) which ruins fruit for wine; and *Clado-sporium cellerae* which grows where wine is stored. (*See also* BOTRYTIS CINEREA, MILDEW and MOULDS.)

FUNGICIDES Chemicals or chemical compounds which prevent fungi attacking plants and fruit and/or kill the fungi. They are used as powders or sprays. Possibly the earliest fungicide used was copper sulphate whose fungicidal properties were discovered by accident. A vigneron sprayed his vines with copper sulphate to stain them blue in an endeavour to prevent his grapes being stolen. The sprayed vines stayed free of mildew whilst the unsprayed vines were ruined. Compounds of copper followed such as Bordeaux mixture, Cheshunt Compound and Collodial copper. With the shortage of copper as a result of the war, substitutes had to be found. These were Captan and Dithane which were more effective in many ways than the copper compounds. Since then the systemic fungicides, Benomyl and Dimethoate, have been formulated and marketed. These latter penetrate into the plant sap and give greater protection.

FUNNEL An inverted cone without a base but with the point extended to form a neck. The neck is inserted into the vessel to be filled and the liquid is poured into the broad end of the cone. Originally funnels were made from metal which was sometimes enamelled but now they are almost exclusively made from plastic, which is impervious both to acid and alkali. They are available in many sizes from 5 cm at the broadest part, to 25 cm.

FUSEL OILS *See* ALCOHOL.

FUSTY Stale smelling, musty; smelling of mould or damp. The odour given off by a dirty cask or jar.

GALLIC ACID A tannin or polyphenol that gives wine astringency.

Catechol and ellagic acid are others. Gelatine combines with gallic acid, so it follows that fining with gelatine only will remove it and leave a less astringent wine.

GALLON   The word is from the old northern French *galon* comparable to the old French *jole* meaning bowl. It is the English cubic measure of capacity and the quantitative measure by which bulk liquid is usually calculated. The capacity of the English gallon is 277¼ cubic inches (4,546 cm³) or 160 fl oz (4,546 ml) of distilled water with a weight of 10 lb. An English gallon contains 8 pints or six standard wine bottles, each holding 26⅔ fl oz or approximately 75 centilitres.

Prior to 1826, the capacity of the English wine gallon was 231 cubic inches—the same as the U.S.A. gallon—although the ale gallon was 282 cubic inches. By Act 5 Geo. IV, passed in 1824 and operative in 1826, however, the gallon was standardized at 277·274 cubic inches and it became known as the 'Imperial' gallon.

GELATINE   This is a yellowish-tinted, transparent, brittle and taste-less collagenous protein that is extracted from animal ligaments, bones and skins. It is obtainable in granulated or leaf form when purified and is used both for making jellies and as a fining agent. For use *see* FINING.

GINGER BEER   Contrary to temperance belief, this favourite drink of children does contain some alcohol when made in the home. It is made by fermenting a weak syrup (500 g sugar in 5 litres of water) with 25 g of bruised root ginger, 2 lemons and 10 g cream of tartar. When fermenta-tion is quite finished and the 'beer' is nearly clear, it is bottled in screw-stoppered bottles and a further 5 g of sugar is added to each bottle. This creates a secondary fermentation, the carbon dioxide from which pro-duces the sparkle of delight when the 'beer' is poured out some two weeks later.

GLASSES   Over the centuries, the half-gourd gave way to the baked clay bowl which was followed by the ceramic vase and later by the silver chalice. In relatively more recent years we have used a glass container from which to drink our wine. This has already passed through many fashions in colour, to hide the murkiness of the wine, and in shape, as well as in decoration. A good wine deserves a pleasing glass so that the brilliance and hue of the wine can be adequately appreciated. A short stem is necessary so that it can be picked up without finger marking the bowl and clearly a good base is required by which to hold it in one's hand or upon which to stand it. The bowl should not only be devoid of colour but also of decoration since this can be a distraction as well as a deroga-tory insolence. It should be tulip-shaped and incurved so that the esters can collect on top of the wine and form a bouquet for our further enjoyment.

Table wine glasses need to be larger than aperitif or dessert wine glasses, as the latter wines contain so much more alcohol and accordingly less of them is drunk. There is no reason why all glasses should not be the same shape, however. The most sensible glasses for general purposes are those known as the 'tall tulip' and made to hold 150, 175 or 225 ml (5, 6 or 8 fl oz Imperial equivalents). Next best are the goblets. For sampling, or judging a wine, the copita-shaped glasses are best. Whether sampling, judging or drinking, the glass should never be more than half to two-thirds filled, since full appreciation of the wine's qualities cannot otherwise be made.

GLAZES Earthenware and pottery glazes are dealt with under EARTHENWARE.

GLUCOSE This is a grape sugar and is a simple sugar of the same atomic combination ($C_6H_{12}O_6$) as fructose, although with a different structure. It combines with fructose to form sucrose (white granulated sugar). Like fructose it is readily fermentable into alcohol and carbon dioxide by the zymase complex of enzymes secreted by wine yeasts.

Glucose from the Greek *glykes* means sweet. It is also known as dextrose because it causes a plane of polaroid light to rotate to the right. (*See also* FRUCTOSE.)

GLYCEROL (GLYCERINE) *See* ALCOHOL.

GLYCOLYSIS The word comes from the Greek *glykes* meaning sweet and *lyein* meaning to loosen. Freely translated, therefore, it means 'the breaking up of sugar' and is in fact the decomposition of glucose or glycogen to lesser compounds.

GOBLET The name given to a glass of a particular shape and size that is used for red table wines. Two kinds are popular, the Paris and the Bordeaux. The Paris has a large tulip bowl on a short stem, the Bordeaux has a spherical bowl on a longer stem.

GRAFTING Where phylloxera exists, vines are propagated by grafting a section of one-year-old stem of the desired variety to a rootstock resistant to the disease. English stocks are frequently used as it is considered that American stocks cause a wine to taste 'foxy'.

GRAPES Although there are around 1,000 different varieties of *Vitis vinifera*, the European grape vine, some are known by different names in different parts of the world, notably such well-known varieties as Riesling and Semillon. Grown in different soil and in different climates the same vine produces more or fewer grapes of better or poorer quality. Indeed, in some parts of France, vineyards are known as 'climats', because the varying micro-climates due to the position of the vineyards on the slopes of a hill, the direction it faces, early morning or late evening shadow, prevailing wind and rainfall, not to mention the soil, all have an effect on the quality of the wine produced from the grapes grown just there.

Experience through 2,500 years has gradually selected certain varieties as being more suitable for one kind of wine produced in a certain limited area than another. Indeed this forms the basis of the European wine laws. The wine must be made from grapes of specified varieties planted no more than a given number to a hectare within a certain clearly delineated area.

No grape makes as good a wine on its own as it does when blended with one or more others. Deciding on the varieties and proportions to use in a given area and in a given year is a matter of experience and judgement. When the different methods of vinification are included, the variables are enormous. Added to this is the time needed for the wine to mature before the results of experiments can be adequately evaluated. Nevertheless, research for better vines continues wherever vines are grown. (*See also* CLONE.)

The advice of local vine growers and winemakers should always be sought and added to a scientific knowledge of what the grape contains and how it is turned into wine. In general terms the grape contains:

between	70	and 85%	of its weight as water
	8	and 13%	glucose
	7	and 12%	fructose
	0·2	and 1·0%	tartaric acid
	0·1	and 0·8%	malic acid
	0·01	and 0·05%	citric acid
	0·01	and 0·1%	tannins

In addition there are important trace elements, such as 21 different kinds of amino acids, several nitrogenous compounds and many vitamins, especially of the B group. There are also traces of a number of minerals, volatile aroma constituents, anthocyanins in black grapes and anthoxanthins and flavones in white. The precise content of each grape variety is slightly different in itself, as well as varying with the area in which it is grown. Some 400 different constituents have been identified but not the flavour element. Current thinking is that flavour is caused by variations in the quantity of the constituents.

GRAPE SUGAR *See* GLUCOSE.

GRAVITY For ease and convenience of working, gravity is often used instead of specific gravity. Gravity is simply the specific gravity with the '1·' omitted.

Examples: Specific gravity 1·030—Gravity 30 (or 030)
　　　　　Specific gravity 1·130—Gravity 130

Thus the equivalent gravity and specific gravity have the same meaning. For example, specific gravity 1·000 and 0 or zero gravity would both refer to pure water.

When the specific gravity is below 1·000 the gravity is referred to as a minus figure.

Examples: Specific gravity 0·999—Gravity −1
                        0·995   −5
                        0·980   −20

See also HYDROMETER and SPECIFIC GRAVITY

GREEN Unripe fruit tends to make wine over-acid and the wine is said to be green. Even when made from some ripe grapes the young wines can have a touch of greenness which later disappears.

GREY ROT *See* BOTRYTIS CINEREA.

GUILDS Many amateur winemakers have associated themselves into guilds or clubs to learn more about the ancient craft of making wine. The first associations were founded in 1954 and gradually spread not only throughout Great Britain but also to Holland, Canada, America, South Africa, Australia and New Zealand. Members meet monthly to hear a talk on some aspect of winemaking or to adjudicate on different wines or even socially to exchange their wines with one another for tasting and discussion.

As a result of these associations better winemaking knowledge is being disseminated and the standard of winemaking is steadily improving. Many guilds now have their master winemakers who act as guides and mentors to the new members. A National Guild of Judges has been formed in Great Britain for the purpose of providing a national standard of adjudication. Entry to the Guild of Judges is by a practical and theoretical examination only. There are members now in all the countries mentioned above. (*See also* JUDGING WINE.)

GYPSUM *See* CALCIUM SULPHATE.

HARD A term describing the feel of a wine that has an excess of acid and tannin.

HARSH A term used to describe a wine that has a coarse, rough and astringent taste caused by excess tannin, either due to over-pressing, bad vinification or a coarse variety of grape or other fruit.

HAZES A wine's first duty is to please the eye, and obviously a wine that is brilliantly clear, or star-bright as it is commonly called, will please the eye more than one containing a haze or looking cloudy and dirty. However, all wines will not clear themselves and the cause of the haze or cloud must be known before they can be rendered brilliant because the corrective measures are different. The causes are:

94

(1) Pectin stabilizing fine particles of material in suspension. For details of tests and corrective action *see* PECTIN.

(2) Starch in suspension. For details and corrective action *see* STARCH.

(3) Metal contamination—coloured hazes and browning, *see* METAL CONTAMINATION and FINING (2) Purification.

(4) Micro-organisms produce hazes which are difficult to identify individually. If a wine becomes hazy after once having been clear, the clouding may have been caused by micro-organisms, including spoilage yeasts. One haze, caused by lactic acid bacteria, can be diagnosed by swirling some wine in a clear glass bottle when the wine will take on a silky appearance. This condition is referred to as oiliness or ropiness. Affected wines should be poured into an open container and whisked thoroughly, then returned to the storage vessel, and 100 to 200 ppm sulphite added. The wine may later need to be fined or filtered if racking is inadequate. The best treatment of wines with all hazes caused by micro-organisms is to treat them with 100 to 150 ppm of sulphite.

(5) Particles of cellulose tissue, protein and other matter which for one reason or another remain in suspension. This form of haze and cloudiness is easily removed by FILTERING or FINING. Refer to those entries for details.

(6) Hydro-colloids. When there are hydro-colloids all with the same electrical charge in a wine, they remain in suspension and cause hazing. *See* FINING for further details.

HEADACHE Some people are allergic to sulphur and experience a headache after drinking white wines that are normally sulphited just prior to bottling. It is thought that the sulphur combines with an element in the blood to cause the pain. Other people suffer headaches after drinking heavy, full-bodied, rich wines. Their remedy is to drink only light wines.

It is said that those who become inebriated by wine do not know how to drink. True oenophiles never suffer from headaches after drinking wine; they know when to stop!

HEAD ROOM *See* ULLAGE.

HEAT SUMMATION The sum of the mean daily temperature above 10 °C (50 °F). It is found by multiplying the number of days with temperatures over 10 °C (50 °F) by the number of degrees over 10. The period covered is from the beginning of growth in the vine to the vintage. Sometimes the figure is referred to as 'day degrees' and the average for Bordeaux is 2,632. The average total number of sun hours and the pattern of the hottest month must also be taken into account. The grape prefers a cool growing period 10 to 25 °C (50 to 77 °F) with a warm ripening period 25 to 28 °C (77 to 82 °F).

HEAT TREATMENT In France, Australia and California much work has been done on the extraction of colour from the skins of black grapes by heat. The bunches of grapes may be exposed to steam, or the grapes may be destemmed and crushed, then heated in a suitable vessel, or some grape juice may be heated and poured over the other grapes. Experimental work at the Australian Wine Research Institute reported by Dr. B. C. Rankine in 1972 indicates that the amount of colour extracted is relative to the length of time the skins are exposed to a given temperature. The lower the temperature the longer the time required and the higher the temperature, the shorter the time required. The lowest effective temperature is 60 °C (140 °F) and the highest safe temperature is 80 °C (176 °F). Above this temperature the grape sugar begins to caramelize and impart an unwanted flavour to the wine. The optimum appears to be 75 °C (165 °F) with a holding time of around 15 minutes depending on the depth of colour required.

This method has been found especially effective in the making of wines from unsound grapes. The resultant wines usually have a better colour, higher alcohol and glycerol content and contain more of the other minor constituents. The wine is more stable and less prone to enzymatic oxidation. Specialized equipment for continuous process as opposed to batch process is now available and the additional cost is covered by the better wine produced and the saving on the other equipment and processes.

After the heat treatment the juice is drained off and the pulp is pressed and then discarded. When cool, the must is inoculated with pectic enzyme and a yeast culture for fermentation. The long period of pulp fermentation is avoided with its alcohol extraction of too much tannin and other harsh tasting constituents.

White grapes are also being treated in the same way and producing higher quality wines less prone to infection and oxidation.

Malo-lactic fermentation usually occurs readily in heat-treated wines since they are not normally sulphited. The heating kills only a proportion of the lactic acid bacteria and those that survive grow rapidly in the warm must during fermentation. (*See also* JUICER, JUICE EXTRACTOR—by heat.)

HEAVY A wine is described as heavy when it has a high alcohol content, over 16% by volume; frequently a fortified wine. Generally wines which are heavy are also full-bodied and are referred to as heavy *and* full-bodied. A wine over-endowed with alcohol and body is said to be 'fat'.

Heavy when used in reference to wine has only this meaning although it is sometimes erroneously used to describe a full-bodied wine.

HECTARE The superficial metric measurement for a piece of land equivalent to 2·47 acres. It consists of 100 ares each of 100 sq metres (approximately 120 sq yds).

96

HECTOLITRE   The metric name for 100 litres of a liquid, equivalent to 22 gallons, approximately 133 standard wine bottles each of 75 cl.

HECTOLITRE PER HECTARE   A term used for expressing the amount of wine produced from a given area of land. One hectolitre per hectare is equivalent to 8·9 gallons per acre, about 54 bottles.

HERBS   Plants whose stems or leaves are used for medicinal, culinary and flavouring purposes. They are usually bitter or aromatic. The addition of herbs to wines and meads can give a tonic effect when chosen for this purpose, they can also add to or vary the flavour of the wine. They need to be used very sparingly since in quantity the taste would be overpowering. Some herbs are distilled and their essences used in the making of liqueurs. Probably the best known is wormwood used with other flavourings in the making of Vermouth.

HEXOSE   Sugars such as glucose and fructose which contain six carbon atoms.

HIPPOCRAS   An ancient wine, one of the most popular of the spiced and herbed types. It was probably made from pricked or sour wine, the spices being added to mask the flavour, together with honey to sweeten it. The name 'hippocras' was taken from Hippocrates' sleeve, a long woollen bag through which it was filtered. The sleeve was named after Hippocrates (460–357 B.C.) known as the Father of Medicine. It is possible that hippocras was given as a medicine or used as a tonic.

Thought by some to be the forerunner of Vermouth, it has also been known as Ippocras and Yprocras.

HISTORY OF WINEMAKING   The grape vine, *Vitis vinifera*, would appear to be one of the first plants to be cultivated by man, probably in the areas south of the Black Sea and to the west of the Caspian, as far back as 6000 B.C. There is strong evidence to show that viticulture was well established in the Tigris/Euphrates area before 4000 B.C. Cultivation of the vine and the making of wine first spread to Egypt about 3000 B.C., to Thrace and Crete about 2000 B.C., to southern Greece and Italy about 1000 B.C., to the Marseilles area about 500 B.C. and to Bordeaux about 50 B.C.

In his famous *Histories* some 500 years B.C., Herodotus described not only the making of wine casks from the wood of the palm tree, but also the making of a wine from dates, the fruit of the palm tree.

Biblical references are numerous and long before the birth of Christ, wine and beer were used as libations such as Vedic Soma, Zend Avesta, Hoama, and certainly among the heathens who worshipped Dionysus, for example. The sacrifices were made to propitiate the gods and to beg for good harvests. The Semitic tribes used wine for religious purposes on

97

the eve of their Sabbath and it was therefore but natural for Christ to choose wine for the Sacrament.

In the warmer regions the wines were no doubt stronger and sweeter than in the more northerly areas, but they were often murky in appearance. Nevertheless, the special characteristics of each wine were noted by Athenaeus, a sort of gossip columnist who lived in Egypt about A.D. 200.

At that time wine from Marseilles was being imported into Britain for the use of the better-to-do, while the common people drank ale, made from wheat. Cider was also well known and the famous orchards in Herefordshire and Gloucestershire were developing.

The drinking of wine in Britain received a great fillip when Eleanor of Aquitaine became Queen of England and brought to King Henry II as a dowry, Bordeaux and its wine-producing hinterland.

By 1568 the drinking of red wine from Bordeaux was thought to be one of the major causes of the ailment of that age—the stone. Accordingly, William Turner, a physician to Queen Elizabeth I, wrote the first book on wine to be published in England. It was called *A New Book of Wines* and advocated the drinking of white wines from the Rhineland as being more conducive to good health.

Monks improved the methods of both viticulture and viniculture and spread the craft wherever they took the faith. Many of the old vineyards of Europe were attached to monasteries; and missionary monks, especially the Jesuits, took the vine to South America and California.

There was much malpractice in the wine trade and wines made in England from cherries, elderberries or gooseberries were often blended with imported wines and sold entirely as imported wine. Probably the English fruit wines improved the imported grape wine, just as today grape juice added to a fruit must improves these wines. The Greeks added pine cones to their wine and the resin prevented souring.

Mead was of course very widely made too, for countless colonies of bees were kept not only to provide honey for sweetening purposes, but also wax for candles. The great houses and farms all made mead as well, and the various recipes were passed from Duchess to Countess and no doubt to the Squire's lady too. In 1669, Sir Kenelm Digby made a collection of these recipes and his book was published very successfully. The flavourings used make fascinating reading; sorrel, balm, violet leaves, strawberry leaves etc., as well as a multitude of spices.

In the eighteenth century the making of fruit wine in England was encouraged by countless books of recipes, but apart from *Vinetum Britannicum* no serious study was published until 1816 when John McCulloch wrote a scholarly treatise for the Caledonian Horticultural Society. Like others before him McCulloch criticized the addition of brandy to these wines and said that they were far too sweet. He also advocated racking wines in 'dry cold weather, as it is only then that wines are clear'. This advice had been published nearly 200 years earlier in the *Mysterie of Vintners* by Walter Charlton and was repeated in 1965 in *Wine Magazine* for the benefit of those who bought their wine in cask and bottled it at home. McCulloch's work was developed in 1835 by W. H. Roberts in a book called *The British Winemaker*. Roberts described and recommended the use of the saccharometer to avoid making excessively sweet wines. His book was extremely popular and sold many editions, proving that a great many of the people who could read were making fruit wines.

The middle of the nineteenth century saw the first golden age of winemaking in the English home. By 1885 however, social conditions were changing and except for a few places in the heart of the country, winemaking in England almost disappeared. It began to revive in 1945, however, and is currently in the midst of a second golden age. The making of fruit, flower, cereal and vegetable wines flourishes widely in Great Britain and has spread to the U.S.A., Canada, Rhodesia, Australia, New Zealand and many other countries too.

Northern Germany, Yugoslavia, Poland and other nations, including France, have a long tradition for making fruit wines among the people of the countryside. Indeed, in every country in the world some fruit, vegetable or cereal is fermented into a beverage to gladden the heart.

More recently the cultivation of the vine has become a hobby among those with large enough gardens and there has been an upsurge in the making of grape wines in the home to provide for family needs. This activity, too, is world-wide and is, no doubt, related to higher standards of living, more time for secondary activities and improved educational facilities.

At the same time there is a marginal decline in drinking of wine in some countries, caused partly by propaganda programmes encouraging car drivers not to drink alcohol of any kind before driving and partly to concur with the social and medical effects of alcoholism, although this disease is more often associated with spirits than with wine.

In Europe as a whole and especially in France, there is an over-production of wine, particularly of the poorer quality.

HOCK   The generic name given to the golden wines produced along the banks of the river Rhine. It is an abbreviation of the name of the town of Hochheim. Hock is produced primarily from the Riesling grape blended with the Scheurebe, Müller-Thurgau or some other variety, especially in poor seasons. Chaptalization is necessary for all but the very best wines in the Qualitätswein mit Prädikat category. The wines are usually sweetened with sterilized grape juice called *süss reserve*.

HOMOGENEITY   A wine is said to be homogenous or to possess homogeneity when all its constituents are intimately blended and integral. The *Shorter Oxford Dictionary* gives the definition of 'uniform nature or character throughout'. A wine lacks homogeneity when you can see, smell or taste separately any of the component parts. For example, if grape brandy is newly added to a wine, one can always smell and taste it separately until it has had time to integrate. Similarly when sugar syrup is newly added to a dry wine to sweeten it, one can see the swirl of syrup before it has been completely integrated.

HONEY There are countless varieties of honey, depending on the flowers from which the bees gathered the nectar, for example heather, clover, orange blossom, eucalyptus and so on. The chemical composition remains fairly constant, however, and is as follows: sugar, 77% and water, 17½%. The remaining 5½% consists of salts of iron, phosphorus, lime, sodium, potassium, sulphur and manganese with traces only of citric, formic, malic, succinic and amino acids together with dextrin, pollen, oils, gums, waxes, fats, yeast enzymes, vitamins, albumen, protein and ash.

Before use honey should be pasteurized. It is the basic and only ingredient of true mead.

HOT BOTTLING Bottling wine immediately after pasteurization while the wine is still hot. Used only for everyday wines it prevents all bottle ailments.

HOT BOX This is a FERMENTATION CHAMBER which has been constructed as a box and is capable of being transported for use wherever it is required.

HYBRID A hybrid is the result of crossing two varieties of fruit and even re-crossing. By hybridization and selective breeding, new varieties are obtained which combine the better characteristics of the parents. Overall quality can be improved with better disease resistance. Hybrid grapes, for instance, have been one method of combating phylloxera. In France, hybrid grapes have been given the name of the hybridizer plus a serial number, e.g. Seibel 5279, but elsewhere various names have been given causing some confusion. It is not always appreciated, for example, that the well-known Müller-Thurgau vine is the Riesling/Sylvaner cross.

HYDRO-COLLOIDS The colloidal particles in wine that are surrounded by a film of absorbed water.

HYDROGEN ION Hydrogen in solution changes by ionization and the solution becomes acidic. The unit of measurement of hydrogen ions is pH.

HYDROGEN SULPHIDE A colourless foetid gas, sometimes described as having the smell of rotten eggs, or skunk. It occasionally occurs in young wines, usually from the reduction of elemental sulphur, residual from fungicidal sprays on fruit, or from the old practice of burning sulphur candles in casks. Imperfect sulphiting to terminate fermentation can also result in the reduction of sulphur dioxide to hydrogen sulphide by the yeast. Indeed, certain yeasts are more prone to hydrogen sulphide production than others.

Traces of metal present in wine are also believed to be a cause of hydrogen sulphide, tin from contact with tin vessels being one example. March (1959) suggested that aluminium reduced sulphur dioxide to hydrogen sulphide and Ribereau–Gayer (1935) believed that an unknown reducing agent reduced cupric ions to cuprous and this in turn reduced sulphur dioxide to hydrogen sulphide. This could explain the presence of the latter in a bottle of wine which has been sulphited. Leaving a wine too long on its lees is believed to be another cause of its formation.

Hydrogen sulphide in a wine can react with alcohol to form mercaptans which have a most objectionable odour and flavour.

HYDROLYSIS/HYDROLYSE From the Greek *hydro*, water and *lyein*, loosen. It is the reaction caused by an enzyme between a chemical compound and water, resulting in other compounds. An example of hydrolysis is the conversion of sucrose (white sugar) to glucose and fructose, caused by the enzyme sucrase (invertase) and as shown in the schematic below:

$$\text{sucrose} \quad \text{water} \qquad\qquad\qquad \text{glucose} \quad \text{fructose}$$

$$C_{12}H_{22}O_{11} \;\text{plus}\; H_2O = \begin{bmatrix} C_{12} \\ H_{24} \\ O_{12} \end{bmatrix} \;\text{sucrase (invertase)}\; C_6H_{12}O_6 \;\text{and}\; C_6H_{12}O_6 = \begin{bmatrix} C_{12} \\ H_{24} \\ O_{12} \end{bmatrix}$$

HYDROMETER This is a scientific instrument for measuring the gravity' (the density or weight) of a liquid in which it is floated. In winemaking it is used solely for measuring the quantity of sugar in any given must or wine. It has long been known for this purpose. The earliest and most rudimentary form was an egg which was floated in a must and the quantity of sugar varied by addition or dilution until 'but the measure of a groat do show'. In 1835 W. H. Roberts described the saccharometer which he had been using for many years; it was much the same as the hydrometer in use today.

A hydrometer consists of a short glass or plastic bulb containing material such as lead shot, wax etc. as a weight. The bulb is attached to a comparatively long stem. If glass, this stem contains one of a number of graduation charts. If plastic, the stem is graduated outside. For winemaking purposes the graduations denote sugar content, potential alcohol or specific gravity. Some have dual scales for specific gravity/potential alcohol or specific gravity/sugar content. Whichever the scale, the ranges are between 0·980 and 1·300 specific gravity, with the most commonly used being 0·990 to 1·100 and 1·100 to 1·200 or 0·990 to 1·170.

In America a Twadell scale is used, so graduated that 1 degree Twadell is equivalent to 5 degrees specific gravity. The Balling scale, however, is becoming increasingly popular in everyday use although it is identical with the Brix scale.

On the Continent and in Australia there is a Baumé graduation indicating the potential alcohol content of the must if fermented to complete dryness. In the U.S.A a Brix graduation indicates the percentage sugar content of the liquid being tested.

A hydrometer is used by standing it in a trial jar and pouring into the jar a quantity of the liquid to be tested. When the hydrometer floats, a reading is taken off the chart at the point at which the meniscus, or surface of the liquid, cuts the chart. The following table comprises the best known graduations:

Specific gravity	Degrees Baumé	Degrees Twadell	Degrees Brix/Balling
1·005	0·7	1·0	1·3
1·010	1·4	2·0	2·5
1·015	2·1	3·0	3·8
1·020	2·8	4·0	5·3
1·025	3·5	5·0	6·5
1·030	4·2	6·0	7·8
1·035	4·9	7·0	9·0
1·040	5·5	8·0	10·3
1·045	6·2	9·0	11·5
1·050	6·9	10·0	12·5
1·055	7·5	11·0	13·8
1·060	8·2	12·0	15·3
1·065	8·8	13·0	16·3
1·070	9·4	14·0	17·5
1·075	10·0	15·0	18·5
1·080	10·7	16·0	19·8
1·085	11·3	17·0	20·8
1·090	11·9	18·0	22·0
1·095	12·5	19·0	23·0
1·100	13·1	20·0	24·2
1·105	13·7	21·0	25·3
1·110	14·3	22·0	26·4
1·115	14·9	23·0	27·5
1·120	15·5	24·0	28·5
1·125	16·0	25·0	29·6

The specific gravity of a liquid varies with different temperatures due to alteration in density. For this reason, hydrometers are calibrated at a particular temperature which should be stated on the scale, it is normally, but not always, 15 °C (59 °F). When testing a must, then, an adjustment should be made for any substantial temperature variation in order to obtain a true specific gravity. The following table sets out these adjustments.

Temperature of liquid		Correction to		
degrees C.	degrees F.	Specific Gravity		Gravity
10	50	Subtract 1·0006		0·6
15	59	No correction necessary		
20	68	Add	1·0009	0·9
25	77	Add	1·002	2·0
30	86	Add	1·0034	3·4
35	95	Add	1·005	5·0
40	104	Add	1·0068	6·8

By using a hydrometer the following information can be obtained about a must or juice:

1. An approximation of the weight of the sugar present.
2. How much sugar must be added to produce a wine of a required percentage volume of alcohol (approximately) when fermentation is completed.

By frequent use of the hydrometer and the recording of the readings it is possible to follow the progress of the fermentation and calculate the percentage volume of alcohol in a finished wine.

In a pure sugar solution, the specific gravity would indicate the amount of sugar present. In a grape juice or other fruit must, however, the dissolved but non-fermentable solids, such as acids, salts and pectin, cause the hydrometer to give a variable reading up to 10 degrees higher than for the sugar content alone. Thus the sugar content can only be approximated, although the approximation is usually sufficiently close to be only of minor consequence to the winemaker unless some specific standard has to be achieved.

Theoretically, 51·1% of the weight of sugar could be fermented to alcohol. In practice, it is unlikely to exceed 47·5% and will probably be a little less. This is the real potential alcohol. The loss is accounted for by small amounts of sugar being metabolized to glycogen and/or carbon dioxide/water; the formation of by-products; and the loss of alcohol during fermentation.

These primary factors are also relative to secondary factors such as the availability of oxygen to the yeast, the amount of sulphite present and the rate and temperature of the fermentation. Furthermore, there is a slight decrease in the overall volume from the loss of carbon dioxide and a small contraction from the mixing of the alcohol and water. The final factor is the amount of unfermented sugar in the finished wine. For these reasons, the calculation from a must gravity of the possible alcohol

103

content of a finished wine can only be an approximation, although this can be quite close.

The following tables are sufficiently accurate for differences to be of little consequence to most winemakers. Being statistical, any variations are likely to be greatest at the beginning and the end, with the closer accuracy in the 10 to 14% volume alcohol—the most commonly used range.

Specific Gravity	SUCROSE SOLUTION					MUST	
	Sucrose *in*		Sucrose *added* to		Potential alcohol*	Possible alcohol	Gravity
	1 gal	5 litres	1 gal	5 litres			
(1)	(2)	(3)	(4)	(5)	(6)	(7)	(8)
1·005	2¾ oz	85 g	2¾ oz	85 g	0·75%		5
1·010	4¾	150	4¾	150	1·6	0·4	10
1·015	7	220	7¼	225	2·3	1·2	15
1·020	9	285	9¼	290	3·0	2·0	20
1·025	11	350	11½	360	3·8	2·8	25
1·030	13¼	415	13¾	430	4·6	3·6	30
1·035	15½	485	16	500	5·4	4·3	35
1·040	17½	550	18	560	6·0	5·1	40
1·045	19½	615	20¼	630	6·8	5·8	45
1·050	21½	680	22¾	710	7·5	6·5	50
1·055	23¾	745	25¼	785	8·2	7·2	55
1·060	25¾	810	27¾	865	8·9	7·9	60
1·065	27¾	875	30¼	945	9·6	8·6	65
1·070	30	945	33	1030	10·4	9·3	70
1·075	32	1010	35½	1110	11·1	10·0	75
1·080	34½	1075	38½	1200	11·8	10·6	80
1·085	36½	1140	41¼	1285	12·6	11·3	85
1·090	38½	1205	44	1370	13·4	12·0	90
1·095	40¾	1275	47	1465	14·2	12·7	95
1·100	42¾	1340	49¾	1550	14·9	13·4	100
1·105	44¾	1405	53	1645	15·6	14·2	105
1·110	47	1475	56	1745	16·3	14·9	110
1·115	49	1540	59	1845	17·0	15·6	115
1·120	51¼	1605	63	1965	17·7	16·3	120
1·125	53¼	1675	67	2090	18·5	17·1	125
1·130	55½	1740	71	2215	19·2	17·8	130

* Assuming 47·5% conversion of sugar to alcohol.
Note: 2 lb sugar increases the volume of a liquid by 1 pint
1 kg sugar increases the volume of a liquid by 0·62 litre

To find the approximate weight of sugar present in a must or juice, first take a hydrometer reading. From this reading deduct the arbitrary figure of 7 to allow for the presence of solids other than fermentable sugar. Using this figure as the specific gravity, note the amount of sugar shown in the appropriate line in column 2 or 3.

Example: Specific gravity of must or juice   1·072
          Deduct   7
                                            ———
                                           1·065
                                            ———

Specific gravity 1·065 = 27¾ oz/gal or 875 g/5 litres

To find the amount of sugar to be added to give (approximately) a required alcohol content in a finished wine, first find the required alcohol content in column 7 and note the corresponding gravity in column 8. Take a hydrometer reading of the must or juice and note the specific gravity. Deduct the gravity of the must from the gravity corresponding to the required alcohol content. The amount of sugar to be added is that shown in column 4 or 5 in line with the difference in gravities.

Example: Required alcohol content 12% (col. 7) = Gravity 90 (col. 8)
          Specific gravity of must 1·065   = Gravity 65
                                                  ———————

          Difference   Gravity 25
          Gravity 25 (col. 8)= 11½ oz/gal or 360 g/5 litres
                         of sugar to be added.

The alcohol content of a finished wine that can be expected from the specific gravity of a must, is that shown in column 7 in line with the specific gravity or gravity, columns 1 and 8.

Example: Specific gravity of must 1·075 = Possible 10% volume alcohol.

The progress of a fermentation is indicated by the difference between recorded regular hydrometer readings. When the fermentation is vigorous, the specific gravity drops rapidly. As the fermentation slows down, the difference between the readings becomes smaller and smaller. When the same reading is obtained more than once over a few days, the fermentation has stopped. If the specific gravity indicates a considerable sugar content when it becomes constant, then the fermentation has stuck. The difference between the specific gravity of the must and the final specific gravity of the wine is a good indicator of the volume of alcohol present.

There is no factor for calculating the exact alcohol content of a wine but an approximation can be obtained by dividing gravity drops by an arbitrary decreasing factor. Gravity drop is the difference between the specific gravity of a must and the specific gravity of the resulting wine, e.g.

Must	1·090
Wine	1·015

Gravity drop   ·075

The following table gives the approximations of alcohol content:

Gravity drop	% v/v alcohol
50	6·75
60	8·25
70	9·75
80	11·25
90	12·75
100	14·25
110	15·75

HYDROMETER JAR   Normally a glass cylinder with a foot and a lip. There is a range of sizes of 3·5, 5 and 6·5 cm in diameter and from 15 to 35 cm in height. The size of jar to be used is that which is the nearest larger than the hydrometer, i.e. if the hydrometer has a bulb of 2 cm diameter and an overall length of 25 cm the jar used should be 3·5 cm in diameter by 30 or 35 cm in height. These are the most popular sizes used by winemakers.

HYGIENE   Many people, when talking about hygiene in connection with winemaking, think in terms of laboratory sterility. This is by no means necessary although it is essential to take at least as much care in preparing wine as you do in preparing food. Equipment, utensils and vessels should always be washed and dried, then put away clean after use. Absolutely all items which come into contact with the wine should be washed before use and as far as practicable should be rinsed in a sulphite solution. (*See* SULPHITE.)

Bottles should be washed thoroughly, drained and rinsed with a little of the solution. The solution may be poured from one bottle into another bottle for the same purpose. This process should also be followed with gallon jars and, of course, casks. Corks should be soaked in the solution before use. The tap to a barrel should be washed in the solution before the cask is broached and so on. If wine or must is spilled it should be wiped up, and the place wiped over with a sulphite solution. When not in use everything should be kept clean, tidy and as far as possible free from dust and, of course, dry, since moisture and dust encourages moulds. It is not necessary, however, to bake bottles, equipment etc. in the oven to sterilize them as is sometimes stated. Use of a sulphite solution is simpler and just as effective. Indeed, apart from the risk of breakages, by the time the equipment is cool enough to use, it could become re-infected from air-borne bacteria.

INDICATOR A chemical that changes its colour when there is a change in the pH or acidity. Indicators are mostly used in the form of impregnated papers or solutions and the colour change is assessed against a colour chart.

INHIBIT In the context of winemaking, to inhibit means to render organisms inactive so that they are unable to function. This refers particularly to bacteria, moulds, spoilage yeasts and oxidasive enzymes.

INHIBITOR The safest and most effective inhibitor of spoilage organisms in the must and during the lag phase, is sulphite. It should be added at the rate of 50 to 150 ppm depending on the acidity of the must. It is assisted by the acids which are also inhibitors when the pH is 3·2 or lower. During fermentation, carbon dioxide acts as the inhibitor. After fermentation, 50 ppm sulphite inhibits oxidasive enzymes and spoilage organisms in wines with less than 12% alcohol. Alcohol acts as an inhibitor in stronger wines especially above 13%.

Similarly, a yeast which is in a fermenting wine, can become inhibited from further activity when the alcohol content reaches the maximum that it can tolerate. The yeast is not killed by the alcohol but is inhibited—prevented from further activity. This quantity of alcohol varies from yeast strain to yeast strain. *Saccharomyces apiculatus* for example can only tolerate from 2 to 4%, while certain strains of *Saccharomyces ellipsoideus* can sometimes withstand the presence of 18% of alcohol.

Proof that the yeast is inhibited and not killed can be gained from the sediment of a wine that has been fermented to the stage that it works no longer but in which there is still sugar to ferment. After the wine has been racked off, a fresh and very vigorous ferment can be started in another must by the addition of the sediment containing the inhibited yeast. Alcohol has to be in a concentration of from 50 to 70% to kill a yeast. Benzoic acid was the only legally permitted chemical that could terminate fermentation, but potassium sorbate has now been passed by the Committee on the Safety of Drugs. Either may be used to prevent a wine from fermenting to dryness when a sweet wine is desired. (*See* POTASSIUM SORBATE.)

INSENSIBLE FERMENT After the first vigorous and sometimes frothy fermentation of a new must, there follows a more subdued but still active ferment until the wine begins to clear and all visible and audible signs of fermentation cease. The wine is then racked and put into store.

During the next few months an insensible ferment takes place. There are none of the normal signs of fermentation but nevertheless slight fermentation is proceeding, including perhaps a malo-lactic fermentation. When the jar or bottle is opened a whitish gas may momentarily appear and sometimes a few bubbles will rise for several minutes.

INVERTASE A popular but imprecise name for sucrase, an enzyme secreted by sugar-fermenting yeasts. It acts as a catalyst which hydrolyses or splits di-saccharides, such as sucrose (white granulated sugar). The result is a molecularly equal mixture of glucose (also called grape sugar) and fructose (fruit sugar), which are simple sugars or monosaccharides.

By its very presence sucrase (invertase) causes sucrose to split into its two components. It is as though a stranger walked into a room where similar twins were entwined. Upon realizing the presence of a stranger the twins separate and move into different positions in the room. The stranger is sucrase (invertase), the twins are fructose and glucose which when entwined become sucrose.

If yeast was unable to secrete sucrase (invertase) there would be no fermentation of white sugar because the enzyme zymase can only ferment simple sugars.

INVERT SUGAR Ordinary white granulated sugar, technically known as sucrose, is a di-saccharide combination of fructose and glucose, which cannot be fermented by the zymase complex into alcohol and carbon dioxide. Sucrose must first be hydrolysed by the enzyme sucrase or by dilute acid, to invert sugar which has a molecularly equal mixture of glucose and fructose—single or simple sugars, or monosaccharides.

Sucrase like the zymase complex is an enzyme that is secreted by wine yeasts and there would appear to be no advantage in adding invert sugar to a must as opposed to ordinary sugar or sucrose, except for a slightly faster fermentation.

Sucrose can be hydrolysed to invert sugar by boiling it for twenty minutes in water to which has been added a small quantity of acid. (5 g citric acid in half a litre of water is sufficient to invert 1 kg of sugar.) This solution may be added in place of dry sugar or syrup. (*See also* SYRUP and SUGARS.)

Invert sugar is produced commercially and usually sold in blocks which are soft. It is made by first hydrolysing sucrose with acid, then removing the acid and finally evaporating as much water as possible. This is only about 80%, so the blocks contain approximately 20% water. 1 lb/1 kg invert sugar is, therefore, the equivalent of 0·8 lb/800 g of glucose and fructose.

Invert sugar is so called because sucrose is dextro-rotatory but when hydrolysed the resultant equimolecular mixture is inverted and becomes laevo-rotary. The enzyme that causes the inversion is commonly called invertase, but is correctly called sucrase since it acts only on sucrose.

IODINE   Used in connection with winemaking to detect starch in hazy wine. Only the ordinary brown iodine will react with starch, the colourless or decoloured will not. Details of test and reactions are given under STARCH.

IONIZATIONS   The dissociation in solution of an atom causes the atom or its radical, to become electrically charged. The ions of hydrogen predominate in an acid solution and it is these ions that are measured by pH.

ISINGLASS   This is obtained from the air or swim bladder of freshwater fish, especially the sturgeon, and is a form of gelatine. It is used mainly for making jellies and glues but sometimes by the winemaker as a fining agent to clear hazy wines, more especially white wines. For use *see* FINING.

JUDGING WINE   In addition to the message from the mouth and nose regarding the flavour and bouquet of a wine, there are other factors that influence an opinion: messages from the ears, eyes and memory.

Opinions of other people expressed within hearing can influence an assessment against the evidence of the other senses. This is particularly so if the other person (or persons) is considered to be more experienced.

Through our eyes we can be led into thinking that wine from one bottle is better than from others even if all the bottles contained the same wine. The sole reason for doing so being the presentation and clarity. For example, the flavour quality of a brilliant wine in a clear, well-labelled, polished bottle will be assessed as better than that of other bottles of the same wine, in dirty (outside) bottles, badly labelled and coloured with a flavourless dye or made hazy. The flavour quality would actually remain the same in each.

In assessing the quality of a flavour the memory can play a part in influencing judgement by past association. An unpleasant or particularly pleasant experience, unconsciously or consciously associated in the memory with a certain aroma, can bias judgement when the aroma is again smelt. Likewise the memory of a particular experience with a flavour.

Most people can, in general, distinguish between poor, better and best wines without any training. But to be a judge of wine, that is, to be able to assess properly the differences between wines of poor quality only, between wines of medium quality only, or between wines of the highest quality only and define the differences, requires training in order to dissociate everything from the judgement except the evidence of the eye, nose and mouth.

A wine is judged by pouring a little into a glass, assessing its clarity and hue, gently swirling the wine, then inspiring the aroma/bouquet and making an assessment. This is followed by sipping the wine which is allowed to trickle over the tongue and into the throat where it is 'chewed'; all the while the mouth is held slightly open and air gently inspired through it. (This operation is at first difficult and requires practice.) An assessment is made, then the wine is spat out and a pause made with the mouth slightly open for inspiration, to appreciate the after flavour. The final judgement is then reached by the overall result of the assessments of clarity, hue, aroma/bouquet, flavour and aftertaste.

All wine judges need a substantial knowledge of wine technology, considerable experience of tasting and evaluating wines, good health, a calm mind and good conditions in which to work. It is preferable to taste wines in the following order: dry before sweet; white before red; young before old; low-alcohol before high-alcohol.

It is desirable to use a thin, plain, colourless glass shaped like a truncated egg. The optimum size is 155 mm high—including a short stem—with a base diameter of 46 mm. Such a glass has a capacity of 215 ml and needs to be half-filled so there is sufficient both to be able to evaluate the colour and clarity of the wine and to enable a good bouquet to develop. The incurved shape of the glass will retain the bouquet.

There are various scoring systems, although the end result is similar.

The Office International de la Vigne et du Vin (OIV) prescribes the following allocation of points:

Colour	2
Condition	2
Bouquet	4
Taste and general impression	12
	—
Total	20

The wine scoring 17·1 or more points receives a gold medal award, 15·1 to 17·0 a silver and 13·1 to 15·0 a bronze.

The Department of Oenology at the University of California recommends the following allocation:

Appearance	2	Colour	2
Aroma and bouquet	4	Volatile	2
Total acidity	2	Sugar	1
Body	1	Astringency	2
Flavour	2	General quality	2
Total 20			

110

A wine scoring 17 to 20 points is outstanding, 13 to 16 is standard, 9 to 12 commercial with a noticeable defect, 5 to 8 below commercial acceptability, 1 to 4 completely spoilt.

In Australia a 20-point scale is used:

Colour and clarity	3
Bouquet	7
Palate	10
	—
Total	20

A wine scoring 18·5 points or more is awarded a gold medal, 17 to 18·4 a silver and 15·5 to 16·9 a bronze.

Major international competitions sometimes provide individual wine profiles or descriptions for each class of wine as a guide to their judges and competitors. For example, rosé wine: 'A still, light and tart wine with a slight tannin finish and a fresh, fruity flavour, but without muscat character. Colour pink—not light red or tawny. It should contain not more than 0·50% reduceable sugar and the alcoholic strength should be between 9·7% and 13·7% by volume.'

In the U.K., the strong amateur winemaking movement uses a 30-point scale thus:

Presentation	2
Colour and clarity	4
Bouquet	4
General impression	20
	—
Total	30

Another U.K. system has been devised by A. Massel, the founder of Club Oenologique that organizes an international wine and spirit competition in London. The system is called the Massel Quality Index. A panel of tasters may award a maximum of 54 points, whilst a maximum of a further 76 points may be awarded as the result of an analytical evaluation. The figures are related to wines and spirits within specified categories for which average analytical data have been collated. Scoring is as follows:

Tasting	Appearance	4
	Colour	4
	Bouquet	8
	Palate	24
	Persistence	14
		—
	Total	54

Analysis		
	Alcohol content	10
	Sugar-free extract content	15
	Sugar content	5
	Volatile acid content	5
	Total acid content	10
	Free SO_2 content	5
	Total SO_2 content	5
	Iron content	3
	Copper content	3
	Microscope examination	15
	Total	76

The following quality scale is applied: less than 70, unsound; 70–80, poor; 80–90, medium; 90–100, good; 100–110, very good; over 110, exceptional.

JUICER, JUICE EXTRACTOR There are two distinct types of equipment called juicers or juice extractors. One extracts the juice by heat and the other mechanically. There is a second type of mechanical extractor but it is referred to as a PRESS or WINEPRESS, under which heading it is described in detail.

Extraction by heat To extract by heat, a double container is used. The lower or outer part is for water and the upper or inner container is for the raw material. From the latter protrudes a long spout through which the juice can run. By applying heat to the water container, controlled heating of the raw material is achieved and overheating prevented. As the water boils the raw material is heated, breaking down the cells and the juice from them runs out through the spout. This method is used almost exclusively for experimental quantities of fruit. A safe maximum temperature is 80 °C (176 °F) with 75 °C (167 °F) as the optimum.

If the temperature is maintained for more than 15–30 minutes, the pectin may gel and the protein become denatured, thus causing a hazy wine. A pectolytic enzyme should always be used when the must is cool. (*See also* HEAT TREATMENT.)

Extraction by mechanical means The oldest version of a juicer, but still used, is rather like a hand mincing machine with the underpart perforated to allow the juice to run free. There is a screw which controls the compression of the pulp. Another version is a rotating, perforated drum with an inner shredding drum into which the raw material is pressed.

Both the methods described are efficient for small quantities of raw material but, today, electrically operated juicers are more frequently used. These are more efficient and by far the quickest. Different manufacturers sell their own versions, all of which vary to some extent, although all work on the same principle. The electric motor drives a fast rotating perforated drum. At the base of the drum is a shredder on to which the raw material is forced. The raw material is shredded very finely and is flung into the side of the drum by the speed. Juice is extracted by centrifugal force just as water is extracted from clothes in a spin dryer.

A disadvantage of this method is that a very considerable quantity of fine particles of pulp is present in the juice. It is therefore, advisable to add sulphite and allow the juice to stand for 24 hours or longer until the particles have formed a sediment. The clear juice is then siphoned off and the sediment allowed to drip through a filter bag. (*See also* PRESS and PRESSING OF GRAPES.)

JUICES and EXTRACTS   It is the general practice to steep or ferment pulp and after a few days to squeeze or press it to make the maximum extract. This may be economical, but without doubt pure juices obtained by pressing or by extractor produce the better wines, particularly for dessert purposes. A common argument is that pure juices are too strong in flavour, or too acid, or have other faults. Rarely is this true with fruit picked at its peak. In fact, steeping or pulp fermentations produce the stronger flavours and often bitterness or other off-flavours, as a result of breaking down the pulp tissues and cell walls, particularly of the skins. The result is an extract of flavourings and chemicals, both desirable and undesirable in the quantities released. The amount of water used when making certain fruit wines dilutes them, but everything else is also diluted, causing other deficiencies. Pure juices do not suffer from these defects. If the flavour of a pure juice is strong, blending with a juice of little flavour will normally remedy it without affecting other factors. Excess acid can be reduced with calcium carbonate and excess tannin with gelatine. Generally, all that needs to be added to pure juice is sugar. Pure juices should of course, be sulphited to inhibit any unwanted micro-organisms they may contain.

There are three separate methods of making pure juice extracts. These are (1) by compression in a press, (2) by electrical or hand-operated juice extractor, and (3) by heating. Pressing may be the more laborious, but is probably the best method. (*See also* PRESS and JUICE EXTRACTOR.)

KLOECKERA   One of the most common of the apiculate yeasts—so called because they are pointed at both ends. These wild yeasts settle on fruit and can ferment sugar to about 4% alcohol before being inhibited. There is some doubt that they cause any spoilage and some belief that they produce good fruity esters. Unfortunately they are always accompanied by other micro-organisms that do cause spoilage. All are susceptible to sulphite.

KOUMISS   Fermented milk. A beverage still made by the herdsmen in Mongolia, Siberia and Tartary. The milk of mares is mainly used, but camel's milk and sometimes cow's milk is used instead. Milk sugar known as lactose can only be fermented by *Saccharomyces fragilis* and indeed this yeast only produces 2% of alcohol. But all the other goodness of milk remains, and clearly Koumiss is not only a tasty but also a beneficial drink for the wandering herdsmen of the great plains of central Asia.

LABELS Professional winemakers always use fancy labels and collars on their bottles to make them look attractive and to give essential information about the wine inside.

Amateurs as a whole tend to neglect this side of presentation on the grounds that they are serving their wines in their own homes, probably in a decanter, anyway. There are some, however, who buy and use charming, coloured labels indicating the type and variety of the wine and the date of the vintage. Some have even designed and printed their own labels rather like the book plates of old. Even if you do not go to this length it is most important to affix some sort of label to every bottle. Months and years afterwards it is impossible to remember details which you will wish to have when you serve them. The minimum information is the name of the main ingredient and the date, but generally speaking the more information you record the greater will be your satisfaction at the time of consumption.

All vessels used from the preparation of the must to the bottling should be properly labelled with at least the details of the ingredients and the date of initial preparation. More advisedly the labels should bear the record number of a separate data sheet or else more details should be recorded on the label of weights and measurements, dates and operations throughout the production. (*See also* RECORDS.)

LACTIC ACID A by-product of fermentation and therefore present in wine in small quantities. Larger amounts are produced by lactic acid bacteria. In low-acid wines this causes spoilage, but in high-acid wines it is an advantage to have some of the malic acid converted to the less sharp lactic acid.

LACTIC ACID BACTERIA (LACTOBACILLI, LEUCONOS-TOC, PEDIOCOCCUS) The lactic acid bacteria are acid-tolerant micro-organisms that originally were referred to as *bacteria gracile* (*gracile* from *gracilis* meaning slender rod). By the use of the pure culture technique of Koch (1881) the organisms have been gradually classified but even today there may be as many unclassified as classified. They are normally in the form of long rods, but they can also be of a short rod form or spherical. In the absence of air they produce lactic acid together with (a) one or more of acetic acid, ethyl alcohol, carbon dioxide, glycerine and mannite from sugar and (b) carbon dioxide from malic acid.

Pasteur recognized four types of spoilage in wine: (1) acetification (vinegar taint), (2) bitterness, (3) slimy spoilage (ropiness), (4) tourne, (4a) pousse (a gaseous type of tourne—flat, slightly sour and cloudy wine with a blackish tinge). For a considerable time these were all thought to be caused by separate specific bacteria, as were also the malo-lactic fermentation and the formation of mannitol, but it is now known that all, or some, of the conditions can be caused by each of several different species of lactic acid bacteria.

Of the cocci, the heterofermentative spherical form, which can also sometimes be short oval, has been named *Leuconostoc mesenteroids*. It has a tolerance of 10 to 14% alcohol, and in low-alcohol wines may produce ropiness by causing the formation of dextran or laevulan from sucrose. From dextrose it forms acetic acid, carbon dioxide, ethyl alcohol and lactic acid. From laevulose it forms mannite. The homofermentative cocci have not yet been classified and have provisionally been placed in the genus *Pediococcus*.

The homofermentative, rod-like bacteria, Lactobacilli, convert dextrose and laevulose to lactic acid with little or no production of carbon dioxide. Both citric acid and malic acid are also fermented to lactic acid with little or no production of carbon dioxide. Both citric acid and malic acid are fermented to lactic acid by most strains, although some prefer malic acid, which others cannot ferment at all.

The heterofermentative Lactobacilli convert dextrose to acetic acid, alcohol, glycerol, lactic acid and mannite plus the production of carbon dioxide. Citric and malic acids are fermented to lactic acid and carbon dioxide. Some species can produce a mousy smell and taste in wine. They have an alcohol tolerance of up to 18%.

Several research workers have found lactic acid bacteria in many unspoilt wines and it is therefore concluded that the wines have remained sound because the conditions were not suitable for attack. Sulphur dioxide at the rate of 100 to 150 ppm will inhibit the bacteria in a must, and a pH of 3·6 or below will prevent growth. Trace growth factors from the autolysis of dead yeast cells are required. Thus the prevention of wine spoilage by the lactic acid bacteria can be achieved by adjusting a must to pH 3·6 or below, by early and regular racking and by adding 50 ppm sulphite to the finished wine.

The lactic acid bacteria which cause disorders in green olives, pickles, various sauces and sauerkraut can become acclimatized to grow in, and spoil wine.

LACTOSE Milk sugar which is not fermentable by wine yeasts. It can therefore be used for sweetening any wine without fear of further fermentation. It has only one-third of the sweetness of sucrose.

LAEVULOSE Another name for FRUCTOSE.

LAG PHASE   The lag phase is the period of time which an organism takes to develop into a colony that constitutes a critical concentration. In winemaking this particularly applies to bacteria, fungi, moulds and yeasts. The lag phase of spoilage organisms can be prolonged by heating or by the addition of sulphite to a must. Controlled experiment has shown that a must has to be maintained at a temperature of 50 °C (122 °F) for at least half an hour to ensure complete sterilization. Shorter periods only prolong the lag phase, for although many of the living organisms are killed, some survive and could eventually develop into a colony. This applies to the concentration of sulphite which has to be limited to 150 parts per million (ppm), so as not to affect the wine yeast as well.

The term lag phase, however, is more commonly used in winemaking to refer to the period of time taken by an active yeast to build up a colony to the concentration necessary to start a visible fermentation after it has been added to a must. This period can be from a few hours to three or four days, depending on the acidity of the must, the nutrient and sugar available, the concentration of sulphur dioxide, the temperature and the concentration of yeast added, as well as other factors. A dormant yeast will obviously take longer to regenerate and grow than one that has already been activated. (*See* STARTER BOTTLE.)

During the lag phase, the must is susceptible to contamination by spoilage organisms unless it has been properly sulphited and all air is excluded. It is essential, therefore, that the lag phase be kept to a minimum by inoculating a sterile must with an adequate concentration of activated yeast cells.

LAYING DOWN   The putting of wine into store for ageing or maturation. The term probably originated because bottles are stored on their sides to keep the corks moist and swollen.

LEAD   Wine that has been in contact with lead is toxic. The poison is cumulative; that is, it does not pass from the body and each dose adds to previous doses no matter how long it is between them. It is an insidious poison which does not show itself until the accumulated total is critical. The first signs, blue lines round the gums, are not usually recognized by the victim as poisoning, and the stomach pains are thought to be something else. Must and wines should be kept completely free from contact with lead in any form at all times. This includes pottery with a soft glaze—lead slip. (*See* EARTHENWARE.)

LEAVEN   The word leaven comes from the ancient French *levare* meaning to raise up, and since pre-biblical times it has been thought of as a substance added to dough to produce fermentation, or a raising up of the bread. At the time of each baking a portion of dough would be reserved for mixing with the next batch of dough to be made. In almost all countries pure cultures of *Saccharomyces cereviseae* are now used for making both bread and beer, although at one time of course, fermenting dough would have been added. Some old recipes for making meads, cider and wine recommended the addition of a few tablespoonfuls of flour since it was known that ground grain possessed fermentative powers.

A sour fermenting dough is still used in the making of black bread in certain countries. Its main fermenting agents are different lactic acid bacteria which produce both a sour and an aromatic flavour in the bread. Lactic acid bacteria protects the dough from other fermentations that might cause off-flavours, so the bread remains wholesome. *Saccharomyces panisfermenti* are also present together with other varieties of yeast including *cereviseae* and *torulopsis*. The latter yeasts are smaller than wine yeast cells and are round and rich in albumen, adding to the nutritive value of the bread.

LEES During fermentation and maturation wines throw a sediment of insoluble matter which collects at the bottom of the vessel. These sediments can be light or heavy but are usually heaviest at the end of fermentation. During fermentation the settling matter includes dust or dirt and cellulose tissue from the ingredients, dead yeast cells, dead bacteria, tartrate, pectin and other solid matter. After fermentation the first sediments contain mainly dead yeast cells, but once the wine has more or less cleared the deposits are largely the result of chemical changes. If, however, the wine is diseased, the after-fermentation deposits will contain dead bacteria and matter resulting from their activity.

Lees left in a wine slowly decompose and the yeast cells autolyse, thus producing off-flavours in the wine. In addition, the autolysis of the dead yeast cells produces trace growth factors necessary for the development of spoilage micro-organisms. Thereby, wines left on their lees not only produce off-flavours but also are very prone to further spoilage by bacterial action. It is therefore essential that wines should be racked as and when deposits form at the bottom of their containers. The exceptions to this rule are wines under a Sherry flor and wines which throw a deposit during bottle ageing.

LEGAL REQUIREMENTS It is an offence under the Civil Code of most countries:

(1) To distil spirits without a licence from the appropriate Government Office.
(2) To dispose of beer or wine for gain without a licence.
(3) To sell beer or wine wholesale without a licence and the payment of tax or duty.
(4) To call wines Port, Sherry, Champagne etc., without the name of the fruit or the country of origin as a prefix. These words are trade names protected by the laws of their country of origin.

Whenever there is an occasion that the law may be transgressed, it is recommended that legal advice be obtained from the appropriate Government Office.

LEMONS   Frequently used both as a source of citric acid and for flavouring. A small lemon contains the equivalent of approximately 3½ g of citric acid. For flavouring only, the finely pared zest or coloured skin should be used. The white pith gives off a most unpleasant bitterness and should never be added to wine.

LIGHT   Light in its sense of daylight or sunlight has an effect on wine. Red wines which are exposed to light, especially sunlight, will gradually lose their colour and turn brown. This is the reason why dark coloured bottles are always used for red wines. Exposure of partly filled bottles of wine to sunlight will cause slight oxidation but the results are not considered equal to normal ageing. Pasteur actually obtained a patent for the rapid ageing of wine by sunlight but it never became a commercial success.

LIGHT WINE   A light wine is one that has a low alcohol content, making it easy to drink. Although nicely balanced, it usually has little, although pleasing, flavour and is somewhat thin. When served, nicely chilled, these wines are far more appealing in hot weather than fuller-bodied and heavier red wines. Notable commercial examples are rosé wines from the Touraine in France and many of the less expensive wines from Germany.

LIQUEUR   A corruption of the French *Liqueur de dessert*, a strong alcoholic liquor, sweetened and flavoured with fruit and aromatic substances and intended to be drunk after a meal. There are many varieties with an alcohol content ranging from 24 to 40% by volume. They are made in one of three ways.

(a) DISTILLATION   A fruit wine is made and distilled, or herbs or fruits are macerated in spirit and then distilled. The process is an expensive one and only suitable for certain fruits and herbs.

(b) INFUSION   Fruits or herbs or seeds are steeped in spirit, which is then filtered and sweetened. Many of the fruit brandies are made in this way, since it is the only way of incorporating their flavour.

(c) ESSENCE PROCESS   The addition of synthetic flavourings to sweetened spirits. This process is widely used in the home. Vodka—a colourless and flavourless spirit is often used. The best essences are made in France. The addition of some glycerine—25 ml per litre—improves the richness, whilst some tincture of capiscum—25 drops per litre—adds warmth. The vodka is usually diluted to the appropriate strength with a bland white wine.

LIQUEUR DE TIRAGE   A mixture of wine and sugar used for dosing a still wine for bottle fermentation when producing sparkling wine. (*See* SPARKLING WINE.)

LIQUEUR D'EXPÉDITION   A mixture of old wine and sugar which is added to Champagne and other sparkling wine after disgorging the sediment from the bottle fermentation. The amount varies according to the sweetness required in the finished wine. It is so called because it is the last operation, apart from corking, before the sparkling wine is despatched.

LIQUOR   In the *Shorter Oxford Dictionary* this word has many meanings. For winemakers, however, it generally means a liquid containing alcohol, wine for example. In brewing beer the liquid at all stages, including the water, is called liquor.

LITMUS PAPER   An absorbent paper, usually in strips 5 cm long and 1 cm wide, soaked in a solution of litmus, a material of organic origin, and used to indicate the presence of acid or alkali, depending upon the colour to which it changes when dipped in a liquid to be tested. If the liquid contains acid, the colour of the litmus paper turns red, if the liquid is alkaline, the colour of the litmus paper turns to blue. This only indicates whether the solution is acid or alkaline. For the approximate degree of acidity or alkalinity, pH papers or colour change indicators should be used. (*See also* PH PAPERS.)

LITRE   The volume of one kilogramme of pure water measured at a temperature of 4 °C (39 °F); equivalent to 1·76 imperial pints. A standard wine bottle holds ¾ of a litre, i.e. 75 centilitres.

LIVELY   A wine is said to be lively when it stimulates the palate by its pleasant, but not dominant, acidity.

MACERATE   To extract flavour, colour and goodness, from fruits, flowers, herbs, spices, seeds etc. This is usually done by steeping in spirit or steeping in liquid.

MADEIRA   A fortified wine usually made from the Malvasia grape, although the Bual, Sercial and Verdelho are also used. It is made in the solera system but the new wines are first lightly fortified then matured for a few months in an estufa, where the temperature is slowly increased to a temperature of 50 °C (122 °F) (and then equally slowly returned to normal—around 20 °C (68 °F)). The wine is then additionally fortified and further matured in the solera. The finished wine has a highly individualistic caramelized flavour.

MADERIZE, MADERIZATION   When a white or rosé wine develops a brownish tinge, a peculiar musty smell and a woody taste, it is said to be maderized. It has become oxidized and has 'gone over the hill' due to too long storage. The term is also applied to the process of exposing certain wines from the Midi, in their casks, to the sun for a year or more. The wines are then supposed to resemble Madeira, although very inferior.

MAGNESIUM SULPHATE More commonly known as Epsom salts, magnesium sulphate is another yeast nutrient. Its presence in very small quantities in the must is necessary for yeast growth and development. (*See* NUTRIENTS.)

MALIC ACID *See* ACIDS.

MALO-LACTIC FERMENTATION Malic acid is a natural acid present in most fruits and vegetables varying from a trace (oranges, lemons, figs etc.) to about 2·5% (plums, damsons etc.). It is a sharp acid, which in the absence of air and sulphite, is fermented by one of the rod forms of the lactic acid bacteria to carbon dioxide and lactic acid that is less sharp. The titratable acid is reduced and the pH increased. The process is known as the malo-lactic fermentation and is common in high-pH wines containing malic acid.

Although malo-lactic fermentation occurs in some wines and not in others, it can be induced in a wine to reduce acidity. A little of a wine that has a malo-lactic fermentation can be added to a too acid wine. It should only be attempted in a dry wine, never in a sweet, because the wine will be spoilt by lactic acid bacteria fermentation of the sugars, producing mannitol etc. (*See* BITTERNESS and LACTIC ACID BACTERIA.)

To secure an adequate malo-lactic fermentation, the wine must be high in malic acid and relatively low in alcohol. It must also be free from sulphur dioxide. Autolysis of yeast and the release of amino acids aid the growth of the bacteria, and for this reason high-acid wines are left longer on the yeast lees before racking if the malo-lactic fermentation is desired. A temperature of 24 to 26 °C (75 to 80 °F) is helpful, the fermentation being delayed correspondingly at 15 °C (60 °F) and below.

Juices of extreme acidity can be treated with ascorbic acid instead of sulphite to encourage malo-lactic fermentation to occur alongside the yeast fermentation.

Some malo-lactic fermentations can produce an unwholesome, thick and cloudy appearance in a wine due to the large amounts of mucilage being formed, although they do not affect the flavour. Other fermentations, in addition to destroying malic acid, spoil the flavour by producing metabolic end-products. Nevertheless it is considered indispensable for the great wines of Bordeaux to undergo malo-lactic fermentation, resulting in changes in colour and softening of taste.

The prevention of malo-lactic fermentation can be achieved by early and regular racking and the maintenance of 100 ppm of sulphur dioxide. Air is also harmful to the fermentation.

When this type of fermentation occurs in bottles, the wine becomes petillant, that is, the wine will have a slight sparkle. This petillance is found in many commercial, high-acid grape wines today, e.g. the Vino Verdhe wines of Portugal. It is thought that the first wines produced as sparkling wines were actually the results of malo-lactic fermentations.

MANNITE INFECTION   A wine disease caused by bacteria which supplant the yeast when fermentation temperatures are too high. Rarely occurs in northern European viticultural areas but was common in the Midi and Algeria. Affected wines have a peculiar, sickly, sweet/sour taste. Known in France as *ferment mannitique*. Prevention is to keep the fermentation temperature down. In Australia, South Africa and California winemakers have to resort to some form of refrigeration.

MANNITOL   A sugar produced when low-acid sweet wines are attacked by one of the lactic acid bacteria which reduce fructose to mannitol. The mannitol so produced is very bitter and causes wine to have a bitterness which cannot be removed. Prevention is the use of sulphite and correct acidity. Mannitol is sometimes formed during a malo-lactic fermentation, especially when it is allowed to continue too long.

MARC   The pips, skins and stalk of black grapes after pressing. The solid matter from other fermentations is called pulp.

MARINADE   Wine is an important ingredient in cooking meals that are out of the ordinary. It is also used extensively in preparing a pickle consisting of wine, vinegar, herbs and spices in which meat and fish are steeped. If stewing beef, mutton chops and the like are soaked overnight in such a pickle containing a dry red wine, they are thereby rendered tender and more flavoursome. The acids and the alcohol begin the breakdown of the tougher tissues, which is continued in the subsequent cooking. Fish can be marinaded in dry white wine with similar success and a notable example is kippers. Soaked in dry white wine overnight, boneless kippers can be skinned and served on crisp buttered toast as a canapé. No further cooking is necessary.

The flavour of fresh fruit is greatly enhanced by marinading it in a sweet white wine for some hours before serving. Raspberries, strawberries, fresh fruit salad and so on become enriched and yet more digestible after marinading.

MARRYING   The mixing together in the must of different varieties of grapes or other fruit, to obtain a better balance of acidity, aroma, body, flavour and sugar. All grape varieties make better wine when 'married' with other varieties.

MASHING   This is the very first stage of winemaking, when the colour, flavour and goodness are extracted from the basic ingredients to form the must. It can be done in several different ways: carbonic maceration, heat treatment, juice extraction or pulp fermentation. Refer to these individual headings for full details.

MATURATION The process of ageing a wine until it is in peak condition and ready for drinking. Although it is well known that all wines improve during the process of maturing, the causes and chemical reactions are still not completely understood. It is known, however, that malic and succinic acids are reduced to esters, that acetic acid is formed in very small quantities, that some tannin is oxidized, that there is a reduction of fusel oils to acids and aldehydes and that acetals, which are very aromatic and form an important part of the bouquet, are produced from the combination of the aldehydes and alcohols. In red wines, some tannins precipitate, some become oxidized and some join with other components of the wine, including proteins. Time, whether short or long, is the main factor. Efforts to speed it up by ion exchanges, by oxidizing and other agents, by electrical discharge, by exposure to the sun, by heating and by other methods have all failed to produce the quality of age. White wine and light table wines require the shortest time, from a few months to a few years, but the time increases with wines that have a greater body, alcohol and sugar content. Red wines need longer depending on the amount of acid, body, alcohol, sugar and, more especially, tannin that is present.

There are two stages of maturation. The first, by free air oxidation, whilst stored in bulk. This is achieved commercially by storing in cask for one to three years when the air permeates through the staves and slowly oxidizes the wine. White wines require a shorter time in cask than red and the smaller the cask the more carefully must they be watched for over-oxidation. In five-gallon casks the maximum period for white wines could well be as little as three months or even less. Amateurs using stoneware or glass jars can achieve bulk oxidation by frequent racking, but again care must be taken not to over-oxidize.

The second stage is by chemical reaction (the redox reaction) which occurs in the bottle when the wine is sealed from contact with air. Again, red wines require longer in bottle than white. After a period of bulk storage nearly all wines improve during a further period in a bottle.

The achievement of the best results is by slow redox reactions, allowing time for the new compounds to marry with the old. A cool storage around 10 °C (50 °F) is needed. Higher temperatures cause the reactions to be too rapid for quality. A slightly higher, but steady temperature, however, is preferable to one that fluctuates widely around 10 °C (50 °F). The storage should be free from vibrations and bright light. The precise time required varies with each individual wine.

MAURY This is the name given to a variety of *Saccharomyces ellipsiodeus* from the dessert wine district of Maury on the Mediterra nean border of France by the Pyrenees. It is regarded as one of the most suitable yeasts for fermenting a honey solution into sweet mead.

MAZER An ancient wooden drinking vessel, frequently carved from bird's eye maple and traditional reserved for the drinking of mead. It sometimes has two handles and may be decorated with silver mountings. The vessel was passed from one to another for each to take a sup.

MEAD The first fermented drink, prickly with fermentation and cloudy with yeast and insoluble waxes and the like, was undoubtedly mead, which it is thought has been known to man for nearly twelve thousand years. Basically, mead is the matured produce of the fermentation of a solution of honey in water. The flavour of the honey depends on the flowers from which the nectar is gathered by the bee and this in turn produces meads of different flavours.

Light-coloured and mild-flavoured honey makes the best mead. Dark honey has a pronounced flavour and the resultant mead has a somewhat overpowering and sometimes unusual flavour, expecially for the sophisticated palate. Because of its rather sweet bouquet, mead should preferably be served on the sweet side of dry, a specific gravity of 1·000 is about as low as it is desirable to go. Below this figure there appears a contradiction of sweet bouquet and dry flavours. Mead should always be served cold and best accompanies fish and chicken or is drunk independently as a beverage. Spiced mead, metheglin, is one of the very few wines that can be drunk and appreciated with curries.

Mead has long been mixed with other fruits to vary the flavour, e.g.: cyser is mead mixed with apple juice, pyment is mead mixed with grape juice, melomel is mead mixed with other fruit juices and hippocras is mead mixed with spiced grape juice. Either spices or herbs may be used for flavouring metheglins and these can be delicious when served sweet and hot (60 °C/140 °F).

From 1 to 2 kg of honey is needed to make five litres of mead and as honey contains neither acid nor nutrient, these essential ingredients to fermentation must always be added. Fermentation is started with 1 kg of honey and more is added in stages if a higher alcohol content is required. There is some controversy still between the 'boilers' and the 'non-boilers'. Traditionally the honey has been boiled in three times its quantity of water and this has served to cause wax and other impurities to rise to the surface as scum, which has to be removed. It has also undoubtedly sterilized the honey from all infections from bacteria, fungi and wild yeasts. On the other hand, the 'non-boilers' rightly argue that the delicate esters and flavours are lost in the boiling and that the quality of the ensuing mead is thus impaired. With the more advanced technical knowledge now available there is little doubt that the best method is as follows:

The honey is dissolved in warm water and 3 g of acid per litre of must is added, together with sulphite at the rate of 100 ppm. The vessel must be tightly covered and left for 24 hours. Tannin, yeast nutrient, in double the quantities used for wine, and an active wine-yeast culture are then added. After seven days the mead is racked, again after fourteen days and then at four-week intervals until fermentation ceases. If fermentation slows and almost stops while the mead is still sweet, a little extra nutrient must be added to continue the fermentation to near dryness. When the mead is a year old and stable it may be sweetened as required with fresh honey.

Honey can be quite expensive to buy and both beehive cappings and washings are sometimes used for making mead, especially after they have been sterilized. They generally produce rather odd-flavoured meads. Honey can sometimes be bought more cheaply in bulk, but the source of nectar should be ascertained if possible. Orange-blossom honey makes superb mead but the flavour of mead made from mixed or blended honey derived from unsuitable sources, e.g. the flowering Eucalyptus, can be less pleasant unless it is finished quite sweet.

Mead needs slow fermentation and sometimes takes six months or longer. Maturation is frequently equally slow, sometimes taking from three to five years. Six months or so in a cask is a great help. Conversely, some light meads are delicious when very young indeed—six to eight weeks.

MEASURES

	U.S.A.	Imperial	Metric
half pint	8 fl.oz	10 fl.oz	284 ml
pint	16 fl.oz	20 fl.oz	568 ml
quart	32 fl.oz	40 (2 pints)	1·136 litres
gallon	128 fl.oz	160 (8 pints)	4·546 litres
half bottle wine		13⅓ fl.oz	(37 cl)
bottle wine		26⅔ fl.oz	(75 cl)
one litre wine		35½ fl.oz	(100 cl)
Magnum		2 bottles	(1·5 litres)
Jeroboam		4 bottles	(3 litres)
Rehoboam (1 gallon)		6 bottles	(4·5 litres)
Methuselah		8 bottles	(6 litres)
Salmanazar (2 gallons)		12 bottles	(9 litres)
Balthazar		16 bottles	(12 litres)
Nebuchadnezzar		20 bottles	(15 litres)
hogshead	varies from	46 gallons to 65 gallons	(210 to 300 litres)
butt (Sherry)		108 gallons	(491 litres)

pipe (Port)	115 gallons	(523 litres)
pipe (Madeira)	92 gallons	(418 litres)
pipe (Marsala)	93 gallons	(423 litres)
Tun	210 gallons	(955 litres)

(All cask sizes vary slightly as they are still handmade)

100 U.S.A. gallons equals 83⅓ Imperial gallons
Hectolitre equals 22 Imperial gallons
Hectare equals 2·47 acres
Hectolitre per hectare equals 8·9 gallons per acre

MEDICINAL FLAVOUR Wines lacking in acid and tannin are soft, flabby and insipid on the palate. They are said to have a medicinal flavour.

MEDICINAL QUALITIES The tonic and therapeutic qualities of wine have been known and used for thousands of years. Hippocrates, the father of medicine, gave his name to a mixture of mead and wine, which he no doubt prescribed for many of his patients. Apothecaries used to mix herbs and potions with wine to mask the flavours. In 1568 William Turner wrote the first book on wine to be published in England, in which he recommended drinking white wine from the Rhineland as opposed to red wine from France, so as not to suffer from stone in the kidneys or bladder—a very common ailment of the day.

Sometimes wine is still prescribed in its natural state, for example, a glass of dry sherry before lunch or a glass of burgundy with lunch for someone convalescent is by no means uncommon. Sometimes too, wine is still used as a vehicle for mineral salts, such as Phospherine and is taken three times a day as a tonic. Thus the practice of the centuries is still continued today.

Wine in a moderate quantity is beneficial to all people and harmful to none, unless suffering from a fever or taken with drugs. Even diabetics may drink very dry wines, although not sweeter or dessert wines. To the young it gives vitality, to the middle-aged it relaxes tensions and strain and to the old it gives comfort and peace. Young children, even from a few months old, may be given a few sips of wine, especially if it is diluted with a little water. Simply because it is customary and not forbidden, no craving is then experienced by the adolescent and the excessive consumption of liquor that causes harm is thus avoided in later years.

In moderation wine stimulates the appetite, aids digestion, relaxes the nerves and gives a graciousness to living that is too often neglected. (*See also* ALCOHOL.)

MELOMEL This is a mixture of mead and fruit juices. The ancient Greeks were such seekers for variation in their drinks that they tried mixing everything! Melomel can be made either by replacing with honey some or all of the sugar in a recipe for mixed fruit wine, or by adding some crushed mixed fruit juice to a fermenting mead. A blend of mead and mixed fruit wine is a splendid drink when served just slightly sweet. Melomel, like mead, can be unpleasant when too dry, but a good melomel is an excellent wine.

MENISCUS   Derived from the old Greek word meaning crescent. The meaning of meniscus as applied to winemaking is the convex or concave upper surface of a liquid column which is caused by capillary action. The word meniscus is particularly applied to the surface of a must or wine, in a hydrometer trial jar. The liquid forms a concave surface, between the stem of the hydrometer and the side of the glass jar. The reading of the hydrometer has to be taken at the hollow of the surface of the liquid, not at the edges which would give a slightly inaccurate result.

MESO-INISTOL   A vitamin required by yeast and readily available in malt. Hence the use of a solution of malt extract in yeast starter bottles.

METAL CASSE   *See* CASSE.

METALS and METAL CONTAMINATION   Metals can cause contamination of wines which range from the harmless, albeit unpleasant, to the positively poisonous. The general symptoms are an unpleasantly harsh or metal flavour and hazes or a darkening when exposed to the air.

Lead, including lead glaze on pottery, zinc and antimony are poisonous and must be completely avoided. Antimony is used in enamels and all enamel vessels should be avoided except those which are vitreous enamelled. Vitreous enamel is inert to acid but the vessels should not be used if chipped, as the acid will attack the metal where the surface has been broken. Contact with brass, copper and iron does not render a wine harmful but it does spoil the wine. Aluminium pans may be used for heating ingredients to make an extraction provided there is little or no acid in the ingredients. Slight contamination with copper, as from Bordeaux mixture on the fruit before fermentation, can be lost during fermentation. The same amount of contamination after the wine is stable will produce astringent and unpleasant flavours and white wines are given a greenish haze. Iron contamination at any time affects the flavour and causes darkening, although the darkening can be cleared by the use of citric acid.

To test for iron contamination, a little of the darkened or hazy wine is put into a glass and a pinch of citric acid is added. The wine will be clear after some hours if the cause is iron. The bulk of the wine could then be treated with citric acid at the rate of 1 oz in 10 gallons/30 g in 50 litres. Although the appearance will be improved the taste will not. Treatment with 90 g fresh wheat bran mixed thoroughly into the wine, left 24 hours and then filtered, can improve the flavour. Generally, however, wines which are metal-contaminated are best thrown away.

Stainless steel is the only metal which is safe to have in contact with musts or wines and all other metals should be kept away from them.

For other causes of hazes and darkening see BROWNING and HAZES. (*See also* LEAD.)

METHANOL This word is derived from methyl and from alcohol. It is normally used in reference to synthesized methyl alcohol but is sometimes used for the spirit which has not been so produced. (*See also* ALCOHOL.)

METHEGLIN Many people like spicy drinks and foods as much as their forebears did. Metheglin is an old Welsh word meaning a 'healing liquor' and is used in connection with spiced mead. The variety of spices was and is legion and according to your own particular palate. Apart from ginger, cloves, nutmeg, cinnamon and so on, herbs such as rosemary, balm, sorrel, strawberry leaves etc., were also used to vary the flavour of mead. The spices and herbs are usually placed in a muslin bag and steeped in the honey solution either while it is brought to the boil or during fermentation. Metheglin is an acquired taste, not to everyone's liking and is best served sweet rather than dry.

MÉTHODE CHAMPENOISE *See* SPARKLING WINE.

METHYL ALCOHOL *See* ALCOHOL.

METHYLATED SPIRIT A mixture of ethyl and methyl alcohol to which has been added pyridine and colouring—supposedly to prevent people from drinking it, although some alcohol addicts do drink it. It is primarily used as a fuel. It is used in winemaking to test for pectin in a sample of a hazy wine. (*See* PECTIN for details.)

METRIC VOLUME Measurement of small volumes which in the past have been known as 'cc' and later 'ml' is now known as 'cm^3'. They are the same volume, i.e. 1 cc = 1 ml = 1 cm^3.

MICRO-FLORA The lowest form of plant life.

MICRO-ORGANISMS A general term used to cover any single-celled animal or plant. Too small to be seen individually with the naked eye, they can be clearly seen only when magnified many times under a microscope. They include bacteria, fungi, viruses and yeasts. These micro-organisms can be present in the air, on ingredients or equipment. If allowed to develop into colonies they could be responsible for the spoilage of wines and wine ingredients, varying from off-taints and odours to complete ruin. The best insurance against unseen micro-organisms is good hygiene and the use of bactericide and fungicide, to which topics also refer.

MILDEW There are two common varieties of fungus that attack vines and fruit bushes and trees.

(a) POWDERY MILDEW—OIDIUM This is seen as a greyish white powder that develops on leaves, shoots and fruit as though the plant had been dusted all over with cement. Without remedial action the leaves dry up and fall and the fruit remains small, sometimes turning brown and dropping. Fruit skins that have been attacked remain rough and corky. The remedy lies in dusting the plant regularly throughout the season with sulphur powder or treating with a proprietary brand of fungicide. The disease was first noticed on grapes in 1878 and was referred to as 'powdery mildew'. It is thought that it came from America with the replacement vine stocks required to combat phylloxera. When it attacks gooseberry bushes it is referred to as 'American blight'.

(b) DOWNY MILDEW—PERONOSPORA This is even more insidious. This fungus just creates white or yellow patches on the leaves of the plant and then moves on to the developing fruit which it ruins. If untreated the vine itself will eventually die. It can be prevented by regularly spraying the vines throughout the season with copper sulphate, Bordeaux mixture, or the newer fungicides Captan and Dithane or the more recent systemics such as Benomyl and Dimethoate. (*See also* FUNGICIDES.)

The effects in wine of mildew or moulds (fungi) on fruit other than grape does not appear to have been properly investigated. Spoilage is the most probable result but some instances may be beneficial. In one instance, gooseberries that split due to the weather developed mould in the split, but not on the skin, during ripening. Wine made from these berries when fully ripe, developed a great similarity to Sauternes as it matured.

MILK A simple source of casein in solution. The fining of wine with milk has been practised for a very long time but is now superseded by the use of casein, especially for large quantities of wine. (*See also* CASEIN and FINING.)

MINERALS In musts and wines there are very small quantities or traces of different inorganic constituents. They are required in the alcoholic fermentation and are part of the redox reactions. There are electro-negative elements (anions) and electro-positive elements (cations). The negative elements include boron, bromide, chloride and fluoride. When fluoride is present in amounts of 200 mg or more per gallon, it prevents fermentation. Also present are iodide, phosphates (a necessity for fermentation), silicate and sulphate. The latter results from plastering and also from the oxidation of sulphurous acid, although Schanderl (1959) reported that the reverse could happen, i.e. sulphate being reduced to sulphurous acid during fermentation.

The positive elements include aluminium, which is present in higher quantities in red wines than in white, calcium from fruit, from plastering and from filtering aids, copper, necessary for fermentation, and iron that is reduced by up to half its amount during fermentation. Schanderl found iron to be in or on yeast cells. Also present are magnesium, manganese, more in red wines than white, molybdenum, rubidium, sodium and potassium, the latter constituting up to three-quarters of the total positive elements.

All these minerals are present in musts and also in finished wines. They are originally derived from the soil and from the chemicals sprayed on the fruit during growth. Although present in minute or only trace quantities, the amounts vary even in the same ingredient when grown in different soils.

Other minerals can be present in finished wines, such as tin, lead and cadmium, causing off flavours and toxicity. They result from contact with vessels containing them. Iron or copper, necessary in the very small amounts present in the ingredients, cause taints, hazes and poisoning, if the content is increased through the must or wine coming into contact with iron or copper vessels or utensils.

MOELLEUX A French word meaning soft, usually applied to a wine that is slightly sweet without undertones of sharpness due to acidity, and has not quite enough tannin to give it bite. The word is derived from *moell* meaning a marrow and also the soft marrow of one's bones.

MORDANT A term applied to a wine with an excess of acid, an excess of tannin, or an excess of both. Wines that are mordant are excessively sharp, astringent or with excessive bite, giving the sensation of being corrosive.

A little mordant wine added to a soft, flabby one will produce a very marked improvement in both of them.

MOSEL, MOSELLE The generic name given to the greenish/gold wines produced along the banks of the rivers Mosel, Saar and Ruwer. Produced primarily from the Riesling grape the bouquet and flavour of a Mosel wine is fresher, lighter and more delicate than a Hock. The wines are often chaptalized and sweetened although, even then, their alcohol content varies from only 8·5 to 10%.

MOULDS There are countless varieties of botanical cells classified under the heading 'fungi', as moulds, which appear in one or two forms—as fine powdery particles, often coloured, or as hair-like threads. They need moisture, warmth, air and some shade for growth, but the cells individually are so minute that they float in the air and settle on growth mediums to develop into a colony of many millions before they become visible. Once they have developed on raw materials or on a must, they impart an unpleasant flavour to the finished wine that cannot be removed.

Since moulds need moisture and shade for growth all fruits should be gathered on dry sunny days, wherever possible, and processed immediately, they should not be allowed to stand about. For the same reason musts should not be left uncovered or without being properly sulphited. During fermentation the carbon dioxide will inhibit mould growth, though clearly mould-infected ingredients should never be used for making wine.

Moulds on vessels and utensils or equipment can be easily inhibited with sulphite and can be prevented from growing by simple cleanliness and storage in a dry place. A final rinse with a sulphite solution just before use is always a well-worthwhile safeguard. Wine poured into vessels containing moulds develop a mouldy, musty smell, dank and dirty. Whilst the wine may not be pathogenic, the smell and taste is so unpleasant that it is best to throw the wine away.

Moulds that could be responsible for spoiling wine are those of the *Penicillium* genus, which are the cause of 'corked' or 'corky' wine, and the *Aspergillus*, *Oidium*, *Sclerotinia*, *Botrytis*, *Mucor* and *Rhizopus* genera. All are harmful to wine except *Botrytis cinerea* which in dry warm weather on grapes produces the characteristics of Sauternes. In humid conditions, even this has a deleterious effect on grapes. If fruit is used on which moulds have already developed, the wine is likely to smell and taste mouldy.

MOUSSE When applied to wine this word means the foam, or conglomeration of bubbles which briefly forms on the top of a glass of sparkling wine and in the bottle. The pressure in the bottle should not on its own push out the cork, nor should foam gush from the bottle. Either denotes faulty production. The mousse should be plentiful and light and quickly disappear from the surface of the wine in the glass. It should leave a continuous rising of small beads or bubbles of carbon dioxide. The mousse should remain in the bottle for some time.

MOUSSEUX A sparkling wine not made in Champagne, but in some other region of France.

MOÛT The French word for the must. Sometimes called *moût de goutte* and *moût de presse*. (*See also* PRESSING GRAPES.)

MOUSY An unpleasant and sometimes revolting odour and taste in a wine, mainly as an aftertaste, due to the presence of acetoin and acetaminde from infection by lactic acid bacteria. This infection frequently develops when the wine has been left too long on its lees. The dead yeast cells in the lees autolyse and release trace elements necessary for the growth of the bacteria. Wines that are regularly racked at intervals not exceeding 10 weeks and as often as lees are deposited, rarely suffer from this infection. Affected wines have a smell and taste that some people liken to the odour of breeding mice. Others consider it to be more like a 'high' cheese. The smell and taste cannot be removed. Affected wines should be thrown away and the container thoroughly cleaned and sterilized.

MUCILAGE   A gummy viscous substance present in various parts of vegetable organisms including fruit, which in small quantities helps to give body to a wine, but when present in too large a quantity can cause considerable difficulty in clearing.

MULLED WINE   Wine which has been warmed, spiced and sweetened. It makes a perfect 'night-cap', gets a party 'going' and is a most warming drink before going out on a cold winter's day. Only poor wines need be used and for something that offers so much, mulling is simplicity itself. The rules of production, if they can be called such, are:

(1) Never use a good wine. The poor or even slightly contaminated wine, as long as it is clean on the palate, is quite suitable.
(2) Keep tasting the mull during the warming to make sure that the spice, the sugar and the wine all contribute and blend as a whole, without any one ingredient overshadowing the others.
(3) Do not allow the temperature to rise above 60 °C (140 °F).
(4) For a basic recipe *see under* PUNCH which is akin to mulled wine, but vary ingredients and quantities and make other recipes to suit your own palate.

The only equipment required is a saucepan, preferably made from stainless steel, but aluminium is also suitable and a wooden or plastic spoon. The wine is put into the saucepan with the sugar and spices and gently heated, stirring to dissolve the sugar. Strain out the solids when pouring into a glass. As the glass can become quite hot, it is best to place a silver spoon in the glass to absorb some of the heat. Glass mugs with handles should be used when available so as not to burn your fingers when holding the glass. China mugs are not really suitable as the colour and appearance of the mull cannot be seen. A porcelain or silver bowl and a ladle are agreeable and pleasing vessels from which to serve the mull.

MUSELET   The wire network or cage used to fasten the domed cork or plastic stopper to the projecting rim at the top of the neck of a Champagne or sparkling wine bottle.

MUST   This is the name given to fruit juice extracts or liquor, with or without pulp, prepared for alcoholic fermentation. In grape wine it is the freshly pressed grape juice, with or without skins and pips, depending upon whether red or white wine is to be produced. In fruit, flower, cereal and vegetable wines etc., it is the juice, extract or the liquid prepared from the mashing, either by heating or steeping, that is ready for the addition of the yeast. By definition (*Shorter Oxford Dictionary*), the must does not become wine until fermentation is complete and the new wine is racked from the lees. Others take the view that must ceases to be must at the onset of the production of alcohol.

To make wine of quality it is necessary to prepare the must carefully. It should contain a variety of ingredients that will give a correct balance, including appropriate quantities of acid, tannin, sugar, body and flavour suitable for the type of wine to be made. The must should be sulphited and protected so that no bacteria, moulds or wild yeasts can develop and spoil the flavour of the finished wine. Few grape varieties make excellent wine by themselves and experience proves that a blend of different varieties make a better wine.

MUSTINESS   A rank odour emanating from a vessel which has been put away damp. Microscopic fungi have developed in the moisture and given off the foetid odour. All vessels and equipment used in wine-making should always be put away clean and dry and stored in a dry place. Even so, before using they should be rinsed in or with a sulphite solution and 'nosed' to make sure that they smell clean and wholesome.

MUTAGE   The stopping of fermentation by adding alcohol of 90% volume, to give about 10% volume in the wine. Some fruits, particularly muscat grapes, lose their fruitiness during fermentation and mutage is practised to retain the bouquet and flavour of the grape in the finished wine.

MYCODERMA ACETI, MYCODERMA VINI   Mycoderma is a name that has been used in connection with bacteria, moulds and yeast. It is from the Greek words *mykes* meaning fungi and *derma* meaning skin. Thus mycoderma is a skin of fungi and refers to the films or pellicles of alcoholic fermentation.

Originally the vinegar bacteria was called *mycoderma aceti* and was accepted as the sole cause of vinegar. It is now known that there are several species of bacteria and yeasts that can acetify a wine or produce a vinegar taint. These are various species of *Acetobacter*, some of which produce a film and some do not, certain lactic acid bacteria and some wild yeasts. The term *mycoderma aceti*, if used now, should only refer to the film or skin as a whole, or, as it is sometimes called, 'the mother of vinegar'. The bacteria or yeasts are defined by their individual designations, some details of which are given under vinegar bacteria and vinegar taint.

Mycoderma vini was the term by which the films, other than the vinegar film, were known. The common name was 'flowers of wine'. This designation of yeast films is, however, very loose, covering several genera, and is falling into disuse. The yeasts are individually identified, the most common being *Candida mycoderma*.

Mycoderma has also been identified as the film or scum that forms on the top of pickle brines, but here again the scum contains many species of yeast and bacteria.

NITROGEN An important element in protein and cell structure. Yeasts build the protein they require from nitrogen in the must or ammonium salts (nutrient). If a must is deficient in nitrogen the yeast obtains it from dead cells and so produces fusel oils.

NOBLE ROT *See* BOTRYTIS CINEREA.

NORMAL SOLUTION All chemicals have a chemical weight. The molecular weight of a chemical in grams per litre of solution is a normal solution. A deci-normal solution has only one-tenth of the chemical per litre. The terms are used to describe the strength of acid or alkali solutions.

NOSE The term used for the combined smell of aroma and bouquet of a wine.

NUTRIENTS A nutrient provides nourishment or sustenance to an organic organism. By general usage in reference to winemaking, certain chemicals have become known as yeast nutrients. This is a somewhat loose term since the real requirement of wine yeasts are substrates. The so-called nutrients, however, have to be added for the sustenance of yeasts in musts which have been prepared with a quantity of water. Undiluted grape juice or fruit juice contains all that is necessary to nourish the yeast and does not need the addition of nutrients.

Wine yeasts, being a low form of plant life, require much the same 'food' as higher plants growing in a garden and, without it, will cease to cause fermentation. This is one of the causes of 'stuck ferments'. In addition, in the same way that some plants need an acid soil and others an alkaline one, so wine yeasts require an acid solution for maximum growth and activity.

The wine yeasts' requirements are certain amino acids, vitamins of the 'B' group and inorganic salts. In more detail these are:

(a) AMINO ACIDS These are present in sufficient quantity in all grape and fruit musts but should be added to honey musts.

(b) VITAMINS Known as 'B_1' and sold by chemists as Aneurin or Thiamine. The usual requirement is 3 mg per gallon.

(c) INORGANIC SALTS Many trace elements are required such as iron, copper, zinc, boron etc., but these will normally be present in the must and it will only be necessary to add the major chemicals. These are ammonium sulphate or ammonium phosphate, potassium phosphate and magnesium sulphate. Quantities naturally present vary from must to must, but a formula based on one originated by the British Beekeepers' Association is as suitable as any for general use:

Ammonium sulphate	428 mg	
Potassium phosphate	214 mg	} per litre of water used
Magnesium sulphate	57 mg	

If a quantity of the mixture is purchased to this formula, the quantity to use would be 700 mg per litre of water. For honey musts, which are very deficient, use a double quantity.

There are many commercial nutrient powders or tablets on sale. These should be used in accordance with the manufacturer's instructions.

Sugar is also necessary for the sustenance of wine yeast, but is not generally referred to as a nutrient, although the yeast obtains energy from it.

OAK   Used for casks, barrels etc., oak has proved to be the best wood for the purpose for many centuries. Not only is it strong, but it allows air to permeate slowly through its pores and so oxidize the wine. This is also true of other woods which are sometimes used, but none of them cause the improvement in wine, by some chemical reaction as yet not defined, as does oak. That oak has this particular quality is confirmed by the fact that wine stored in a glass tank to which oak chippings have been added, matures in the same way as in oak casks.

ODOUR   An odour is a pleasant or unpleasant smell. The quality of wine is in its fine aroma and bouquet and any other odours that are present are unwanted and undesired. The most common of unwanted odours that occur in wine are those produced by lactic acid bacteria, vinegar souring, sulphur dioxide, and that of acetates produced by spoilage organisms. Sound wines stored unsealed can acquire unwanted odours if stored with strong-smelling commodities, such as creosote or paraffin.

OENOLOGIST   A person who is experienced in matters concerning wine and winemaking.

OENOLOGY   The study of wine in all its aspects, preparation, fermentation, maturation and consumption.

OENOPHILE   A person who loves wine in the aesthetic sense. One who deeply appreciates the appearance, bouquet and flavour of good wine, has 'feeling' for wine, and is always anxious to learn more about wine.

OFF-FLAVOURS   These are the unwanted flavours in wine which are noticeable either in the first or in the aftertaste. Invariably they are the result of bad or careless winemaking in any one or more of a number of ways.

(1) Acetification or the presence of acetic acid (*see* VINEGAR and LACTIC ACID BACTERIA). Sour taste, resulting from exposure to air.
(2) Aldehydes formed to excess. Over-exposure to air. 'Greenish' oxidized flavour.
(3) Asbestos pulp—a taste like paper or cardboard, due to the use of improperly cleaned asbestos pulp when filtering.
(4) Autolysis of yeast—mousy or cheesy taints resulting from inefficient and infrequent racking.
(5) Bitterness—inclusion of too many stalks, or crushing a few too well. Also from the formation of acetamide and mannitol by bacteria as a result of insufficient racking and the non-use of sulphite.
(6) Boiling and thereby the extraction of unwanted compounds causing off-flavours.
(7) Burnt taste from the use of brown sugars and from fermentation at too high a temperature.
(8) Corky—a corky taste caused by corks attacked by moulds.
(9) 'Flowers of wine' causing conversion of alcohol to carbon dioxide and water, the result of exposing low-alcohol wines to air through faulty corking.
(10) Fusty from use of dirty jars or casks.
(11) Maderized—the heavy, flat smell and taste of excessive age. The wine is also said to be 'over the hill'.
(12) Metal contamination—metallic taints from contact with metal.
(13) Mouldy, musty flavour—from mould in casks and on raw materials, utensils, vessels and in the must, but very rarely in the wine.
(14) Tourne—flat and often a little sour, from lactic acid bacteria.
(15) Over-oxidation—a 'greenish', flat taste, due to over-exposure to air.
(16) Volatile acidity—causing a taste of acetic acid formed by spoilage organisms.

OIDIUM *See* MILDEW.

OILINESS Another name for ROPINESS, under which details are given. Not to be confused with the thick appearance of wines containing a high quantity of glycerine.

OINOS The Greek word for wine from which it is believed that many other words for wine have been derived, e.g. *vinum*, *vin*, *vino*, *Wein*, *guino* and others. There is, however, a following for the belief that all words, including *oinos*, come from the Sanskrit word *vena*, meaning a drink-offering (to a god).

OSMOSIS When two solutions are separated only by a semi-permeable membrane, water will leave the weaker solution in an endeavour to equalize the differing strengths of the solutions. Thus when too much sugar is dissolved in a must, water leaves the yeast cell through its semi-permeable exterior membrane. Since 65% of the yeast cell is water, the cell caves in as it dries up, metabolic activity ceases and the cell eventually dies. This is one of the causes of a stuck ferment when large quantities are added to a must. At the time of inoculation with an active yeast, it is best that the must should not contain more than 200 g sugar per litre, equivalent to a specific gravity of about 1·075. If a high alcohol content is required, sugar syrup should be added in small doses when the gravity has fallen considerably. Sauternes yeast is one that can tolerate a high sugar concentration, although fermentation is slow.

OVER-FINING   The fining of wine is a very effective method of clarification when correctly applied. When used in excess, many fining agents cause further hazing instead of clearing the wine. This is known as over-fining. *See also* FINING and especially TRIAL FININGS.

OXIDASE   An enzyme present in fruit, especially very ripe fruit, that causes browning that can taint a wine.

OXIDATION, OXIDIZED   In the life of every wine oxidation must occur in different forms but always within limits. It is absolutely essential to the development of the wine. (*See* MATURATION.) Only when the limits are exceeded does it become a fault. Frequently it is then erroneously described as 'oxidized' although in fact it is over-oxidized.

Certain wines, however, such as Sherry and Arbois types have an excess oxidation that give them their individual flavour and character without fault. They are correctly referred to as oxidized wines.

The fault of being over-oxidized occurs when the wine has been allowed to absorb too much oxygen from the air and there has been dehydrogenation of the alcohols, so forming an excess of aldehydes. It is the result of exposing stable wine to air by leaving it too long in the cask, in an imperfectly covered vessel or in a covered container only partly filled, i.e. too much ullage. Over-oxidized wines have a distinct, flat, 'greenish' off-odour and taste that once experienced is not forgotten. The colour of the wine is not affected.

Confusion sometimes occurs between over-oxidation and browning. Browning of young wine is caused by enzymes combining oxygen from the air with tannins. This is enzymic oxidation, the result of leaving crushed fruit, must, or even newly finished wines, exposed to air. The wine develops a brown tint but the smell and flavour is not affected. Enzymic browning and over-oxidation can occur together, however, in very young wines but never in crushed pulp or must. It is only in these very young wines that colour, smell and flavour are affected.

After wine has matured by a proper amount of air oxidation, as in the cask, it is bottled and further develops by another oxidation. This is the oxidation and reduction between the wines' components in the absence of air, that develops bouquet and flavour. If the wine remains in the bottle too long it again becomes over-oxidized, although this over-oxidation usually causes a wine to be described as maderized.

No quantitative or time-factor can yet be given for any of the oxidations; because there are so many variables involved, each wine is individual. Generally, red wines require much longer than whites. Certain white wines benefit from up to one year in cask, but many red wines usually require at least two years or more. When wines should be bottled can be judged only by taste. Certain white wines can require up to 3 or 4 years in bottle to reach their best condition. Many reds need at least 4 years in bottle and some even more than 10 years. Again taste is the only decider as to when the wines have reached their peak of perfection. Sweet wines usually require longer than dry.

OXIDIZED WINES Wines of the Sherry and Arbois types which have been subject to excess oxidation without developing fault.

OXYGEN Oxygen from the air plays a considerable part in the production of wine and is both wanted and unwanted at various stages. This is best illustrated by considering its desirability from the must stage to the fully matured wine.

When fruits and some other materials are cut or crushed and also with the fine particles of pulp in juices, enzymes use free oxygen to oxidize the tannins in the pulp and so turn the material or juice brown. If this is allowed to occur, the resulting wines will be from light to dark brown. Here, free oxygen from the air is unwanted, but its exclusion is not always practicable. The best preventative is the correct use of sulphite as an anti-oxidant in the must. (*See* BROWNING.)

During fermentation oxygen is not required for low-alcohol wines, as the initial yeast crop is sufficient to ferment to dryness. For high-alcohol wines with larger amounts of sugar to be fermented the yeast crop must reproduce itself. To do so, the yeast requires oxygen which can be introduced into the ferment by stirring, or preferably by frequent racking. (*See* YEAST and AIR CONTROL.)

After fermentation free oxygen from the air is required for the first stage of maturation. This can be supplied by either storing the wine in casks, or by regular racking of wines stored in glass, stoneware or stainless steel vessels impervious to air, care being taken not to over-oxidize the wine. (*See* OXIDATION.)

Finally, the wines are bottled and, for this stage, free oxygen has to be excluded in order that maturation is completed by oxidation and reduction (*see* REDOX REACTIONS) between the sugars, acids and other constituents of the wine. In order to exclude oxygen from large vessels and long pipelines to be filled with must or wine, nitrogen or carbon dioxide is first pumped into them to push out the air containing oxygen.

PALATE Biologically, the palate is the roof of the mouth of vertebrates, but in connection with wine the word refers to the senses of smell and taste together with their mental appreciation. A person is said to 'have a good palate', implying that he has a keen sense of flavour appreciation, whereas on the palate, texture and taste only can be assessed: i.e. a wine is smooth and clean or is acid, bitter, salt, sweet. (*See also* AROMA, BOUQUET, FLAVOUR, JUDGING WINE, SMELL, TASTES and TEXTURE.)

PARAFFIN WAX *See* WAX.

PASTEURIZATION The raising of the temperature of a must or wine (or for that matter any liquid) in order to kill yeasts and bacteria. In commercial winemaking one of two methods is used—(a) flash pasteurizing by raising the temperature to about 80 °C (185 °F) for one minute; (b) slow pasteurization to stabilize white table and dessert wines by heating them to about 60 °C (140 °F), adding bentonite, then holding a temperature of from 50 °C (120 °F) to 55 °C (130 °F) for one to three days. The wine is then bottled. In America, fruit wines are heated to 60 °C and bottled hot. Fine wines are never pasteurized, and the wines that are pasteurized never reach the standard of those that are not. Pasteurization, nevertheless, saves poor wines from complete spoilage and makes them a saleable proposition.

PEARSON'S SQUARE A method of calculating an unknown quantity. There are two primary uses for it in winemaking:

(1) to calculate how much alcohol should be added to give a particular fortification; (*See* FORTIFICATION.)
(2) to calculate how much syrup should be added to a must to give a specific gravity.

The Pearson's Square is formed thus:

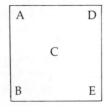

and the method of use is as follows:

(1) For adding spirit to fortify a wine

	Example	
1. At A write the alcohol content of the spirit	Spirit	40%
2. At B write the alcohol content of the wine to be fortified	Wine	15%

3. At C write the alcohol content required in the fortified wine — Fortified wine 18%
4. Subtract B from C and write the answer at D — $18 - 15 = 3$
5. Subtract C from A and write the answer at E — $40 - 18 = 22$
6. D is the parts of spirit to be added to E, the parts of wine — 3 parts of spirit to 22 parts of wine

Therefore, to each 22 litres of wine of 15% alcohol, 3 litres of spirit of 40% alcohol must be added to increase the alcohol content of the wine to 18%.

(2) For adding syrup

Example

1. At A write gravity of the syrup to be added — Syrup at S.G. 1·300
2. At B write the gravity of the must (or wine) — Gravity of must 25 (S.G. 1·025)
3. At C write the desired gravity after adding syrup — Desired gravity 80 (S.G. 1·080)
4. Subtract B from C and write answer at D — $80 - 25 = 55$
5. Subtract C from A and write answer at E — $300 - 80 = 220$
6. D is the parts of syrup to be added to E the parts of must (or wine) — i.e. $\dfrac{55}{220}$ equals $\dfrac{1 \text{ syrup}}{4 \text{ must}}$

Therefore, to each of 4 litres of must 1 litre of syrup should be added to raise the specific gravity from 1·025 to 1·080.

PECTIC ENZYMES These are enzymes which degrade pectin. They are naturally present in fruits but often in insufficient quantity to degrade all the pectin in a must. Preparations of the enzymes are sold under various trade names usually beginning 'Pect—' for adding to musts or wine. They contain the enzymes polygalacturonase and pectin-methyl-esterase. (Also refer.)

PECTIN Formed in fruits from pectose as the fruit ripens, pectin is a soluble, gum-like carbohydrate that gels or clots with heating. Desirable in jam and jelly making because it is the setting agent and causes the gel, pectin is unwanted in winemaking. It is one of the causes of failure for a finished wine to clear. Filtering is also made difficult. It is therefore advisable to avoid heating, even by the use of boiling water, any materials which contain appreciable amounts of pectin, unless a pectin-destroying enzyme is also used.

A guide to the pectin content of fruits is the rule of thumb, 'Fruits which set well in jam are high in pectin; fruits which set badly are low.' Vegetables can also contain pectin, and parsnips are one example of high content. Shoots, leaves and flowers are usually devoid of pectin.

Precipitation of pectin caused by naturally present enzymes occurs

139

during alcoholic fermentation. If a must has a high pectin content, however, there can be too much for the natural enzymes to degrade particularly if the must has been heated. Up to 70% of the pectin can remain in suspension in a finished wine from such a must and the wine will be hazy unless a pectin-destroying enzyme is used in the must.

To test a must or hazy wine for pectin, add three parts methylated spirits to one part must or wine in a bottle. Shake well, leave for a while, then hold the bottle to the light. Small amounts of pectin will be seen as jelly specks floating in the liquid. If the bottle is left standing for some time the specks will settle to the bottom as a whitish deposit. Larger amounts of pectin will be seen as clots or chains of jelly. The more pectin present the larger the clots.

The only method of removing the pectin from a must is the use of pectin-destroying enzymes, pectin-methyl-esterase (P.M.E) and poly-galacturonase (P.G.) which can be obtained under various trade names such as Pectozyme, Pectasin, Pectolase, Pectinol etc. The clearing of a pectin-hazy wine is by the use of enzymes followed by fining after a period of time. Treatment of the must or wine should be according to the directions provided by the manufacturers of the enzymes.

It is recommended that polygalacturonase and pectin-methyl-esterase be added to all musts. They will assist in juice extraction during pulp fermentation and prevent hazes in the finished wines. Methyl alcohol in a wine is primarily derived from hydrolysis of the pectins naturally occurring in the raw ingredients.

For other cause of hazes in wines *see* HAZES.

PECTIN-METHYL-ESTERASE   An enzyme which is present in fresh fruit. Its function is to reduce pectins. Heating above 65 °C (150 °F) destroys P.M.E. and for this reason it is essential to add P.M.E. to musts which have received heat treatment. Pectin molecules are long chains of galacturonic acid with side chains of the methoxyl group. It is these side groups which the P.M.E. removes as methyl alcohol and so reduces the pectin to pectic acid which can react with calcium from hard water to form a jelly. Nevertheless without the action of P.M.E. either from the fresh fruit or synthetic addition, the enzymes of the yeast cannot cause further degradation. (*See also* PECTIN and POLYGALACTURONASE.)

PEDIOCOCCUS   *See* LACTIC ACID BACTERIA.

PELLICLES   A pellicle is a film, membrane or skin. The word is nor-mally used in winemaking to refer to the films or skins which can form on the surface of wines. The film that forms on Sherry is called the Sherry flor. 'Flowers of wine' is used to describe the films formed by spoilage yeasts and lactic acid bacteria; acetic acid bacteria films are the so-called 'mother of vinegar' but all of these would be correctly referred to as pellicles.

PENICILLIUM   A species of mould that can be identified by its blue, green and white, hairy growth. It attacks damaged fruit and will grow on any ripe fruit if not processed quickly. It can also grow on musts during the lag phase, if the must has not been sulphited. If fruit or must is attacked, the mould should be removed and sulphite should be added at the rate of 150 ppm. After 24 hours, the must should be racked and re-yeasted.

PERCENTAGE ALCOHOL   Method used to measure by volume the alcohol content of a wine or spirit. Measurement is also by other means. (*See* PROOF SPIRIT.)

PERLANT   A wine with some bubbles in it. Between a still wine and petillant.

PERRY   The fermented juice of fresh pears. As with cider, in which special cider apples are used, so with perry, special pears are crushed and macerated for a day to reduce the tannin content. Only the juice is used.

Dessert varieties of pears are not really suitable for making perry and it is preferable to use such pears, before they are quite ripe, for making a pear wine. Alternatively they may be blended with somewhat acid cooking apples to make an excellent white table wine.

PETILLANT   Originally a French word, it is now widely used to describe wines that contain a little gas, causing a prickle in the mouth. Very small bubbles rise in the glass, but not in sufficient quantity to form a mousse. It can be caused by a bottle malo-lactic fermentation or the tail-end of a sugar fermentation. The classic examples are the *Vino Verdhe* wines of Portugal. Wines that contain only a few bubbles of carbon dioxide are called PERLANT. (*See also* SPRITZIG.)

pH   This is the measure of the hydrogen ion concentration or of the active acidity/alkalinity. In other words it is the degree of acidity (or alkalinity) of a solution and not a measurement of the total amount of acid present in it. (*See* TITRATION.) It is considered by leading authorities, however, that humans taste acidity by its degree (pH) and not by the quantity of acid present.

The negative value or neutral point is a pH of 7. The higher the reading above 7 the greater the alkalinity and the lower the reading below 7 the greater the acidity. Thus a solution with a pH of 3·2 is more acid than one with a pH of 4·0. This figure, particularly in winemaking, would give no indication of the quantity of acid present (by parts per thousand for instance) because musts and wines are complex solutions containing buffers which cause little change in pH with comparatively large increases in acid content. The optimum pH range for musts and wines is 3·1 to 3·4, but some wines are as low as 2·7 and others as high as 3·9.

The measurement of pH can only be made really accurately with electronic pH meters, but readings of sufficient accuracy for winemaking can be obtained by the use of colour indicators. Colour indicators can be obtained in two forms. The more accurate form consists of a number of sealed tubes of liquid of a definitive colour, each with an individual pH value.

For a white or clear must, a measured sample is put into a tube and a measured amount of colour-change indicator is added according to the instructions with the kit. The colour of the solution is then compared with the sealed indicator and the tube placed in a comparator block with a sealed tube of distilled water. Sample tubes of the must or wine are also stood in the block with sealed indicator tubes. By this means the indicator tubes are viewed through the same density as the sample of wine containing the colour-change solution and a reasonably accurate pH reading can be obtained.

The second and less accurate form of colour change indicator is the pH paper. These are small books of paper 5 cm × 1 cm which when dipped into a solution change colour. There is a wide range of these papers, but the only ones of any use in winemaking are the narrow-range papers with pH values 2·5 to 4·0. The pH indications will be approximate but near enough for practical purposes. Tests with musts and wines have shown that the following colour changes are reasonably accurate:

	Bromophenol Blue Colour Changes
Bright yellow	pH 2·9 or below
Dirty yellow	3·1
Dirty yellow with mauve tint	3·2
Pale mauve	3·4
Dull mauve	3·6
Intense mauve	above 3·6

Controversy sometimes exists between winemakers concerning the relative importance of pH, and titratable acidity. This is probably because titratable acidity is easily and accurately adjusted, whereas pH is not, being affected by buffers. Furthermore, the titratable acidity can sometimes vary considerably from wine to wine for the same pH. Nevertheless, pH affects factors in the wine that the titratable acidity does not and these factors are important. Lactic acid bacteria and others cannot grow in wine below pH 3·4 (Fornachen 1943) but above 3·5 there is always a grave danger of spoilage. Thus a low pH is important in preventing bacteria spoilage. The lower pH is also important in fining and to the effectiveness of sulphite, and there is less calcium pick-up from filter aids. Amerine and Cruess recommend that to produce the best wines the pH has to be between 3·2 and 3·4 and this was confirmed by a panel of expert wine-tasters. They were given samples of Sherry and unanimously gave the highest score to ones with pH 3·2. Those with 3·4 and 3·6 were second and those with pH 4·0 were given a very low rating.

PHENOLPHTHALEIN   The major colour-change indicator which is used in assessing the total acid content of a must or wine by titration. The neutralization of the acid occurs at pH 8·5 or slightly higher, and it is therefore necessary to have a colour-change indicator which changes near this end point. Phenolphthalein undergoes a sharp and distinctive change from white to pink at pH 8·6 and thus clearly indicates the end point. It will hold this pink tint for at least one minute and cannot be discharged by shaking or swirling the solution.

When using phenolphthalein care must be taken to ensure that the must or wine being tested contains no dissolved carbon dioxide (CO_2), to which it is very sensitive. An inaccurate high acid reading is otherwise given. When testing ferments or wines containing CO_2 it is always necessary to boil the samples so that the gas is driven off. (*See also* TITRATION.)

PHYLLOXERA   A very small aphid (*Phylloxera vastatrix*) commonly called a plant louse. It attacks the root of a vine from which it sucks the sap. The plant soon dies. It was accidentally imported into Europe in 1864 with some oidium-resistant vines. The aphid spread across Europe and wiped out almost every vineyard. It resisted all attempts to kill it and resource had to be made to grafting the European vine (*Vitis vinifera*) on to the phylloxera-resistant, American root stocks (*Vitis ruparis* and *Vitis rupestris*). More recently, hybrid varieties have been developed that are phylloxera resistant.

PIPETTE   A length of tubing, usually glass and sometimes with a bulb about midway, or lower in its length. It is most frequently used in winemaking for removing a sample of wine from a cask or jar. The pipette is placed in the wine, allowed to fill and the top end then closed with a finger. With the end still closed, the pipette is lifted from the wine and the sample is transferred to a glass or other vessel. As soon as the finger is removed from the end of the pipette the wine runs out.

PIQUETTE   A wine made from marc and water. Also a derogative term for a wine low in alcohol and high in acid. (*See also* PRESSING GRAPES.)

PITH   When pith is mentioned in winemaking, it usually refers to the white pith of citrus fruits (lemons, oranges, grapefruit etc.). This pith, if present in a must during pulp fermentation will produce an excess bitterness that can make a wine unpalatable. Care has, therefore, to be exercised to exclude it from all musts.

PLASTERING   The addition of gypsum (calcium sulphate) to a must to increase the active acidity and to lower the pH. When crushing grapes

143

it also lowers the viscosity. Extensively practised in the production of Sherry, it has been advised for use in musts intended to produce Sherry-type wine from different ingredients. The recommended quantity to use varies from 15 to 30 g of gypsum per 5 litres of must. The variations appear to be a matter of preference in amateur winemaking, but in the production of Sherry the variation is from 1·25 kg to 6·75 kg per 1,000 kg of grapes, according to the district, the method of pressing and the shipper.

PLASTICS, PLASTIC CONTAINERS   There have been many arguments between winemakers 'for and against' the use of plastics. Whilst there are reasons against the indiscriminate use of plastic vessels, with precautions and with intelligent application, they are very satisfactory in use, particularly for fermentation and initial storage. Containers of the right type have the advantage of being light, compact and easy to handle.

There are a very few containers made from P.V.C. which, because of the plasticizers they contain and for other reasons, are unsuitable for winemaking. The majority are now made from virgin polythene and sometimes sold under a trade name such as Alkathene. They are inert to acids and any chemical reaction from wine and contain no plasticizers. Polythene is sold in two grades, 'low density' (L.D.) and 'high density' (H.D.). Both grades are liquid proof but not vapour proof. Esters and other volatiles can escape through the walls of a closed container. Low-density polythene is by far the worst in this respect and should be completely avoided for the storage of wine. High-density polythene containers may be used for short storage while the wine clears but is not recommended for the longer storage during maturation. High-density polythene is suitable for fermentation vessels in the form of tubs, bins and wide-necked jars or for lining other containers used for fermentation.

Polythene will retain smells and taints from any liquids or materials that the vessels have contained. Therefore, only new vessels should be used and they should be kept solely for winemaking. Second-hand containers may be used if the previous content is known to have been only fruit juice or some other foodstuff which would not leave an unwanted smell or taint.

Plastic bags, which are normally made from polythene, are sometimes used in winemaking. They are invariably made from low-density polythene and whilst quite suitable for fermentation, when supported in some other container, wines should not be stored in them after fermentation. More recently, laminated plastic bags have been produced containing a middle layer of nylon. These bags are vapour proof and quite suitable for storage or distribution purposes. These plastics are also suitable for lining concrete and other tanks and containers. New possibilities are being opened up by blow moulding co-extruded plastics into diverse shaped containers that are said to be gas-tight and prevent oxidation.

POLYGALACTURONASE (P.G.) A yeast enzyme which reduces pectic acid. After P.M.E. (*see* PECTIN-METHYL-ESTERASE) has reduced pectin to pectic acid, P.G. repeatedly splits in half the pectic acid chains until they are single or near single units. Jelly cannot be formed by these units to maintain a haze. Thus, wines with hazes caused by pectins are cleared by the use of P.M.E. and P.G. enzymes. (*See* PECTIN.)

POLYPHENOL Originally only substances that tanned (caused browning) were called tannins. Later substances which did not tan but were of similar construction were also called tannins. Both are now often referred to as polyphenols.

Phenol has one −OH group attached to a benzene ring. When several −OH groups are attached to the benzene ring, as have tannins, it is called polyphenol.

POLYTHENE *See* PLASTICS.

POLYURETHANE This is a synthetic finish for woods and other surfaces. It is tough, resistant to heat and completely seals a wood surface, but more important, it is inert to fruit acids. Applied in two or more coats it is the ideal finish for all wooden utensils used in connection with winemaking, such as crushing tubs, wooden stirring spoons, presses etc., made from woods other than oak. It is liable to peel from oak after a period of time.

Because polyurethane completely seals the surface, it prevents the wood from absorbing any juice, sap or other liquid whilst the utensil is in use. A polyurethane surface dries very rapidly. For these reasons the growth of moulds and other micro-organisms is inhibited and possible contamination of future musts or wine prevented, provided the utensils are thoroughly washed.

Moulds will appear in crevices and joints if the utensils are inefficiently washed. This is due to particles of matter being left in such places and the mould grows on the particles, not on the polyurethane surface. The mould and matter can be removed easily by wiping with a cloth which, for anti-contaminant reasons, should be wetted with a sulphite solution.

PORT WINE Technically, a fortified sweet red wine is not Port unless it bears the Portuguese Government seal of authenticity and has been shipped out of Oporto. It is made in several different styles primarily from the Maurisco grape. Each wine is fortified during fermentation to prevent further attenuation. The finished wine contains up to one-third of its original grape sugar, but never tastes cloyingly sweet. It is, nevertheless, usually drunk as an after-dinner wine.

(a) RUBY PORT   A medium to dark red wine, full bodied and fruity, but well balanced with comparable acidity and tannin. It is a blend of wines from different vintages and different years.

(b) TAWNY PORT   Also a blended wine, usually a paler red with a distinct amber tinge. The bouquet is fruity and aromatic and the wine seems lighter, smoother and even drier than ruby port. These qualities are achieved by long years in cask.

(c) VINTAGE PORT   A deep ruby in colour, full-bodied, fruity and superbly aromatic. Although firm it has no astringency and shows the mellowness of long age in bottle. It is an outstanding wine from a single very good year. To drink a good vintage Port is to experience one of the greatest gifts that wine has to offer.

(d) LATE-BOTTLED VINTAGE   A wine of similar quality but matured in cask and bottled when it is about eight years old.

(e) CRUSTED PORT   A good blended wine bottled at two years of age and kept for six to eight years in bottle.

(f) VINTAGE CHARACTER PORT   Similar to crusted Port in quality but matured in cask and bottled when it is about six years old.

(g) A WHITE PORT   Also made in the same style but the juice is fermented without the skins of the black grapes. Some white Ports are not fortified until fermentation is finished and the wine is served dry as an aperitif.

POTASSIUM CARBONATE   Is used to reduce the acidity of too-acid wines made from grapes, or other too-acid wines which contain a high proportion of tartaric acid.

Make a solution for this purpose by dissolving 28 g B.P. quality potassium carbonate in 170 ml water. To test if a wine will react, add 3 drops of the solution to 170 ml of wine and leave for twelve hours. If crystals develop, the bulk of the wine can be treated by adding 6 ml of the solution to each litre. Chill, and when crystallization ceases, test the wine for acidity. If still too acid, a second dose of the potassium carbonate solution can be added. No more than a total of 12 ml per litre should be added or an excess of soluble potassium salts of other acids may be left in the wine. The wine should be siphoned from the crystals. The chilling causes the crystal to develop the more rapidly.

POTASSIUM HYDROGEN TARTRATE, POTASSIUM BITARTRATE   If potassium bitartrate forms in wine, it will precipitate out of its own accord in the form of sand-like crystals commonly known as cream of tartar. Potassium hydrogen tartrate is the intermediate compound between soluble tartaric acid and potassium bitartrate. It remains in suspension until the wine is chilled, when it precipitates.

POTASSIUM METABISULPHITE See SULPHITE.

POTASSIUM PHOSPHATE Another yeast nutrient. Some has to be present in every must to encourage the growth of wine yeasts. (*See* NUTRIENTS for further details.)

POTASSIUM SORBATE *See* SORBIC ACID.

POTENTIAL ALCOHOL This is the theoretical amount of alcohol that could be produced by fermentation from a given amount of sugar by wine yeasts. Theoretically it is 51·1% of the amount of sugar but practically it is only 90 to 95% of the theoretical, due to variable factors. The variable factors are the amount of by-products produced, the amount of sugar used by the yeasts, sugar used by other organisms, alcohol lost by evaporation or entrainment, which partly depends on the temperature of fermentation, presence of air, stirring, straining, racking or other movement of the ferment, plus other factors. (*See* HYDROMETER for tables of potential alcohol.)

POTTERY When pottery is used in winemaking care must be exercised to ensure that the vessel has a salt glaze and not a lead slip. (*See* EARTHENWARE.) Unglazed pottery is not suitable for winemaking.

POUSSE A gassy form of tourne. In other respects they are similar. (*See* TOURNE.)

PRECIPITATE Two soluble compounds joined together to form an insoluble compound. The insoluble compound ceases to remain in suspension and falls out in the form of a deposit, called a precipitate.

PRECIPITATED CHALK Also used to remove or reduce the acidity of a must or a wine. The grade used is that which is known as B.P. quality. It is also known as CALCIUM CARBONATE under which reference details of its use are given.

PRESSES An instrument used since ancient times to extract as much juice as possible from crushed grapes and fruits. Force was originally provided by heavy stones, then levers and finally screws turned by men or by mules. Later hydraulic force was used. More recently the air-bag press has been developed. This consists of a long cylinder of perforated stainless steel containing a deflated rubber bag. The cylinder is filled with crushed grapes, the bag inflated and the pulp pressed against the perforations through which the juice escapes into a container beneath.

To produce better wines, modern winemakers use tall stainless steel containers fitted with a perforated plate. The pulp is poured into the top of the cylinder and the weight of the grapes alone, extracts 'free-run' juice, considered to be best for quality wine.

PRESSING GRAPES For white wines the grapes are de-stemmed, crushed and pressed as quickly as possible after picking. The free-run juice from the crushed grapes is called the *moût de goutte* and is sometimes fermented separately to make the highest quality wine. The juice extracted when the pulp is pressed is called the *moût de presse* and is either used to make an everyday wine or is mixed with the free-run juice. To prevent white grapes being pressed too much for wine, French law requires vignerons to distil the last pressing and sell the alcohol to the State.

For a very light rosé wine (*vin gris*) the black grapes are de-stemmed, crushed and pressed immediately after picking, in the same way as white grapes, but they are pressed more slowly so that a little of the colour from the skins is also extracted.

In the vinification of red wines, the grapes are crushed and the juice fermented with the pips, skins and sometimes even the stalks as well, to extract both colour and tannin. For lighter red wines the stems are removed. The wine when run off is the *vin de goutte* and it leaves behind the marc of skins, pips and pulp. The marc is pressed for the *vin de presse* which has a lower fixed acidity but a higher volatile acidity and tannin content than the *vin de goutte*. How much *vin de presse* is added to the *vin de goutte* depends on the type of wine required. The surplus *vin de presse* is sold as everyday wine or sent for distillation. Some marc is pressed only once so that the stalks are not crushed, since this would cause an excess of tannin in the wine. The first pressing is often made in a cylindrical air-bag press and the second in a traditional 'basket' press.

The real rosé wine of good colour is at first vinified in the same way as red wine but fermentation on the pulp only proceeds for a few hours varying from 5 to 48 depending on the grape varieties and depth of colour required. The must is then run off and fermentation is completed.

The marc is, of course, pressed but the *vin de presse* is too deep a red for rosé wine and is blended with red wines.

Sometimes water is added to the marc left from the *vin de presse*, and fermented for up to 15 days. This produces a rough wine frequently drunk by the vigneron's family and workers, but sometimes distilled into a brandy. The wine is called *piquette*. (*See also* JUICER, JUICE EXTRACTOR.)

PRICKLE The slight prickly or tingly feeling in the mouth from wine containing a small amount of carbon dioxide. A wine can produce a prickle in the mouth without bubbles appearing in the wine or in the glass. It is acceptable when not in excess. It can be caused by a wine that is fermenting slightly or by an earlier slight fermentation in the bottle, by yeast or bacteria which have released a little gas into the wine. (*See also* PETILLANT and SPRITZIG.)

PRIMARY FERMENTATION From the time an active yeast culture is added to a must there is some fermentation taking place unseen and unheard while the yeast colony multiplies. This is the lag phase. Following the lag phase is the primary fermentation, when hosts of bubbles rise rapidly through the wine. They can be seen rushing to the surface where they burst causing a very audible hiss, or even cause frothing. This stage is also known as the audible, tumultuous, violent or visible fermentation. Its duration is normally a matter of days in an optimum temperature, and is followed by the quiet, steady secondary fermentation.

PROLONGED FERMENTATION A fermentation can be prolonged to produce the maximum amount of alcohol that can be tolerated by the yeast simply by adding small quantities of sugar at intervals of several days. The initial specific gravity should not exceed 1·075. When the must has been attenuated to, say, S.G. 1·010, some sugar syrup is added, say 60 ml per litre. The process is repeated until fermentation ceases. By adding the sugar in this manner a total alcohol content in excess of 17% can be obtained. The method is especially helpful in the production of Sherry-, Port- and Madeira-style wines.

PROOF SPIRIT Levying a tax on beer, wines and spirits has long been a profitable source of income to countless governments, all over the world. In the U.K., Proof Spirit is a spirit solution which weighs $\frac{12}{13}$ of an equal amount of distilled water at 10 °C (50 °F). Thus it contains 48·2% alcohol by weight, or 57·0% alcohol by volume, which at 15 °C (59 °F) would be 49·28% by weight and 57·10% by volume. The alcohol content of liquids used to be measured by a Sikes hydrometer on which 100 was proof. Thus an alcohol is said to be proof, or under proof, or over proof. For example, a spirituous liquid with a reading of 70 was said to be 30 under proof, one of 140 was 40 over proof. A pure spirit that is 100% by volume is 175 ° proof.

Canada and the U.S.A. have different ratings as indicated in the following table. In Europe the Gay Lussac Scale is used, 1 ° of the scale equals 1% of the spirit by volume.

U.K.	Canada	U.S.A.	% alcohol by volume Gay Lussac
0	100 U.P.	0	0
25	75 U.P.	28	14·3
50	50 U.P.	58	28·6
70	30 U.P.	80	40
75	25 U.P.	86	43
87	13 U.P.	100	50
100	Proof	114	57·1
125	25 O.P.	143	71·5
140	40 O.P.	160	80
175	75 O.P.	200	100

To translate U.K. Proof Spirit into % alcohol it is only necessary to multiply by 4 over 7. Thus a wine of 25° proof contains 25 times 4 over 7 which equals 14⁴⁄₇% alcohol. Conversely a wine containing 12% alcohol is equivalent to 12 times 7 over 4 which equals 21° proof.

PROPIONIC ACID   A cause of bitterness in wine as a result of tourne. The bacteria break down the tartaric acid to propionic acid.

PROTEIN   Present in the nuclei of all animal and vegetable cells. It is essential to life and vital to reproduction characteristics. Protein can cause a slight haze in some wines. It can be removed by casein or bentonite.

PULP, PULP FERMENTATION   Pulp is the name given to any solid matter of fruit, vegetables, roots or other raw ingredients when prepared for the must. Pulp fermentation is, as the name implies, fermentation of a must which contains this solid matter. Traditionally, but decreasingly due to new technology (*see* HEAT TREATMENT, and CARBONIC MACERATION), red grape wines, but not whites, have been fermented on the pulp for up to two weeks. Experienced winemakers have varying opinions on how long pulp or fruit other than grapes should be fermented. They are now agreed that the lengths of time previously recommended were, in general, too long for the production of the best quality wines.

Three to four days of pulp fermentation would appear to be the maximum period necessary to extract all desirable matter from the pulp of many fruits. Thereafter, unwanted matter is extracted as well, and this adversely affects flavour and balance. Furthermore, cellulose tissue is often broken down into such fine particles, that clearing becomes very difficult. The recommended practice is:

(1) For table or light and thinnish wines the pulp should be fermented for 24 to 48 hours only, then strained out and pressed very lightly or not at all. The ferment is then tested and balanced.
(2) For heavier and fuller-bodied wines, the pulp is fermented for 2 to 3 days, then strained out and pressed. The ferment should be balanced, if necessary, and continued under an airlock.
(3) For heavy, full-bodied dessert-type wines the pulp should be fermented for 3 to 4 days, strained out and heavily pressed.

When preparing the pulp for fermentation, care should be exercised to avoid, as far as possible, cutting or crushing pips and to avoid cracking stones. It is preferable to remove all stones from fruit, and to exclude them from the must. Similarly, pith from citrus fruits should always be excluded from musts. Stems and stalks, such as those of blackcurrants, grapes and elderberries, should be excluded. During fermentation they can produce a 'green' or 'grass' flavour in a finished wine. Likewise only the petals of flowers should be fermented and the calyx or 'green parts' excluded whenever possible.

Finally it is important to keep the pulp submerged during fermentation in order to extract all the goodness from it and to prevent it from becoming a breeding ground for spoilage organisms.

PULP FERMENTATION VESSELS The best vessels to use are those that readily permit the addition and removal of pulps and that can be cleaned easily. These are:

(1) Vessels with an open top such as high-density polythene bins, wooden, stoneware, or stainless steel tubs and glass- or wax-lined concrete vats. Glass-lined tanks are also suitable for pulp fermentation and can be used without restriction for all musts.
(2) High-density polythene or stoneware jars with wide necks of 10 cm diameter or more and glass jars with wide necks. Large polythene bags may also be used when supported in a wooden or cardboard box. They are especially useful for temporary, emergency or experimental purposes.

PUNCH Punch was first introduced into England in 1655 after Jamaica had been taken from the Spanish. It was at first rum and water, either hot or iced, to which some sugar, and lemon or orange juice was added. Today, punch is a beverage composed of spirits or wine, with milk, tea or water added, together with sugar and fruit juices, herbs and spices. The combination of ingredients from which a punch can be made are innumerable, and everyday wines will be found to make some of the best. Experiments in producing a punch are as fascinating as the drinking can be pleasing. A basic recipe is to heat some red wine in a saucepan to 60 °C (140 °F). Ginger, cloves, thinly peeled lemon skin as well as lemon juice and sugar are added to suit your taste. The wine should never be heated beyond 60 °C (140 °F), otherwise the alcohol will be driven off. At a lower temperature the punch tastes tepid rather than hot.

The derivation of the name is obscure. Some authorities suggest that 'punch' comes from the Indian *panch* or the Persian *panj* meaning 'five', but others say punch was originally the drink of sailors and was their abbreviation of 'puncheon' in which the drink was kept.

PUNT In the context of winemaking this is the indentation in the bottom of the bottle. Much has been said and written about it being put there to hold any sediment and so on, but originally it was formed in the bottle from necessity in the production, not for any useful purpose. The first bottles were blown and had spherical bodies like the present-day Chianti bottle. From these developed the cylindrical bottles which were shaped by rolling them with the aid of an iron rod whilst the glass was still malleable. This rod was known in the trade as a punto. The indentation made by the punto whilst rolling the bottle was thus called the punt.

When machinery was developed to mould bottles they could have been made with flat bottoms. However, the punt does help to hold any sediment and so for this reason as well as for tradition, manufacturers have continued to make bottles with punts. Since many wines are now completely free from any deposit, the tendency is for more flat-bottomed bottles to be used.

PUPITRE   A desk or rack containing holes in which bottles of sparkling wine can be held at any angle during *remuage*. (*See* REMUAGE.)

PURIFICATION FINING   The use of a fining agent to remove colour, taint or tannins from wine. *Refer to* FINING.

PYMENT   The first meads were made with honey and water as true meads are today. Fermentation was probably difficult, as nothing was then known of the need to add acids and nutrients. Later, it was found that better drinks were produced if some grape juice was added instead of water. This brew was called pyment. Thus it is either a mead made with grape juice or a grape wine made with honey, whichever way you wish to describe it.

QARABAS   The name of the large wine jars used in Persia. Whether or not it was in these that Ali Baba and the forty thieves hid, it is certainly from Qarabas that our word carboy has come.

QUALITY OF WINE   Quality in their wines is what all winemakers strive to achieve. Quality is not just one factor, but a multiplicity which basically can be described as:

(a) SMELL   A subtle aroma and bouquet which are perfectly balanced; neither of them, alone or together, being overpowerful. They must be clean, pleasing, enticing, added to a definite vinosity.

(b) FLAVOUR   A perfect, or at least a good balance is essential. There must be a complete harmony of the tastes (acidity, bitterness and sweetness), aroma, bouquet and texture. The tastes, especially, having the right intensity and flavour, being appetizing or satisfying according to the type of wine, e.g. table or dessert.

(c) AFTERTASTE   Must be clean, round and pleasing, without taint, and complementary to the flavour. It should be noted that when wine is taken with food it should be complementary to the food. Under such conditions the wine may appear to have a fuller flavour, be higher in acid and more astringent with some foods than with others.

(d) TEXTURE   A wine's texture should be smooth and caressing, be without harshness or roughness on the palate, and should leave the mouth clean and unencumbered.

(e) NEGATIVES   Factors which must be absent. A wine to have quality must be without contamination of metal, bacteria, moulds, spoilage yeasts and other organisms, and without taint or off-flavour of any kind. It must not be over-oxidized by free air or be 'over the hill' because it has been kept for too long.

RACKING In the language of winemakers the word 'rack' has nothing to do with shelves or framework on which to keep articles. It comes from the Provençal *raca* meaning the stems and husks of grapes. 'To rack', or 'racking' as the action is called, now means the removal of wine from its lees or deposit, which is accomplished by the use of a siphon, or by running-off via a tap.

Racking, like all winemaking, is simple but requires care and attention to detail. Inefficient or infrequent racking can cause off-flavours and spoilage resulting from autolysis of dead yeast cells and decomposition of other matter. The one cardinal rule for racking, is that young wines should not be allowed to stand on their lees for longer than twelve weeks whilst throwing deposits. This is the maximum period and a shorter length of time is preferable.

Wines intended to be light and dry should be racked when the specific gravity drops to about 1·000 and the wine is beginning to clear. It is again racked when the wine is clear, provided the time is not longer than twelve weeks from the first racking. It is again racked as and when deposits form, until the wine is bottled. For these rackings the siphon used should be of small bore and the delivery end placed so as nearly to touch the bottom of the lower or receiving vessel. This is to minimize the agitation of the wine, thereby minimizing the absorption of oxygen whilst at the same time retaining as much as possible of the dissolved carbon dioxide. When wine is run off via a tap, agitation can be minimized by attaching a length of hose to the tap and placing the other end at the bottom of the receiving vessel. If a pump is used it should be of the submersible type to avoid oxidation.

Wines intended to be heavy and sweet should be racked within fourteen days of the start of fermentation. This will not only remove the very young wine from the lees but also provide oxygen for reproduction of the yeast crop necessary for the fermentation to the higher alcohol content required. Further rackings should be made at intervals of five to six weeks, or less, until the wine ceases to throw heavy deposits and is clearing due to the alcohol content inhibiting further fermentation. For these rackings the siphon tube should be of a large bore and the wine should be allowed to fall into, and splash in, the receiving vessel. A large funnel placed in the neck of the receiving vessel will assist and increase the agitation. This falling and splashing increases the amount of oxygen taken up by the wine. After the wine has cleared, further rackings should be made when deposits form but the siphon should have a small bore and be used as described for light dry wines.

Wines intended to be of the oxidized or Sherry type are racked with a large-bore siphon and the wine allowed to fall for all rackings.

Medium and other wines should be racked according to their individual requirements using the light and heavy methods described as guides, remembering that the use of large-bore siphons and splashing is more liable to induce continued fermentation if sugar is present in the wine.

It will be appreciated that correct racking serves more than one purpose. It removes the wine from the lees, so preventing some off-flavours, helps to prevent bacterial infection and provides oxygen for the initial oxidation necessary as part of the maturation of wine. Low-alcohol wines should be sulphited at the rate of 50 ppm after racking.

RAISINS Dried black grapes, which, due to their ripeness and the process of drying them, have a high sugar and a low acid content. Thus, with the addition of acid, they can be made into wine. More important, however, they contain amino acids necessary for rapid fermentation of a must. A small quantity of raisins added to a non-grape must is, therefore, always advantageous. Likewise, the addition of a small quantity of chopped raisins to a must in which fermentation is difficult to start will have a marked effect. On average, two-thirds of their weight consists of fermentable sugars and this should be taken into account before adding sugar to a must. (*See also* SULTANAS.)

RAPID AGEING To commercial wine producers time is money. Also the quicker the wine can be matured the less storage space is required—again a saving of money. Thus a search for a rapid ageing process has gone on for a very long time. Louis Pasteur secured a patent on rapid ageing of wine in partly filled bottles exposed to sunlight. Other methods that have been tried involved the use of hydrogen peroxide, catalysts and ozone, induced oxidation, controlled heating and the addition of oak chippings. All have failings of one nature or another.

All winemakers because of storage problems or the desire to sell or drink their wines quickly, seek a rapid ageing process. So far the mecca has not been reached but maturing can be speeded up although types of the finest quality will not be produced.

To secure early maturation the wine should be racked immediately fermentation ceases and again immediately settling is completed. The wine should then be filtered to make it clear, aerated by stirring it at a low temperature to allow easier absorption of oxygen and then the temperature raised to induce oxidation. Dessert wines should then be stored in temperatures up to 32 °C (90 °F) and table wines up to 21 °C (70 °F) for the most rapid ageing. The lower the storage temperature is under these figures, the slower the ageing. The wines should be regularly checked to see that they are not spoiling.

A rapid ageing process that improves one wine may spoil another.

Therefore the process quoted is one for the most general use. It should not be applied as a 'rule of thumb', for each wine behaves differently. It is the intelligence, skill and care with which the process is applied that will determine the final result. Some wines may be spoilt. The process cannot be advocated; time and patience produce infinitely superior wines.

RAW MATERIALS This term is used as an overall name embracing all major basic ingredients of a must or wine. It is a blanket term that covers not only grapes but also fruits, saps, vegetables, grains, flowers, honey, shoots, leaves, roots and seed pods. In fact anything edible, whether it is fresh, frozen, dried, canned, bottled or preserved, or has been made into a juice or extract, can be a major basic ingredient of wine and is called the raw material.

RECORDS In one form or another, it is very important that records should be kept for every single wine made. The reason for a wine developing a fault can often be traced from a record, something omitted, too much added, too long between rackings and so on. To repeat a single wine that has been successful, it is necessary to have a record. But to keep an incomplete record is a waste of time. To be of use it must be complete in every detail of ingredient, of every process or action taken, of temperatures and conditions of fermentation and storage, and if possible, gravities, pH and titration.

Records are especially important for new winemakers. The grape varieties available, the types and quantities mixed together, yeast cultures used, methods of growing and vinification are all variables affecting the quality of the wine produced.

The form in which the records are kept is of little moment. Some winemakers use filing cards which are hung on the wine vessels until bottling when they are filed. Others use a book, in which they set out their details, sticking only a reference number on the vessel. Others use printed record cards which can be bought from certain suppliers.

REDOX REACTIONS This is the simplified name for the chemical reactions of reduction and oxidation which are inter-related. When one substance is reduced another is always oxidized, and likewise when one substance is oxidized another is always reduced. The reactions were originally so called at the time that it was first discovered that when a substance gained oxygen (oxidation) another substance always lost oxygen (reduction). Later the term was also applied to the loss and gain of hydrogen and also to the loss and gain of electrons, when it was found that these caused what had been considered oxidation or reduction. Thus the term now means: *oxidation*—addition of oxygen or loss of hydrogen or loss of electrons; *reduction*—loss of oxygen or addition of hydrogen or gain of electrons. These oxidative and reductive reactions are collectively called redox reactions.

Oxidation or reduction naturally changes a substance and can be noticed in the interaction between acids and alcohols, resulting in esters that develop the bouquet and flavour of a matured wine.

When wine is in contact with air, only the wine oxidizes, the air loses oxygen. (Excess of this oxidation spoils wine—refer OXIDATION.) This first necessary form of oxidation takes place when the wine is in open vats, and much more slowly when in casks, barrels etc. When the wine is sealed in bottles, oxidation by the air in the neck of the bottle occurs comparatively quickly. Subsequently, oxidation and reduction between the substances in the wine continue for a long time. These redox reactions in the bottle are assisted by the absence of air and produce the finer qualities in bouquet and flavour. This is the process of maturing or ageing in the bottle.

The maturing of wine by a combination of storage in wood for a while and then in bottle has long been appreciated, as instanced by Port, even if the reason for the improvement was not originally understood. The length of time the wine should be kept under these conditions depends on the type of wine, the substances present, their individual quantities, the conditions of storage etc. But all wines benefit from such treatment, although each individual wine varies from another in the length of time required for ageing. Experience is the only guide as to how long a wine should be kept, and tasting is the only proof of when it is reaching its peak.

REDUCTION *See* REDOX REACTIONS.

REFRIGERATION Proteins and other compounds in addition to potassium bitartrate (refer), can be precipitated by chilling wines to near freezing, because they become insoluble at the lower temperatures. Chilling and racking will therefore remove protein and some other hazes from wine.

In hot climates refrigeration may be necessary to maintain storage and/or fermentation temperatures at the appropriate level. Some of the new stainless steel equipment is fitted with pipes containing a flow of cold water or brine for this purpose.

REMUAGE The removal of the deposit that forms during the bottle fermentation of sparkling wine is called remuage. When a sparkling wine has matured sufficiently, the bottle is placed neck first at an angle of 45° in a rack called a 'pupitre'. The bottle is gripped by the base, lifted slightly, given a twist or a quarter turn, knocked gently or given a slight shake as it is returned to its hole with a fractional change towards the vertical. This loosens the deposit from the side of the bottle and encourages it to slide slowly down towards the neck and eventually to settle on the cork. The process lasts between two and three months before the bottles are vertical, by which time the deposit is ready for DISGORGE-

MENT. Remuage is a very delicate operation. The movement must be sufficient to cause the deposit to slide but not sufficient to cause it to rise.

RESIN The crude turpentine which oozes from cuts in pine or similar trees and from sawn pieces of white woods. Resin imparts an unwanted and undesirable flavour to any wine which comes in contact with it. For this reason, resinous woods should not be used for any winemaking vessels, utensils or equipment.

In Greece some wines have for many centuries been flavoured with sundarae resin. These wines, called *retsina*, have a subtle turpentine odour and are not appreciated by those who have not a cultivated palate for them.

RIPE A grape is said to be ripe when its acid content has been sufficiently reduced and its sugar content sufficiently increased by warm sunshine, to a point when both are in balance. In poor seasons, this balance is never achieved in cool climates and the grapes and their ensuing wines remain sharp unless balanced by the addition of some sugar. In warm climates the grapes are too often low in acid and their ensuing wines taste soft. The most advantageous stage of ripeness for picking is the balancing point between sugar and acid content.

ROBE A term used by wine tasters in reference to the colour of a wine.

ROHAMENT P The trade name used for a preparation of pectin glycoside which assists in juice extraction.

ROPINESS This is due to some member of the group of lactic acid bacteria in musts which have not been properly sulphited, but it can also be caused by later contamination. The bacteria hang together in strings and give a shiny viscous appearance to the wine which pours thick like oil. The wine suffers no serious defect in flavour in spite of the unpleasant appearance. When attacked, the wine should be immediately sulphited at the rate of 100 ppm SO_2 to kill the bacteria and then thoroughly beaten to break up the chains. The wine usually clears in a few days and can be racked into a clean vessel. Failure to clear may necessitate filtering. The remedy, however, really lies in prevention by adequately sulphiting the must before the wine yeast is introduced.

ROSÉ WINE This wine is made by a delicate manipulation of a must, usually prepared from black grapes—notably the Cabernet Sauvignon or Grenache. Sometimes a small number of white grapes are mixed in, but quality rosé wines are never made from a blend of red and white wines. After crushing, the grapes should be sulphited, treated with pectic enzyme and left for 24 hours before inoculating with an activated yeast. As soon as the right depth of colour is obtained in the must, it should be run off into a sterilized vessel where fermentation can be continued under an airlock. The wine should be racked at S.G. 1·002 and sulphited at the rate of 100 ppm. It should be finished with a hint of sweetness, a touch of tannin and be both fresh and fragrant from its acidity.

ROUSING, ROUSING STICK   Rousing meant stirring a wine and originally a rousing stick was used for stirring or rousing wine after finings had been added. Now, rousing means any stirring of a must or wine and a rousing stick is any stick, wooden spoon, paddle or other means of stirring.

The general purpose of rousing is thoroughly to mix any addition with the wine or must, or with pulp fermentation to break up the cap and submerge the pulp. During fermentation rousing also serves the further important purpose of introducing air and thereby oxygen into the ferment. This is essential for ferments for high-alcohol wines, the oxygen being necessary to produce greater yeast crops. Whether or not high-alcohol wines are produced by pulp fermentation, they should be roused during the early stages of fermentation, or alternatively should be racked and thereby oxygenated.

In the production of sparkling wines by the méthode champenoise, the bottles are roused in the early stages of bottle fermentation. The cellarman holds the bottles by their necks, in gloved hands, and gives them a thorough shake. This mixes the yeast into the wine and stimulates the fermentation.

SACCHAROMYCES APICULATUS   A sub-group of *Saccharomyces*, which is generally classed as 'a wild yeast'. Often lemon-shaped, these small yeasts occur in abundance during the early stages of winemaking, causing rapid fermentation. They are inhibited by 4% of alcohol, but O'Hara (1959) found 75 parts per million sulphur dioxide had little effect on them and that it required 150 parts per million before they disappeared from a ferment. The 150 parts per million unfortunately, also had an appreciable effect on *Saccharomyces cerevisiae* (*ellipsoideus*).

Originally classified by Rees in 1870, they were later divided into *Hanseniaspora* (sporulating) and *Hansenia* (non-sporulating). *Hanseniaspora* has been retained, but *Hansenia* has been reclassified as *Kloeckera* (Janhe 1924). Three species of *Hanseniaspora* are now recognized and four species of *Kloeckera*.

SACCHAROMYCES BETICUS   The name now used for the Sherry and Arbois yeasts which form a flor. Named separately because of their quite distinct characteristics.

SACCHAROMYCES CEREVISIAE   The name used to refer to bakers' yeast and brewers' yeast. Authorities consider them to be the same yeast with slightly different characteristics. Bakers' yeast used for brewing will gradually assume the different characteristics of brewers' yeast, and *vice versa*. Wine yeasts are strains of the same yeast, but are referred to as *Saccharomyces cerevisiae* var. *ellipsoideus*. (*See also* YEAST.)

SCHIRAZ (SHIRAZ)   A place in Persia that is claimed to be the cradle of viticulture and winemaking. It is most probable, however, that the vine came from much further north and had been cultivated for wine long before it reached Schiraz. Nevertheless, it is possible that Schiraz is the place where Noah planted a vineyard; 'and Noah began to be a husbandman and he planted a vineyard; and he drank of the wine and was drunken; and he was uncovered within his tent' (Genesis 9:20–21). Schiraz is also the name of a variety of black grape, widely used to produce both dessert wines and robust table wines.

SCUDDY   A wine that is thick and cloudy from disturbed sediment is said to be scuddy.

SECONDARY FERMENTATION   When the tumult of the primary fermentation dies down it is followed by a quiet steady fermentation—the secondary—which can continue for a short or a considerable length of time depending on the type and composition of the wine. The secondary fermentation produces the best wine when conducted in a temperature between 12 and 20 °C (55 and 68 °F). The lower temperature is best for white wines and the higher for reds.

The secondary fermentation can be conducted in the same vessels as used for pulp fermentation and for juice or extract fermentation. The narrow-necked vessels are, however, the better type for secondary fermentation when it is advisable to restrict the ullage. It is also easier in a narrow-necked vessel to prevent contamination by micro-organisms by the use of a tight fitting cork containing an efficient air lock.

Casks and barrels are not recommended for use until a wine is stable and clear. This is due to the difficulty of thoroughly cleansing them from the deposits of fermentation. Remains of these deposits can cause contamination of wines subsequently contained in the cask or barrel.

SEDIMENT   Matter which settles to the bottom of a fermentation or wine. The word is used generally to refer to all such formations. According to the stage of a wine's production, however, the sediments are more specifically called (a) lees (during fermentation), (b) deposit (after fermentation) and (c) crust (formed in the bottle during ageing).

SEKT   The German name for sparkling wine, sometimes also called *Schaumwein*.

SELECTED WINE YEASTS   The strains of the sugar fermenting yeasts, *Saccharomyces cerevisiae* var. *ellipsoideus*, which have been specifically selected and bred for the purpose of producing different types of wine. (*See also* YEAST.)

SHERRY A wine made from a mixture of Palomino and Pedro Ximénez grapes, fermented to a high alcohol content with the aid of the yeast *Saccharomyces beticus*. If necessary, it is fortified to between 17 and 20% alcohol and then matured in a cask not quite full to encourage oxidation. A solera system is used in which the wine drawn off from the oldest cask is replaced by wine from the second oldest. This in turn is topped up from the third oldest which is topped up from the fourth oldest and so on. The older wine imparts its flavour to the younger wine. Sherry is therefore always a blended wine and never the product of a single vintage. Only Sherry from Spain may legally be called Sherry. All similar wines must be prefixed with the country of origin, e.g. South African Sherry.

SILICACEOUS EARTH *See* SPANISH EARTH.

SINKER A heavy, perforated plate used for keeping the cap of grape skins and pulp below the surface of the must during fermentation.

SIPHONS and SIPHONING A siphon is a piece of equipment used to transfer wine from one vessel to another, especially when the wine has thrown a sediment. In its simplest form it is no more than a length of flexible hose. More frequently it consists of a piece of rigid tubing bent in the form of the letter 'J' with a flexible hose attached to the top of the long arm. Also popular is a flexible tube blocked at one end, but perforated just above the block. More sophisticated devices include self-priming and flow-control devices.

When the crooked or blocked end of the tube is placed in the wine, the whole tube is filled with wine, either by suction from the other end of the tube or by the priming device. The free end is then held closed until it is placed in the receiving vessel when it is released. Provided the end of the tube outside the vessel is always lower then the end inside, gravity will pull the wine into the receiving vessel. To this end, it is customary to arrange for the vessel to be emptied to be placed in a position above the vessel to be filled. By using a 'J' tube or a perforated tube above a blocked end, the wine is drawn down or across into the tube, thus avoiding any disturbance of the sediment.

If a pump is used to perform the same process, care must be taken to exclude the intake of air since this would cause an excess of oxidation.

SMELL In judging or appreciating a wine, the sense of smell—olfactory sense—is probably more important in assessing a flavour than taste and texture. However, the classifications of odours has proved very difficult. The great Swedish botanist Charles de Linnaeus (1707–78) gave seven categories: (1) aromatic (carnation), (2) balsamatic (lilac), (3) ambrosial (musk), (4) garlic, (5) caprylic (valerian), (6) repellent (bugs), (7) nauseous (putrefying). In 1924 Henning gave six categories: (1) spicy, (2) flowers, (3) fruit, (4) resin, (5) burnt, (6) putrid. This difficulty arises because there are literally thousands of aromas which are detected by only a few different sensors.

Despite the difficulty of classifying them, it is certain that we retain the memory of, and recognize a vast number of various odours and combinations of odours and that the bouquet or smell of a wine is of major importance in assessing its qualities.

The olfactory sensors or receptors are situated in an upper chamber of the nasal passage and are embedded in a mucous membrane. An aroma is detected only when vapour is breathed in and it passes through the chamber and over the sensitive area. Even when the nose is filled with an aroma it will not be detected unless air is inspired. Gentle steady inspiration produces the greater response to an aroma. From deep, rapid inspirations there is an initial response and thereafter the nerve endings are saturated and the aroma ceases to be detected. A scent released into a room is immediately noticeable but after a time it is no longer detected. The inability to respond lasts only a short time so that if the room is left and shortly afterwards re-entered, the scent is again immediately detected. Also, after deep inspiration, a flower appears to have lost its scent with the next inspiration.

The difference in effect of gentle and deep inspiration is exemplified by the seeming difference between a pleasant and an unpleasant smell; the pleasant seems to fade quickly whilst the unpleasant lingers. This is due to the fact that a person's reaction, say to the smell of hyacinths, is to inspire deeply (deadening the responses), whilst near a dung heap he inspires gently trying to shut out the smell (prolonging the time of response and making the smell seem to linger).

SOCIAL WINE Strictly speaking a social wine is any wine which is drunk socially without food other than nuts and savoury biscuits. It can, then, be any wine from the light, dry and thin, to the heaviest and most full-bodied. By general usage the term has come to mean any wine that lacks the full characteristics of any of the classic styles. Usually it is not too dry, well bodied and well flavoured.

SODIUM BENZOATE The more readily obtainable form of benzoic acid used to stop fermentation.

SODIUM HYDROXIDE The strong alkali most commonly used in the titration of wine. It is used as a deci-normal solution (N/10).

SODIUM METABISULPHITE *See* SULPHITE.

SORBIC ACID Although sulphite is effective as an inhibitor of wild yeasts and other organisms and actually kills some, it is not completely effective as a stabilizer with normal dosage of wine because wine yeast cells are only inactivated by it. To remove cells from an apparently clear wine, and it can contain a surprisingly large number, sterile filtration is

161

required through extremely fine filters. Without this the invisible yeast cells can become active again as the sulphur dioxide content of the wine decreases. Any residual sugar would then be fermented thus spoiling the appearance and condition of the wine.

Sorbic acid, usually in the form of its salt, potassium sorbate, is often added, therefore, as a stabilizer for low-alcohol wines that contain residual sugar. It is added in concentrations up to a maximum of 200 ppm equivalent to 10 ml of a 10% stock solution or 1 g in 5 litres of wine. German researchers in the wine industry have found that derivatives from sorbic acid, due to the actions of lactobacilli, can cause a geranium smell in the bouquet of a treated wine. Further research showed that this could be avoided if sulphite was added with the sorbate. It is, therefore, advisable to keep the sorbate concentration as low as possible and to use it only in conjunction with sulphite, i.e. 100 ppm sorbate with 50 ppm sulphur dioxide.

SORBITOL   This is a sugar that wine yeasts are unable to ferment. It is, therefore, useful for sweetening wines that may not have been completely cleared of viable yeast cells. It is occasionally present in fruit wines, especially when apples have been used in the preparation of the must.

SPANISH EARTH   A complex silicate which was originally obtained from the soil of Spain, but is now also dug in the United States and South America. It has the property of absorbing both positive and negative charged colloids and is, therefore, an excellent fining agent.

SPARKLING WINE   A wine that contains enough carbon dioxide from fermentation to give it sparkle. When poured into a glass the wine produces a show of bubbles that initially form a mousse (head of foam). Sparkling wines are known as *mousseux* in France and *Schaumwein* in Germany but although Champagne is a sparkling wine, it is never referred to as *mousseux*. Champagne is exclusively produced in Champagne.

The rural method of producing sparkling wine is the oldest, being in use a long time before the méthode champenoise. It is rarely used today. The primary fermentation is slowed, but not stopped, by repeated racking and filtering. The wine is bottled when the sugar content is judged to have dropped sufficiently low for safety during the conclusion of fermentation in bottle. By this method there is only one fermentation compared with the two fermentations of the méthode champenoise. This rural method can produce excellent wines with very good bouquet but it is an uncertain method and, therefore, dangerous. There can be variations from one bottle to another; bottles can explode from the pressure of too much carbon dioxide; or the sparkle can be almost non-existent from too little carbon dioxide. Although the sediment can be disgorged, the wine can still be hazy from a side-effect of the method.

Some Asti Spumanti is produced by another method employing single fermentation. The juice of Canelli Muscat grapes, which produce wine of a fairly low alcohol content, is stored in refrigeration to prevent fermentation and encourage clarification. It is then transferred off the deposit into hermetically sealed vats, where it is fermented and remains until clear. It is bottled under pressure direct from the vat. By this method the aroma and flavour of the muscat grape is retained in the sparkling wine. When Asti Spumanti is made by the méthode champenoise the delicious aroma and flavour of the muscat grape is diminished.

There are three methods of producing sparkling wine by double fermentation. In order of ascending quality they are:

(a) CHARMAT SYSTEM   This is better known as the cuve close system. Dry, still wine has sugar and yeast added to it in a vat able to withstand high pressure and the vat is sealed. The secondary fermentation takes place in the vat. When completed the wine is forced by pressure through filters and into bottles. This is a cheaper and widely used, but inferior, method of producing sparkling wine. When the wine is poured into a glass the beads—or bubbles—are larger and their duration is shorter than those produced from bottle fermentation.

(b) TANK TRANSFER or GERMAN SYSTEM   This system lies somewhere between the Charmat system and the méthode champenoise. Still white wine is first produced, then sugar and yeast are added and the wine is bottled as for bottle fermentation. There is no remuage or disgorging, but when the secondary fermentation is completed, the sparkling wine is mechanically transferred to a cold stainless steel tank. The wine is chilled and stabilized by nitrogen pressure. Sugar is added for sweetening and the wine is forced through filters into bottles. When the wine is poured into a glass the beads are smaller than from the Charmat system but larger than from the méthode champenoise. They continue to rise for a considerable time.

(c) MÉTHODE CHAMPENOISE   This is the only method permitted by law for wines sold as Champagne and is used all over the world to produce the finest sparkling wine.

The bunches of grapes, both black and white and often a mixture of the Pinot Noir and Chardonnay are carefully picked by hand and are not crushed before pressing. The presses are wide and shallow to force the juice away from the skins before it can dissolve any colouring matter. The presses hold 4,000 kg of grapes which yield 26 hectolitres of juice. The first pressing gives approximately 77% and this is used for the sparkling wine. The second pressing or first 'tailles' gives 15·5% and the third pressing or second 'tailles' gives 7·5%; these are made into other wines. Any further juice that can be extracted from the marc is fermented into wine to be drunk by employees. Finally the marc is fermented for distilling, into *eau de vie de marc*.

The first fermentation is the same as for any still white wine. During the winter the wines are cleared by the cold in open cellars, potassium hydrogen tartrate is deposited and the acidity of the wine is thereby lowered. The clear wines are racked, fined and blended to produce the standard product of the particular firm. Each has its own blend. The aim is to have the blending completed before the cold weather ends, otherwise the mixture of wines can become unstable and cloudy.

In spring, when the blended wines have married, the residual sugar content is accurately measured and the precise quantity of *liqueur de tirage* is added to increase the sugar content to 24 gm per litre, which is 2·4% volume of the wine. This will produce 5 atmospheres of pressure in the bottle after the secondary fermentation. It is a critical process as greater pressure from a little more sugar can burst the bottles. Before it was possible to measure an exact dosage, between 15% and 50% of the bottles used burst; in 1828 it was 80%. The secondary fermentation is made by a yeast that not only can withstand the great pressure from the imprisoned carbon dioxide but also forms a granual deposit easy to disgorge. When the wine is fermenting it is transferred into heavy, especially thick, glass bottles and sealed in by corks double the diameter of the bottle neck. An agrafe is fitted to prevent the cork being forced out by the pressure of the carbon dioxide. More recently crown corks have been used. These are cheaper, easier and quicker both to fit and remove. The bottles are then stacked on their sides in cellars with a temperature between 10 °C and 12 °C so that the sugar in the wine can ferment very slowly. The low-temperature fermentation is considered to produce a better and more persistent bouquet, as well as help the later remuage.

Occasionally the wines are roused, by giving the bottles a good shake, usually when the staff are removing the odd bottle that is weeping, or worse, that has burst. In the early stages it mixes the yeast into the wine, so helping fermentation. Later it assists homogeneity. Eventually the yeast settles in a firm deposit on the lower inner surface of the bottle and the wine is left to age on this deposit as near to the estimated shipping time as possible. During this ageing there are chemical reactions between the components of the wine and with the dead yeast cells causing esterification. Spoilage cannot occur because of the pressure of the carbon dioxide. Bouquet and flavour develop and the wine acquires a greater smoothness. The minimum period for vintage champagne to be left on its lees is 3 years. Non-vintage sparkling wine needs 12 months, but in practice this period is extended. Vins mousseux have by law to be left for a minimum of 9 months in the bottle to receive the 'appellation d'origine' title, and all other sparkling wines are left for at least 4 months. Then follows remuage and disgorgement.

The bottles are transferred into pupitres (desks) neck downwards, at an angle of 45° and the delicate operation of remuage begins. When the sediment has settled firmly on the cork and the bottle is standing *sur point* (on its head) it is ready for disgorging but will keep indefinitely.

Undoubtedly, sparkling wine is at its best if disgorging is delayed until just before drinking, although this is not commercially practicable. The bottles are topped up with dry wine or *liqueur d'expédition*, according to the degree of sweetness required. New corks are then fitted and muselets (muzzles) are wired on. For some sparkling wines, plastic stoppers are now used instead of the bell-shaped corks. Some pink Champagne is made and also some sparkling red wine but in no great quantity. Blanc de Blancs is made exclusively from white grapes, mostly Chardonnay, and never reaches the highest quality of a Champagne made from mixed black and white grapes but is, nevertheless, a splendid Champagne.

Carbonation is the poorest of all methods of giving a sparkle to a still wine. It is simply the injection of carbon dioxide and the result is like fizzy tonic water—a rush of large bubbles that quickly disappear.

SPECIFIC GRAVITY   The relative weight, expressed as a ratio, of a given volume of matter to the same volume of a standard. The standard for liquids is water which at 15°C (59°F) has been given the value of 1 (one), normally written as 1·000. This is measured by floating a hydrometer in water, the temperature of which is 15°C (59°F), and the point at which the stem of the hydrometer is cut by the water is marked on a chart in the tube of the hydrometer at the position 1·000.

The specific gravities which concern the winemaker are those produced by the presence of sugar or alcohol. When sugar is added to water, the water becomes more dense and its specific gravity is increased. A hydrometer placed in the solution will then float with its stem higher above the surface than if it was in plain water, and its specific gravity can be read from the chart. The more sugar that is added the higher the specific gravity will read, e.g.

S.G. of any volume of water at 15°C is 1·000
S.G. of 1 gallon of water plus 1 lb sucrose is 1·035
S.G. of 5 litres of water plus 500 g sucrose is 1·035
S.G. of 1 pint of water plus 2 lb sucrose is 1·300
S.G. of 625 ml of water plus 1 kg sucrose is 1·300

Alcohol is less dense than water, therefore its specific gravity is lower. When alcohol and water are mixed, as in a dry wine, the gravity is lower than that of water, e.g. wine with a specific gravity of 0·990. If sugar is added to water and alcohol, then the specific gravity of the solution is raised. For example—if 500 g sugar is added to 5 litres of wine of S.G. 0·990, the specific gravity is increased to 1·028 approximately. Thus an

165

increase in gravity can indicate an increase in the amount of sugar and a decrease in specific gravity can indicate an increased alcohol in a solution. Whilst specific gravity can indicate the amount of sugar in a must when there is no alcohol present, it cannot indicate the amount of sugar present in a finished wine, unless the alcohol content is known. Following from this it can be seen that the sweetness of a finished wine cannot be solely judged by a single hydrometer reading, it can only be appreciated by taste. Alternatively, the amount of alcohol present in a wine can only be assessed from a single specific gravity if the total amount of sugar in the must and added is known, although it can be calculated if both the specific gravity of the original must and of the finished wine are known. The difference between them or gravity drop as it is called, if divided by 7·5 gives the approximate alcohol content by percentage:

Example: S.G. of must   1·070
          S.G. of finished wine 0·995
          _____
          Gravity drop   75 divided by 7·5 equals
                                       10% alcohol.

Frequently, for ease of working, the specific gravity of water is called zero and the 1 as well as the 0s are omitted. The figure left is then referred to as the gravity.

Examples:

Specific gravity	Gravity
1·000	Zero
1·005	5
1·025	25
1·125	125

If the specific gravity is below 1·000 it is referred to as a 'minus gravity'.

Examples:

Specific gravity	Gravity
0·995	− 5
0·990	−10
0·985	−15

(*See also* HYDROMETER.)

SPIGOT A wooden plug, usually cone-shaped, for stopping the hole in the cask head. A spigot is also the wooden tap which is driven into the cask for drawing off the wine. It should not be confused with SPILE.

SPILE A slightly tapered cylinder of wood, some 7·5 cm long and 1 cm in diameter. It fits into the hole bored into the centre of a bung. When a barrel is broached, it is sufficient to remove the spile so that air can get in to replace the wine as it is drawn off. It is easier to remove the spile than the bung, which is hammered home to fit flush and tight. When checking whether a cask needs topping up it is sufficient to remove the spile and take a measurement of the depth of wine with a glass or wooden rod, to see whether the wine has evaporated sufficiently to need any addition.

SPRITZIG   A German word that has roughly the same meaning as petillant. It is applied to wines that are lively and which contain just a little carbon dioxide, although not enough for the wine to be called sparkling wine. It can be very pleasant in a light wine and is sometimes deliberately produced by the early bottling of a wine that has cleared quickly. The very last stage of fermentation thus takes place in the bottle and causes the lively prickle.

STABLE and STABILIZING   During fermentation a wine is said to be active. After fermentation has completely stopped and the wine becomes still, it is described as stable. The *Concise Oxford Dictionary* describes stable as 'firmly fixed or established—not easily changed'. This definition does not strictly apply to stable wines as they are easily changed and are not fixed or established when they are thought to be. Quite rightly, when fermentation completely stops the wine is said to be stable, but even in brilliant wine, dormant yeast cells are often present. These can start fermenting again for no apparent reason and even though the refermentation is very slow and slight, the wine is no longer stable.

Commercially, wines are stabilized by being passed through filters so fine that they remove all yeast cells, and pasteurization is also practised. These processes are not practicable for the domestic winemaker with limited facilities. To be certain of having stabilized low-alcohol sweet wines, sulphite can be used, but a massive dose of up to 1,000 ppm could be required. This would bleach the colour, cause a high, fixed, sulphur-dioxide content and produce an objectionable odour. However, stabilization can usually be obtained by the use of up to 300 ppm (6 Campden Tablets to a gallon of wine with correct acidity). In practice and for dry wines, 50 ppm is sufficient when coupled with frequent racking. For wines with residual sugar, sorbic acid is added at the rate of 100 ppm together with 50 ppm SO_2. Yeast activity can also be prevented by the addition of benzoic acid. Whatever the dosage and method used, the maximum amount of stabilizer allowed to remain in the wine should not exceed 0·1%.

STAINLESS STEEL   This is the only metal that may be used for all purposes in winemaking. It is inert to acids and alcohols and cannot cause metal contamination. It may be used for crushing and pressing equipment, measuring vessels, fermentation and storage vessels, and utensils of all kinds.

STAR-BRIGHT   Wines which are brilliantly clear and reflect highlights when in the bottle are said to be 'star-bright'. All wines that are

167

entered in competitions or are otherwise exhibited publicly should be star-bright.

STARCH ($C_6H_{10}O_5$) The common carbohydrate found in all plants except fungi, and even stored in their seeds. Wine yeasts are unable to ferment it, and if present in sufficient quantity it will cause a finished wine to be hazy. Fining or filtering will have little effect in removing the haze and the only treatment is by the starch reducing enzyme, amylase. This can be obtained under the trade name Amylozyme 100 and should be used as directed by the suppliers. Wines treated with enzymes should not be tightly corked or sealed down as further fermentation may occur.

To test if a haze in a wine is due to starch, pour a little wine into a test tube and add a few drops of ordinary iodine. If the wine turns blue, purple or black the presence of starch is indicated. If a white wine containing no starch is tested the colour will change to pale brown or a brown tint. Red wines will have brown added to their colour. N.B. Colourless or decoloured iodine is of no use for this test. For other causes of hazes in wines *see* HAZES.

STARTER, STARTER BOTTLE and STARTER SOLUTION The purpose of a starter is to activate the selected wine yeast and provide a sufficient quantity of active yeast with which to start a must fermenting. As it is essential to produce a rapid, visible fermentation in a must, it is obvious that the more active yeast cells that are added, the sooner the yeast colony reaches a critical concentration. There are, however, practical limits, and the generally accepted quantity is 5% of the quantity of must to be fermented, approximately one half-pint of active ferment per gallon of must (50 ml per litre). To obtain this a starter bottle is used. To make a starter for one gallon (5 litres) of must use a one-pint or half-litre bottle; for two gallons a quart or litre bottle; for five gallons (25 litres) a half-gallon or 2½-litre jar; and for ten gallons (50 litres) a one-gallon or 5-litre jar. Oversize vessels are used so that they will be only half full, thus allowing space for air which can provide essential oxygen for the yeasts' reproduction.

The bottle or jar is first thoroughly sterilized and then half filled with one of the following yeast starters:

(1) Pure fruit juice and sugar at the rate of 50 g sugar per litre fruit juice, boiled for five minutes and allowed to cool.
(2) Malt extract, citric acid, sugar and water boiled together for five minutes and allowed to cool. Quantities used are 50 g malt extract, 5 g citric and 25 g sugar per litre of water.
(3) Chopped raisins 50 g and sugar 25 g per litre of water, boiled for ten minutes and allowed to cool.

The selected wine yeast, whether it is in granulated, powder, liquid or culture form, is added to the starter solution when this is cool, around 20 to 21 °C (68 to 70 °F). The neck of the vessel is then plugged with plain, unmedicated cotton wool and the vessel is stood in a temperature of about 24 °C (75 °F). As soon as there is a visible fermentation, the must is prepared and the starter ferment added to it.

If a little of the starter is retained in the starter bottle and further starter solution is added, an active yeast culture can be maintained, particularly if it is stored in a refrigerator. An active ferment can be kept in this manner, but it may not remain a pure culture, as the cells could mutate, and contamination by wild yeasts and other micro-organisms might occur. To obtain the best results a new starter should be prepared for each must, especially if there is likely to be a gap of more than a few days before the starter is used again.

STAVES   The curved lengths of wood which form the side of a cask.

STERILIZATION   Often mentioned in connection with the preparation of musts but musts are rarely sterilized. Action is normally taken only to inhibit the growth of spoilage organisms, but complete sterilization is not achieved. However, all equipment vessels and utensils should be sterilized before use. Boiling, baking and spraying with steam were the old-fashioned methods used, but the use of sulphite is simpler, easier and without the possibility of causing damage. For full details of inhibiting bacterial and similar growth in musts and wines and the sterilizing of equipment etc., *see* SULPHITE.

STERILIZING DETERGENTS   Now marketed under various trade names, they have been formulated especially for the beer, food and wine trade. As the name suggests they are cleaning agents combined with a chemical which in solution produces hypochlorous acid, a powerful bactericide. Sterilizing solutions will both clean and sterilize equipment and are quite harmless when used strictly in accordance with the manufacturers' instructions. These compounds that yield hypochlorous acid have proved to be more effective than sulphite when used to sterilize equipment and have the added advantage of their cleaning action. Many manufacturers claim that it is not necessary to rinse equipment after using a sterilizing detergent. To be on the safe side, however, it is advisable to do so. They cannot and must not be used in the wine. (*See* SULPHITE.)

STILL WINES   Wines which contain no gas or sparkle. Most wines are in fact still wines or are supposed to be!

STILLAGE   A stand for casks usually made of wood comprising two X-shaped pieces joined at their centre by a length of timber. The cask is laid in the upper part of the Xs. It is sometimes called a cask cradle.

STIRRING   *See* ROUSING.

STOCK FERMENT   After a yeast has been activated in a starter solution, the whole is called an active yeast culture. Some winemakers maintain an active culture by never using it all and topping it up with fresh starter solution each time some of the culture is used. When not in use it is stored in a refrigerator. The culture which is maintained in this manner is called a 'stock ferment'.

Whilst the practice of keeping stock cultures has certain advantages, it is not a practice to be recommended. Each time the culture is used and topped up, it is subject to contamination by wild yeast and spoilage organisms present in the air. In addition the yeast cells can mutate and produce strains of yeast with individual characteristics. For both these reasons, stock ferments that are not maintained under laboratory conditions generally decrease in quality the longer they are kept and wines made with them are apt to become contaminated or be of poor quality. (*See also* STARTER BOTTLE.)

STOPPERS   Corks that are sometimes used in place of straight-sided corks for bottling. They are T-shaped in section and are made of: (a) all plastic, (b) all cork, (c) cork stem and wood or plastic cap. Their advantage in use is that they can be easily withdrawn without a corkscrew and replaced. Their disadvantage is that they are not suitable for long storage, unless completely sealed with a capsule or wax. They are most commonly used when bottling wines which will be drunk without storage, or for high-alcohol fortified wines. Light wines for storage are best sealed with straight-sided corks. Stoppers are usually specified for bottles in competitions.

STORE and STORAGE   The method and place of storing wines is most important. Little is known of all the effects that light has upon wine, as different forms of light have various wavelengths which make it a complex problem. Nevertheless, there is little doubt that wines should be stored away from light, either natural or artificial. It will cause red wines to lose their colour and white wines to become cloudy.

Rapidly fluctuating temperatures have adverse effects, as do changes between extremes, thus a wine store should be of an even, or slowly fluctuating temperature preferably around 12 °C (54 °F), though this is not so important as the temperature being even.

Vibration is known also to have an adverse effect on wine. It does not matter, however, whether the place is dry, or dampish, provided all the bottles and containers are properly sealed. To sum up, a wine store should be dark, of even temperature and quiet.

The wines themselves should be in properly sealed containers, whether they be cask, stainless steel, earthenware jar, bottle or other vessels, all with the minimum of ullage. If the sealing is by cork, these will shrink during storage and should, therefore, be waxed to maintain their seal. Bottles of table or low-alcohol wine should be laid on their

170

sides so that the corks remain moist and do not shrink. Bottles containing wines with a high-alcohol content should be stood upright because the suberin which bonds cork together is partly soluble in a high concentration of alcohol. The corks might otherwise become soggy and porous. For vintage Port-type wines that need long bottle storage, the risk of seepage can be minimized by a complete wax seal.

STRAINING The removal of pulp from a must or a fermenting liquid. The main requirement is that the method used rapidly removes all pulp and larger particles. Straining which is slow and prolonged can result in contamination by micro-organisms or help towards over-oxidation. Probably the best method for small quantities is the use of a felt or fine nylon filter bag suspended from a ring and chain. Linen bags can be used but are much slower. Even so, it is preferable to use two or more bags as they quickly clog and the juice stops running. As soon as the flow from the first bag starts to slow down no more liquid should be added to the bag. A second bag is then filled and whilst this is running the first bag is squeezed, emptied of pulp and rinsed in clean water to free the felt of fine clogging particles. It is then ready for use again as soon as the flow from the second bag starts to slow.

STUCK FERMENT This is a fermenting must or wine in which the fermentation has prematurely ceased, for one or more of several causes:

(a) TEMPERATURE When the temperature drops too low, many wine yeasts become dormant, the fermentation becomes sluggish and eventually stops altogether. The wine is stuck. As soon as the temperature rises sufficiently the yeast again causes fermentation. In very hot weather when the temperature of the must exceeds 31 °C (90 °F), the same thing happens in reverse and fermentation does not start again until the temperature falls. Certain yeast strains are unaffected by these low and high temperatures whilst others are 'burnt out' by 30 °C (86 °F).

(b) NUTRIENT If a quantity of water is used in the preparation of a must and no nutrient is added there will be a nutrient deficiency. The yeast may then cease to function and the fermentation becomes stuck. To restart such a fermentation, nutrient is dissolved in some of the wine and well stirred into the bulk. Should the wine fail to referment, a new yeast culture should be added. Correct addition of nutrient to a must which includes added water will always avoid this form of sticking.

(c) SUGAR If the sugar content of a must is too high, added yeast cultures will ferment only for a short time and then stick. Dilution with other fruit juice, juice and pulp or with water is the only satisfactory way of causing refermentation. A new yeast culture may also have to be added for the original yeast will probably have been killed by osmosis. Fermentation will also be stopped prematurely if too little sugar has been added and it has all been converted into alcohol and carbon dioxide. This can be corrected by the addition of sugar or syrup.

(d) BACTERIAL If there is an excessive bacterial development in a must, it can cause fermentation to stick. Sulphiting and subsequently re-yeasting will result in continued fermentation, but the wine has usually been spoilt and is rarely worth re-fermenting. Correct sulphiting of a must will prevent this occurring.

(e) ACIDS If the pH of a must is below 3·0 fermentation is slowed and can become stuck. Likewise, a too high pH can have the same effect. The cure and prevention is to readjust the pH to between 3·2 and 3·6.

(f) CARBON DIOXIDE If an adequate gas release is not fitted, the retained carbon dioxide can inhibit fermentation. The remedy is to pour the wine from one container to another, thoroughly rousing it in the process.

With (b) and (c) above, when it is necessary to add a second yeast culture, it should not be added direct into the stuck wine. First add an equal amount of stuck wine to an active yeast culture. When the mixture is fully fermenting, add another quantity of stuck wine equal to the fermenting mixture. Repeat until all the stuck wine is fermenting.

SUBSTRATES Inert substances which contain or receive a nutrient solution, and upon which enzymes act. Yeasts, living by the action of the enzymes they secrete, thus live upon substrates and only indirectly upon the so-called 'yeast nutrients'.

SUCCINIC ACID The principal acid in the formation of esters that provide the winy aroma and flavour of wine. Very little, if any, is present in unfermented must, but it is formed during the highly complex chemical actions that take place during fermentation and maturation. A small amount may be added to a wine after fermentation to assist esterification. As the esters form during maturation it will take some time to produce an effect.

SUCRASE The correct name of the enzyme that hydrolyses or splits the di-saccharide sucrose into its two component mono-saccharides—fructose and glucose. It is commonly but erroneously called 'invertase' because 'invert sugar' is the name given to the mixture of fructose and glucose after the hydrolysis of sucrose. (*See* INVERT SUGAR.)

SUCROSE The name of the di-saccharide obtained from sugar cane, sugar beets and other sources. It is commonly called 'sugar'. In its white granulated form it is 99·9 pure sucrose. The chemical composition of sucrose remains the same no matter from what source it is produced.

When white granulated sugar is heated to 180 °C (356 °F) it becomes caramelized and a range of brown 'sugars' are produced. (*See also* SUGARS.) Brown sugars are also produced in the refining of raw sugar and they then contain certain impurities that are subsequently removed in the production of white sugar.

SUGARS Carbohydrates fall into two categories, sugars and non-sugars, each of which are sub-divided into groups. Sugars comprise the so-called single or simple sugars, mono-saccharides, such as fructose and glucose; di-saccharides which are built from two molecules of mono-saccharides by condensation and include lactose (milk sugar), maltose (malt sugar) and sucrose (cane or beet sugar); tri-saccharides which are built from three molecules of mono-saccharides and tetra-saccharides from four. The continuance of the process of repeated condensation of mono-saccharides, produces non-sugars, or poly-saccharides, which include pectin, starch and cellulose. Although the simple sugars are the basic units from which higher sugars and non-sugars are constructed, there is a considerable difference between sugars and non-sugars. Sugars are crystalline, soluble in water and possess a sweet taste. Poly-saccharides are shapeless, uncrystallized, insoluble and tasteless.

The complexity of the mixtures of mono-saccharides in fruit and vegetables is not always realized, being overlooked through stressing the abundant carbohydrate. For example, it is generally known that potatoes contain starch, but their sugar content also includes fructose, glucose, maltose, mannose, sucrose and xylose.

Wine yeasts can directly ferment only simple sugars, or mono-saccharides, although they also secrete the enzyme sucrase which inverts sucrose to simple sugars, thus permitting them indirectly to ferment cane or beet sugar. It follows that the only sugars of interest to winemakers are the simple sugars and sucrose. The forms in which these are obtainable are:

(a) CARAMELS Brown sugars (demerara, barbados, pieces, moist etc.). They darken wines and add a caramel flavour. Not suitable for winemaking, unless a caramel flavour is desired as in a Madeira-type wine.

(b) FRUCTOSE (fruit sugar) and GLUCOSE (grape sugar) They are both readily fermentable, 500 g of either is the equivalent of 400 g of sucrose. They are completely suitable for winemaking, but have no advantage over sucrose, except for a slightly quicker fermentation.

(c) HONEY The basic ingredient of mead. Not advisable for use in other wines, unless a honey flavour is desired.

(d) INVERT SUGAR Sucrose which has been inverted and is an equimolecular mixture of glucose and fructose. Invert sugar is readily fermentable and can be used in place of sucrose, but is much dearer to purchase. It can be produced by boiling sucrose with citric acid for twenty minutes. (*See* INVERT SUGAR.)

(e) LACTOSE (milk sugar)   Cannot be fermented by wine yeasts and is, therefore, a suitable sugar to use for sweetening low-alcohol wine.

(f) LUMP SUGAR and PRESERVING SUGAR   Different forms of sucrose. They have no advantage in being used in its place and are dearer to buy.

(g) MALTOSE (malt sugar)   Readily fermentable and used mostly for ales and beers. It is not suitable for wine as the malt flavour is not altogether desirable.

(h) STARCH   Not a sugar and strictly should not be included here, but it is a source of sugar and can be converted to sugar by the enzyme amylase and is then fermentable.

(i) SUCROSE (white sugar)   The common white granulated sugar in everyday use and the cheapest form purchasable. It is readily converted to glucose and fructose by the enzyme sucrase secreted by wine yeast and is then fermented. It is the most suitable sugar for use in winemaking.

The concentration of sugar in a must is of considerable importance. The optimum concentration for the maximum speed of fermentation is between 10 and 20% whilst above 20% it retards fermentation, or causes it to stick. German Trockenbeerenauslese must of 40% sugar and over can take as much as five to seven years to complete fermentation and even then the alcohol content is of only 5 to 9% by volume. Maximum alcohol content is obtained from a total of 25 to 35% sugar which has been fed into the must in small doses and fermented in stages (syrup method).

SULPHITE

General   For many centuries sulphur has been used in the wine industry. Early commercial winemakers knew from experience that unclean casks caused the wine to turn sour. Washing with water was inadequate and resort was made to brimstone. This was fashioned into the form of a match or candle and burned inside the cask. The burning sulphur combined with oxygen from the air to form sulphur dioxide, a powerful disinfectant, that killed spoilage organisms. Today sulphur dioxide is extensively employed as a bactericide and anti-oxidant but it is no longer obtained from burning sulphur.

Sulphite, the accepted contraction for sodium or potassium metabisulphite, breaks down when dissolved in a solution and reacts with the water to produce sulphur dioxide. When acid is added to the water, the amount of sulphur dioxide increases until the solution contains all that was bound up in the metabisulphite. Sulphite is used commercially, but for large-scale operations a cylinder of compressed liquid sulphur dioxide is preferred. The cylinders of sulphur dioxide are not suitable for small-scale operations because the small quantities required at any one time are very difficult to measure. Sodium metabisulphite (cheaper than potassium metabisulphite) or its tablet form—Campden tablets—is more suitable for experimental and domestic purposes.

In must and wine the sulphur dioxide 'splits' into two fractions. One combines with other chemicals to become the fixed fraction, the other does not combine and is the free fraction. It is the free sulphur dioxide that is the disinfectant and inhibits or kills micro-organisms depending on the concentration.

Sterilization of equipment A solution of metabisulphite can be made up and stored for repeated use. Such solutions even with distilled water are not completely stable and the instability increases with the hardness of tap water. The effective life of a solution—the period during which it can be stored and reused without losing its effect—varies with the strength of the solution. A solution of 1% metabisulphite in distilled water takes about 1 hour to 'sterilize' equipment and the effective life of the solution is less than 4 weeks. A solution of 10% in distilled water needs only a few minutes to sterilize and the effective life of the solution is about 20 weeks. The sulphur dioxide can be increased to shorten the sterilizing time by adding citric acid to the stock solution but it could not then be kept for future use.

Probably the most reliable method is the preparation of a 10% stock solution by dissolving 100 g sodium metabisulphite in 0·5 litres of warm water and then making up the quantity to 1 litre with cold water. This stock solution should be stored in a glass container with a good seal. The effective life of the solution could be 4 to 6 months. Each time equipment is to be sterilized, as small an amount as is required is acidified with citric acid. Clean equipment need only be swilled around with the acidified solution which is discarded after use. An alternative method is to dissolve 1·5 g sodium metabisulphite and 1·5 g citric acid in 1 litre of water. This solution should be used for all immediate needs and then discarded. It would be necessary for this solution to remain in contact with the equipment to be sterilized for from 10 to 15 minutes.

Whilst these solutions are reasonably effective, the sterilizing detergents (refer) are more effective in killing certain bacteria, and they have the added advantage of cleaning at the same time. Equipment has to be thoroughly cleaned before it can be sterilized with sulphite. Sterilizing detergents, however, can only be used on equipment. *They must not be used in musts or wine*.

Sterilizing must and wine When sulphite is added to a must or wine, sulphur dioxide is liberated. Some of it combines with other chemicals, and the rest remains free. Thus there occur different reactions with different end results. The sulphur dioxide (1) kills or inhibits spoilage organisms, (2) combines with oxygen ,and prevents browning and over-oxidation, (3) combines with compounds and influences their reactions.

(1A) All fruit is liable to be contaminated by micro-organisms of one kind or another (bacteria, moulds and wild spoilage yeasts), and their concentration is highest on damaged or over-ripe fruit. In the must these micro-organisms have to be killed or inhibited to prevent spoilage. Of the many 'safe' chemicals used for preservation in the food industry, only sulphite is suitable for use in wine. The others not only prevent spoilage but also prevent fermentation by killing or inhibiting the wine yeast. Even so, sulphite should only be used in the long-established quantities. An excess of sulphur dioxide from indiscriminate use of sulphite is very difficult to remove, and in a finished wine can be objectionable.

A concentration of around 50 ppm sulphur dioxide in a must is usually sufficient to prevent spoilage and has no deleterious effect on the wine yeast. In a fairly acid must 100 ppm of sodium metabisulphite provides around 55 ppm sulphur dioxide. But this depends on the acidity of the must which is a variable factor. A further variable is the condition of the fruit—whether it is damaged, over-ripe and/or mouldy. Such fruit has a higher concentration of spoilage organisms and the increased sulphur dioxide binding compounds require an increased concentration of metabisulphite.

The following is a guide to the average dosages required:

High acidity	100 ppm metabisulphite
Medium acidity	150 ppm ''
Low acidity	200 ppm ''

In must from damaged, over-ripe or mouldy fruit,
the ppm metabisulphite should be doubled.

The addition per litre of must of 1 ml of the 10% stock solution of sodium metabisulphite described above provides 100 ppm metabisulphite, producing around 55 ppm sulphur dioxide in the higher acidity. The addition for medium acidity is 1·5 ml per litre and in the lower acidity 2 ml per litre. Each Campden tablet contains 0·44 g sodium metabisulphite producing approximately 50 ppm SO_2 in 5 litres of high-acid must. Additions per 5 litres would, therefore, be 1, 1½ or 2 tablets for high, medium and low acidity, respectively. Wine yeast—*Saccharomyces cerevisiae* var. *ellipsoideus*—is resistant to small amounts of sulphur dioxide in the must, probably because it has strong reducing powers. Their resistance is at its highest when the cells are fully active, yet another reason for adding a pre-activated yeast to the must. The aldehydes formed by the fermentation also assist by reducing the free sulphur dioxide. Herein lies the reason for waiting 24 hours after sulphiting a must and before adding an active yeast. The free sulphur dioxide has to be allowed adequate time to kill or inhibit the micro-organisms before yeast activity reduces it.

(1B) During racking and bottling, low-alcohol (table) and more particularly low-alcohol/low-acid wines are susceptible to oxidation and to infection by wild yeasts and bacteria. It is now standard practice to add sufficient sulphite at these stages to prevent spoilage. For most wines 50 ppm sulphur dioxide (100 ppm metabisulphite) are added at the first racking and again at bottling. If intermediate rackings are required it is only necessary to add 25 ppm sulphur dioxide to keep the level topped up. These amounts should not normally be exceeded since too much sulphur dioxide can result in the formation of too much sulphurous acid which could interfere with maturation.

(1c) Residual sugar, in other than high-alcohol wines, or wines that have not been the subject of sterile filtration, has the potential for fermentation by yeast cells that remain in the wine no matter how clear it may be. Sulphiting, as described in (1B), will 'stun' these cells. The amount does not have to be increased as it will serve both purposes.

This is not a 100% guarantee of stability however, because the yeast might become active again as the result of the diminution of the free sulphur dioxide by the aldehydes. Sorbic acid is now sometimes used in conjunction with sulphite for greater stability. (*See* SORBIC ACID.)

(2) Sulphur dioxide is an anti-oxidant because atmospheric oxygen readily combines with it to form sulphur trioxide which can itself combine with hydrogen to form sulphurous acid. Oxygen dissolved in fruit juice or in a must or in contact with its surface can therefore be denied to the oxidasive enzymes by the presence of sulphur dioxide and so prevent browning.

In finished white wines, sulphur dioxide withholds oxygen from ethyl alcohol and so prevents over-oxidation. This is another function of sulphite when added at the racking and bottling stages. (*See* (1B).) Red wines are themselves sufficiently anti-oxidant to require no sulphiting for this latter purpose.

(3A) Sulphur dioxide combines with chemical constituents which contain carbonyl groups, such as galacturonic acid, pyruvic acid, and xylosone, forming a fixed fraction but leaving a small amount free.

Of all the sulphur dioxide binding compounds present in must and wine, acetaldehyde far exceeds the total of all the others put together. Acetaldehyde is a compound in the chain of normal reactions by which sugar is reduced to ethyl alcohol. When acetaldehyde binds with sulphur dioxide, this chain of reactions is blocked. Fermentation is then completed by other reactions which produce large amounts of glycerol.

Some glycerol, which gives a slightly sweet taste to wine, is formed in all fermentations but the largest amounts are found in wines from heavily sulphited musts such as Sauternes. The Semillon grapes attacked by the 'Noble Rot' have to be heavily sulphited to prevent action by oxydase. These wines can contain up to 2·5% glycerol which contributes to their rich, smooth, quality. Fermentation is inevitably slow and takes up to 3 or 4 times as long as for dry table wines.

(3B) After fermentation, the addition of 50 ppm sulphur dioxide aids the clarification of the wine. (It can be the same addition used at the first racking.) The sulphur dioxide neutralizes electrical charges on suspended colloidal particles, promoting their coagulation and settlement.

SULPHURETTED HYDROGEN This is a term that is now rarely used. It has been replaced by HYDROGEN SULPHIDE, under which details are given.

SULTANAS Dried white grapes which can be used for winemaking purposes as well as for cooking. (*See also* RAISINS.)

SYRUP, SYRUPING and SYRUP METHOD Syrup for winemaking purposes is made by bringing to the boil 1 kg (2 lb) of sugar in 0·62 litres (1 pint) of water. The total volume is 1·25 litres (2 pints) of syrup. It has a specific gravity of 1·300. As the sugar content is high, it is not subject to attack by micro-organisms and can, therefore, be made in large quantities and stored indefinitely until required. It is best to store the syrup in screw-stoppered bottles each of which will contain a precise amount of sugar as syrup. 1 pint of 300 gravity syrup contains 1 lb sucrose and 500 ml contains 400 g. If 5 g citric acid is added to the sugar and the solution is boiled for 20 minutes an invert sugar solution is made (*see* INVERT SUGAR).

The syrup method of fermentation is the best method of producing wines that are high in alcohol, such as dessert wines for which large quantities of sugar have to be fermented. Yeast ferments best in a low sugar solution. The adding of large amounts of sugar to a must is very liable to result in a slow, protracted ferment and even a stuck fermentation due to osmosis of the yeast. The syrup method not only prevents this, but the stirring in of the syrup introduces oxygen and enables a larger crop of yeast to be produced. Furthermore, this method ensures that wines will not be over-sweet when fermentation ceases. Undiluted concentrated grape juice which has a high sugar content may be used instead of sugar when an increase of body is also required.

When the must is prepared the sugar content is checked with a hydrometer. If this is less than 100 g per litre (S.G. 1·035), syrup must be added to increase the sugar content to this amount. The yeast is added and fermentation begins. When the specific gravity drops to around

1·010, syrup is again added, this time to raise the gravity to between 1·025 and 1·035. This process is repeated as often as necessary until the desired alcohol content is reached or the alcohol tolerance of the yeast is surpassed. The inclusion of an additional dose of nutrient salts and vitamin B_1 with the second or third additions of syrup will assist fermentation by nourishing the yeast.

TABLE WINE A term usually applied to unfortified beverage wine which is drunk with meals. Normally, table wine is low in alcohol, 9–12% by volume, so that it can be drunk in quantity. Thinner and more delicate than dessert wine, it usually also has a higher or more noticeable acidity to clean the palate, particularly with fatty foods. As a rule of thumb, red table wines have a higher tannin content than white and are therefore more astringent and take longer to mature. The reds also tend to have a more robust flavour. Red wines are generally drunk with red or strong flavoured meats and white wines with white meats and fish.

TANNINS In early times it was found that some plant substances reacted with skins of animals and tanned them, making them more durable. These plant substances were called tannins and knowledge of them was obtained by trial and error. With the development of chemistry it was found that other compounds had the same properties as tannin, but did not tan, i.e. turn brown. These are now also called tannins. Several are glucosides of gallic acid, which store plant volatile scents and flavours. Naturally present in plants, including grapes, are enzymes which hydrolyse the glucosides and release the substances during crushing and pulp fermentation. Other tannins vary in composition, but all are similarly astringent in character.

Wide variations of tannin content are found in different fruits and in different varieties of the same fruit. The tannin content increases with ripeness and unripe fruit can have a deficiency. Little is present in the juice and nearly all of it comes from pips, skin and stalks. For example, grape juice contains less than 0·05% tannin, the pips contain from 5 to 6%, the skins from 0·5 to 1·5% and the stalks about 3%. White wines average between 0·014 and 0·03% and red wines 0·1 to 0·4% tannin, including colouring. It is the tannin content that makes the palate difference between white and red wines—not the colour. The amount of tannin in red wine depends on the tannin content of the fruit, the amount of pulp, the composition of the pulp (ratio of pips, skins and stalks) and the length of the pulp fermentation. During the pulp fermentation the hydrolysing enzymes break down the glucosides, then, as alcohol is formed, that, too, assists in the extraction.

Tannin is a minor but indispensable ingredient of wine. Its bitter-astringent qualities give wine its 'bite' and character. Wines that lack tannin taste flat and dull. Tannin assists clarification by combining with and precipitating proteins and allied nitrogenous substances which in suspension cause or stabilize hazes. This is the reason why red wines usually clear more quickly than white.

Hydro-colloids consisting of gums, pectic substances and protein are too fine to filter out and can cause persistent hazes. These hazes must be removed by fining with substances that coagulate with tannin and, in falling, enmesh the hydro-colloids and deposit them. (*See* FINING and TRIAL FININGS.)

The high tannin content of red wine improves its keeping quality but increases the time taken to mature it to its peak. During this time the tannins react with other substances to form insoluble tannates that settle out as a deposit. There is a slight loss by combination with aldehydes and protein and by oxidation and the wine becomes smooth and mellow. Red wines high in tannin and somewhat harsh when young require longer to mature than red wines of more even balance, but frequently they mature to superior quality.

Commercially the addition of tannin is a legitimate procedure permitted by law and often necessary in white wines. Wines made by amateurs frequently suffer a greater deficiency in tannin than commercial wines. It should be a standard practice to add some tannin to nearly all wines made from fruits, other than black grapes, elderberries and pears. Unfortunately there is no simple test for tannin, except the palate, yet the content of tannin in musts and wines varies very considerably according to the ingredients. The practice should, therefore, be to add some tannin to a must and some more, when the wine is stable, if this is thought necessary after tasting the wine. Fear of adding too much need not be considered, as few, if any, musts contain sufficient tannin. In any case no harm will result and the tannin content can always be reduced, if necessary, by macerating a little gelatine into the wine. There is more fault in not having enough tannin in a wine than by having too much.

TANNISAGE   The addition of tannin to a must to correct deficiency, or to assist in fining.

TAP and TAPPING   To 'tap' a cask or the 'tapping' of a cask is the fitting of a tap in order to draw off wine. To tap a cask is also known as to BROACH, under which heading fuller details are given.

TARTARIC ACIDS   *See* ACIDS.

TASTE and TASTING   Commonly used but inaccurate terms, because they are generally used to mean appreciation of flavour, or judgement of quality, which is the result of smell, taste and texture. (*See also* JUDGING WINE and TASTES.)

TASTES   Taste is but one factor in the appreciation of wine. We are said to recognize only four tastes: acidity, bitterness, saltiness and sweetness. Charles Linnaeus (1707–78) classified eight savours: bitter, salty, sour, sweet, dry, harsh, fat and viscous; but only the four previously mentioned are accepted today. Fattiness, harshness and viscosity are now considered as texture, whilst dryness and sweetness are degrees of the same taste.

The tastes are recognized by the taste-buds, of which there are several thousand, arranged in patterns over the surface of the tongue and on the soft palate, loosely referred to as 'back of the mouth', or uvula. Whilst some taste buds react to two tastes and most react to only one, all decrease in response when subjected to a constant stimulus of their own type. For instance a sugar/water solution held in the mouth will produce the maximum response for only a few seconds. Thereafter the sensation of sweetness slowly diminishes until the solution will appear to have no taste at all—approximately two minutes. This decrease in response is also the reason why a semi-sweet wine will taste dry if taken immediately after a sweet one, or a sweet one taste very sweet after a dry wine.

With some slight overlapping, the buds detecting sweetness are very near the surface on the tip of the tongue, saltiness is on the tip and edges, sourness on the sides, and bitterness at the back in grooves which can be opened or shut by muscular action. They are controlled by the seventh and ninth cranial nerves and show a slight decrease in response from childhood to middle age, after which there is little change until near the eighties when there is an overall decrease.

The taste buds of individuals do not all have the same responses, due to inherited poor development or to damage. The differences of responses with other factors cause variations in flavour appreciation and are reasons for some people being poor judges of wine.

Of the four tastes, saltiness is rarely encountered in a wine—Manzanilla being one of the exceptions—but the cleanness of acid taste is of importance for all wines and especially for table varieties. Low-acid wines seem flat or insipid. The correct sweetness for purpose is most important whether it is the lack of it, as in dry wines, or its particular evidence, as in dessert wines. Bitterness should be slight in the form of the bite or astringency of tannin. Without it a wine lacks much in character.

TASTEVIN A small shallow silver or pewter cup with a raised and embossed centre to reflect light, and with a small handle at the side. It was regularly used by wine tasters in the past but is now more often replaced by a tasting glass.

There were similar silver cups used by barber-surgeons as bleeding vessels in olden days, and as antiques the two should not be confused.

TEMPERATURE Temperatures play an important part in the life of wine from its preparation in the must to its 'consummation' in the glass.

At 32 °C (90 °F) wine yeast is greatly weakened and at 36 °C (97 °F) and above it dies, although the enzymes secreted during fermentation are not destroyed until a temperature of about 65 °C (150 °F) is reached. Therefore, above 36 °C (97 °F) the fermentafion can continue only for a short while after the yeast cells are dead, just until the enzymes are exhausted.

At the other extreme, wine yeasts cease to cause fermentation when the temperature falls to about 7 °C (45 °F) and below, although there are some special wine yeasts that will continue to cause fermentation at a lower temperature. The cold does not appear to harm the wine yeasts, they just become dormant and will again cause fermentation when the temperature rises sufficiently.

Between the extremes of 7 and 32 °C (45 and 90 °F) lie the best temperatures for purposes connected with wine.

Alcoholic fermentation liberates some heat which in small vessels of one or two gallons can be largely lost by radiation, but the larger the vessel the greater the retention of heat. During fermentation, then, temperatures should be taken from the fermenting wine and not from the air. If needs be, a large fermentation vessel should be fitted with a cooling device, or sprayed with cold water during the heat of the day. It has also been proved by experience that a steady fermentation and storage in a constant or very slowly fluctuating temperature produces the best wine. Rapid fluctuations of temperature during fermentation and storage produce inferior wine.

(a) RED TABLE WINE   The flavour may be damaged at 32 °C (90 °F) and the yeast injured. Fermentation should not be conducted at a temperature above 28 °C (82 °F). The ideal temperature is between 21 and 24 °C (70 and 75 °F).

(b) WHITE TABLE WINE   Bouquet and flavour are damaged at 28 °C (82 °F). Fermentation should therefore not be conducted above 24 °C (75 °F) with the ideal range being between 15 and 18 °C (59 and 64 °F).

(c) DESSERT WINES   The initial fermentation should be conducted at 21–24 °C (70–75 °F), followed by secondary fermentation at 15–18 °C (59–64 °F).

(d) SPARKLING WINE   The bulk fermentation should be conducted as for white table wine. The bottle fermentation should be by cold-acclimatized yeast in a temperature not exceeding 15 °C (59 °F) preferably about 13 °C (55 °F). The higher the bottle fermentation temperature, the less satisfactory the absorption of carbon dioxide in the wine and the quicker the wine goes flat after drawing the cork.

(e) SHERRY   To produce a flor, the Sherry yeast *Saccharomyces beticus* appears to require an optimum of 20 °C (68 °F). The range is possibly between 18 and 21 °C (64 and 70 °F). Above the latter, the flor becomes steadily scarcer.

(f) MADEIRA This wine benefits from a period of storage during which—over a period of three months—the temperature is slowly increased to 50 °C (122 °F) and then reduced at the same rate to normal. The caramel flavour is thereby enhanced.

(g) TOKAY Tokay yeast is an exception to the rule that high temperature fermentation causes spoilage. It is normal to ferment at temperatures between 32 and 35 °C (90 and 95 °F) and fermentation is complete in 14 days. To produce in a wine the individual flavour of the Tokay yeast it appears necessary to conduct fermentation at the high temperature.

(h) LOW TEMPERATURE There are specially bred yeasts which it is claimed ferment in temperatures as low as 4 °C (39 °F). White table wines fermented at low temperatures often produce better results than at higher temperatures. The wine certainly would not suffer spoilage from the low temperature, but fermentation naturally takes longer.

(i) AGEING The lighter and thinner wines are best aged and stored in a temperature between 10 and 13 °C (50 and 55 °F) that is as constant as possible.

The heavier and more full-bodied wines, such as dessert, age better in slowly fluctuating temperatures which aid the absorption of the oxygen necessary for maturing in a cask or similar bulk container. The higher the temperature range, the quicker the ageing, but quality appears to be best preserved when the wine is aged in temperatures between 15 and 20 °C (59 and 68 °F). After ageing, it is best kept at a lower temperature to retard chemical changes.

(j) DRINKING There is some controversy as to the temperatures at which wines should be drunk. It is, however, generally accepted that white table wines are best chilled and that robust red table wines are best at room temperature, 17 to 20 °C (63 to 68 °F). Whilst it is not harmful to chill white wine by placing the bottle in a bucket of ice or in a refrigerator (ice should never be put into the wine), it is harmful to red wine to warm it quickly. A red wine, either sweet or dry, from a cold cellar should be stood in the room where it will be drunk until it has naturally assumed the right temperature. This may take some hours in a cool climate. In very hot weather it may even be necessary slightly to refrigerate red wines not stored in a cool cellar.

Delicate wines should not be chilled so hard that they become 'dumb' and lose their bouquet and flavour. Around 12 °C (54 °F) would seem adequate. Rosé wines should be treated the same way.

Medium- and full-bodied sweet white table wines and tawny Sherries and Madeiras are also best served cold. (See also CHAMBRÉ and FRAPRÉ.)

Sparkling wines need to be chilled a little more, to 8 or 9 °C (46 or 48 °F) in order to maintain a slow release of bubbles whilst the wine is in the glass and to prevent the unpoured wine going flat too quickly. It is normal practice to keep the bottle in ice until the last of the wine has been poured.

TÊTE DU CUVÉE   Literally the head of the vat or cask. Normally used to refer to the first pressing, or extraction from raw materials. It is also used in the Côte d'Or (France) to mean an outstanding growth of grapes. Sometimes, however, it means the wine in the upper third of the cask which is frequently slightly better than the rest.

TEXTURE   Texture is the chemical reaction between the tannin of wine and the proteins of the mucous membranes in the mouth. Thus young wines of high tannin content are said to be astringent, i.e. to dry in the mouth. As the wine matures, the astringency ameliorates until, in a properly matured wine, the texture is smooth. Texture is also the arrangement of the constituent parts or structure which is part of the 'body' in wine.

There are other forms of texture, such as greasiness, that are of no concern in the composition of wine. Greasiness of food does, however, have direct bearing on the type of wine that should be drunk with it. With very greasy food the wine must obviously be acid to help clean the palate and rather high in tannin, partially to counteract the feeling of the grease in the mouth.

THIAMINE   Contraction for thiamine hydrochloride, better known as vitamin B_1.

THIN   The word used to describe a wine that is lacking in body. A thin wine has a low content of soluble matter, oils and unfermented fruit juice. Commercial thin wines are, generally, also light. Thin wines made by amateurs can be very variable in their alcohol content.

TITRATION   The determination of the quantity of a given constituent by observing the quantity of a standard solution required to cause a change in form. In winemaking it is the quantity of total acids that is determined by titration.

All acids present in a must or wine are weak acids, that is they ionize only partly and reversibly in aqueous solutions. When titrated, a weak acid is neutralized by a strong base (alkali) at alkaline pH values, with a sudden rise between pH 7 and 11. The strong base used to neutralize the acids of a must or wine is sodium or potassium hydroxide as an N/10 solution, and the end point is about pH 8·5. If a 10 ml sample of must or wine is used, then half of the volume of the base required to reach the end point is the total acid content, as parts per thousand sulphuric (sulphuric as the reference standard). Parts per thousand citric acid can be calculated by multiplying the figure by 1·43 and for tartaric acid by multiplying the figure by 1·53. The acidity expressed as parts per thousand sulphuric is a more simple and convenient reference standard.

(*See* the ACID COMPARISON TABLES.) It is more accurate to repeat the titration and take the mean of the two readings.

Two methods for indicating the end point are in use. One uses an electronic pH meter (not pH papers) and the other, a colour-change indicator. Phenolphthalein is a most suitable colour-change indicator as it changes from colourless to pink at a pH of 8·6, an ideal point.

To titrate with an indicator the following items are required:

One 10 ml pipette
One or more 100 ml conical flasks
Solution of 1% phenolphthalein in methyl alcohol in dropper bottle or
  with separate dropper
One 25 ml burette
One burette stand
Decinormal solution (N/10) sodium hydroxide
Distilled water

To titrate, 10 ml of must or wine are taken up in the pipette and run into a flask. Then 25 ml approximately of distilled water (quantity is not critical) and 2 drops of phenolphthalein are added. The burette is filled with sodium hydroxide, making sure that there are no air bubbles, then zeroed by running off the excess. The flask is then stood under the burette and sodium hydroxide slowly run into it whilst gently agitating the flask. Pink tints will be seen in the solution which disappear with agitation. The end point is reached when a permanent faint pink tint is assumed and not altered by the agitation. A brilliant pink indicates that the end point has been overshot. The quantity of sodium hydroxide used is noted and half the figure is the ppt, as sulphuric, of total acids present in the must or wine.

Three points should be noted. Phenolphthalein is sensitive to carbon dioxide which causes an abnormally high indication of acid content. Fermenting, sparkling or other wines containing carbon dioxide have to be boiled, to drive off the CO_2 before attempting to titrate. Anthocyanins, the red pigments in wine, change colour with altered pH and tend to obscure the end point. Normally a grey colour develops at various pH before the end point and this is an indication that the end point has nearly been reached. A careful check for the end point must then be made. If the flask is stood on a screened light the end point of red wines can more clearly be seen. When titrating red must, it is of considerable advantage first to filter the liquid before titrating it.

To use the pH meter for titration, place 10 ml of the must or wine in a beaker and run in N/10 sodium hydroxide from a burette until pH 8·5 is recorded. The volume of sodium hydroxide used is noted. Half this figure is the ppt, as sulphuric, of total acids in the must or wine.

The acid content of must and wines should be between 3·5 and 5·5 ppt as sulphuric, with table wine between 3 and 4 ppt and sweet wines between 4 and 5 ppt. With an acidity below 2·5 ppt a wine tastes insipid and off-flavours develop.

Equivalent acidities are:

Sulphuric	Citric	Tartaric
2·5 ppt	3·575 ppt	3·825 ppt
5·5 ppt	7·865 ppt	8·415 ppt

(*See also* the ACID COMPARISON TABLES.)

TOKAY, TOKAJ, TOKIER Wine made mainly from the Furmint grape grown in the small viticultural area of Tokaj–Hegyelia on the banks of the Bodrog in north-west Hungary. Two styles are produced.

Szamarodni is the dry or semi-sweet Tokay. As its Polish name means, it is made 'as it comes'. That is the whole grape crop from one picking is pressed, but this happens only in poor years. It is also made by adding over-ripe grapes to the others in the press.

Aszu is the wine made from selected 'noble rot' grapes collected and left standing in wide open tubs, called puttonyos, to the end of the vintage which is often December. The juice which was squeezed from the grapes solely by their own weight was once collected to make the fabulous Essenz which Hungarian law no longer allows to be made. The 'noble rot' grapes are ultimately trodden and, due to the break-down caused by the 'noble rot', become a paste, or sort of dough, which is called 'the heart of the wine'. This 'heart' is added to juice previously pressed from normally ripe grapes and then fermented. Aszu is graded by the number of puttonyos (25 litre) added to a fut (136 litre) and is labelled accordingly: 'Aszu——puttonyos' with the number varying from 1 to 6. The more puttonyos the better the quality of the wine and the higher the price, with 5 normally being the highest.

TOPPING-UP The filling of casks, jars or other storage vessels as near to the closure as possible with extra wine or liquid. During fermentation, carbon dioxide is produced and this being heavier than air will form a layer on top of the wine if undisturbed. This layer prevents contamination by spoilage micro-organisms as it keeps away air necessary for their well-being. During this stage vessels may be only partly full, but after fermentation when the carbon dioxide has been dispersed, air must be reduced to the minimum by keeping the vessels as full as possible to prevent contamination. In larger wineries, carbon dioxide or nitrogen is pumped in and maintained. After each racking there is a small loss, producing an air space at the top of the storage vessel. This air space has to be filled, or as it is said, the vessel has to be 'topped-up'. This topping-up can be done by adding sound wine of the same or a similar kind, or syrup (if it is desired to make the wine sweeter). When the wine has been made from fruits, the topping-up can be by the strained and sterilized juice of the same fruit. Grape juice is frequently used in this way in the making of slightly sweet table wines.

TOTAL ACIDITY and TOTAL ACIDS   The total amount of the fixed non-volatile and the volatile acid content of a solution. It is normally measured by TITRATION (*See* page 184) with phenolphthalein as the indicator.

TOURLOPSIS   A slime-forming spoilage yeast that attacks unsulphited low-acid musts and wines.

TOURNE   A wine disease caused by certain lactic acid bacteria has been called 'tourne' when there has been no production of gas, and 'pousse' when gas has been produced. Wines that are affected become slightly cloudy with a blackish tint to their colour. They taste flat and are often a little sour and bitter due to the formation of proprionic acid from the breakdown of tartaric acid. Only wines low in acid and alcohol are usually attacked. Adequate acid and sulphite prevent infection.

TRIAL FININGS   Over-fining of wines can detract from their quality and cause haze. To prevent this, trial finings are made to ascertain the minimum quantity of fining agent that will clear a wine. For this purpose, percentage solutions/suspensions, as detailed under FINING, are used, so that dosage can be accurately measured. Into each of a number of identical vessels (they can be small bottles) place 100 ml of the wine to be fined. Varying volumes of the fining agent are then added, well mixed in and allowed to stand for 24 hours. If four vessels are used, the volumes of the fining agent are added as 1 ml, 2 ml, 3 ml and 4 ml, but it is preferable to use six vessels adding 0·5 ml, 1 ml, 1·5 ml, 2·0 ml, 2·5 ml and 3 ml.

After standing 24 hours it should readily be seen which sample has fallen clear with the least quantity of fining agent. Dosage for bulk can then be calculated and the wine treated accordingly.

Should none of the samples clear properly further action is taken depending on the fining agent that has been used:

(1) If the fining agent is one that does not require tannin for reaction, another fining agent has to be tried.

(2) If the fining agent is one that reacts with tannin, the trial fining is repeated with 2 ml of 1% tannin solution also added to each sample. After mixing well the samples are again left for 24 hours. Action for clearing bulk wine is as previously stated with the addition of tannin. If this second trial fining also fails to clear the wine different fining agents should be used for further trial fining.

For trial finings the volumes required are so small that it is not practical to

make them in fluid ounces, but treatment of the bulk wine can be so
made and the equivalents are as follows: ~

Trial Fining	Additions to Bulk Wine
0·5 ml in 100 ml	5 ml per litre = $1\frac{1}{2}$ fl.oz per 2 gallons
1·0 ml in 100 ml	10 ml per litre = $1\frac{1}{2}$ fl.oz per gallon
1·5 ml in 100 ml	15 ml per litre = $2\frac{1}{4}$ fl.oz per gallon
2·0 ml in 100 ml	20 ml per litre = 3 fl.oz per gallon
2·5 ml in 100 ml	25 ml per litre = 4 fl.oz per gallon
3·0 ml in 100 ml	30 ml per litre = 5 fl.oz per gallon
3·5 ml in 100 ml	35 ml per litre = $5\frac{1}{2}$ fl.oz per gallon

For small volumes of bulk wine it is not always practicable to add dry
fining agents direct to the bulk. Percentage solutions have to be used. For
additions, where practicable, the dry weight can be calculated from the
following table.

Trial Fining with 1% concentrations	Dry weight of fining agent to bulk wine
0·5 ml in 100 ml sample	0·25 gm per 5 litre = 0·45 gm per 2 gallons
1·0 ml in 100 ml sample	0·50 gm per 5 litre = 0·45 gm per gallon
1·5 ml in 100 ml sample	0·75 gm per 5 litre = 0·68 gm per gallon
2·0 ml in 100 ml sample	1·00 gm per 5 litre = 0·90 gm per gallon
2·5 ml in 100 ml sample	1·25 gm per 5 litre = 1·14 gm per gallon
3·0 ml in 100 ml sample	1·50 gm per 5 litre = 1·36 gm per gallon
3·5 ml in 100 ml sample	1·75 gm per 5 litre = 1·59 gm per gallon
4·0 ml in 100 ml sample	2·00 gm per 5 litre = 1·81 gm per gallon
4·5 ml in 100 ml sample	2·25 gm per 5 litre = 2·04 gm per gallon
5·0 ml in 100 ml sample	2·50 gm per 5 litre = 2·28 gm per gallon

When higher than 1% concentrations are used for the trial finings the dry
figures in the table are multiplied by the higher percentage. For example
1 ml of 5% concentration in 100 ml sample equals 0·50 gm × 5 = 2·5 gm
per 5 litre and 0·45 × 5 = 2·25 gm per gallon. (*See also* FINING.)

TRIAL JAR This is another name for a HYDROMETER JAR.

TWADELL A graduation of a hydrometer frequently used in America
with only one-fifth of its unit equal to one degree S.G. One degree
Twadell is therefore equal to five degrees on the British scale. (*See also*
BAUMÉ, BRIX and HYDROMETER.)

ULLAGE The space in a vessel that is unoccupied by wine, or the
amount a vessel lacks in being full, sometimes loosely referred to as
'head room', is called ullage. 'On ullage' is the term applied to a bottle
from which wine has escaped because of a faulty cork. 'On ullage' refers
to any wine which does not fill its vessel to the closure. For instance if
there were only 40 litres of wine in a 45 litre cask, the wine would be said
to be 'on ullage'.

During fermentation wines can be on ullage without harm due to the presence of carbon dioxide gas. After fermentation, the ullage should be at its minimum, or, in other words, the space between wine and closure should be as small as practicable. If a stable wine, particularly when low in alcohol, is left on an appreciable ullage it can become contaminated by spoilage micro-organisms or will oxidize excessively. The greater the ullage, the more likely are these spoilages to occur. For these reasons casks and barrels should be constantly topped up to make good losses by evaporation. In a dry atmosphere, water evaporates from a cask of wine. In a humid atmosphere alcohol also evaporates and must be replaced.

UTENSILS   Winemaking utensils are any instruments or containers that are used in connection with the production of wine. They are not specific items and can be anything from a teaspoon to a hydraulic press. Whatever the utensil is, it should conform to certain specifications regarding all parts which will be in contact with fruit juices, acids, musts, fermentations and wines.

(1) All parts, if constructed of metal, should be of stainless steel or so treated as to be inert, such as vitreous enamel, but not enamel containing antimony. The one exception is the use of an aluminium vessel when used for boiling raw materials to produce extracts. Even so it is not advisable to add acid before or during the boiling. (*See* METALS.)
(2) Parts constructed of wood should be of a non-resinous variety. When resinous wood has been used the surfaces should be thoroughly sealed with polyurethane. (*See* WOOD and POLYURETHANE.)
(3) Other parts should be of an inert material, such as glass or salt-glazed stoneware or of synthetic materials of a polythene nature.

Within the limitations of the usability or purpose, the utensils can be of any type or construction according to their availability and the user's own preference.

VARIETAL WINES   The generic name given to wines that are described by the name of the grape from which they have been made. A wine described as a Cabernet, Marsanne, Riesling, Shiraz, Zinfandel etc., however, need not be made exclusively from the variety named. No variety makes as good a wine on its own as it does in combination with others. The name of the main variety is, therefore, used. In the U.S.A., the variety named must have been at least 51% of the grapes used, in Europe and Australia, the proportion is 75%. In South Africa, the proportion was raised to 50% in 1976 and will be 75% by 1983. The use of varietal names is increasing with the wider production of wines throughout the world, because wines called Claret or Burgundy or Hock are totally different from the classic wines, when they are made in Australia, South Africa or California or even in Spain.

VAT   A modern word for a large vessel, used for fermenting, storing or blending wine. It was formerly made of wood but now is more often made from glass-lined concrete or stainless steel.

VELVETY   A wine which feels very smooth due to a low acidity and a high glycerol content.

VENDANGE   The French word used to describe the grape harvest. The precise date of the harvest varies with location, soil, climate and variety of grape. It also depends on the type of wine to be made. To make a dry table wine, grapes are usually picked just before they are fully ripe to ensure a pleasant total acidity. Sweet wines are made with over-ripe grapes often deliberately left hanging on the vines. The picking of grapes has to be done carefully and quickly at the right point of ripeness so that they can be taken without oxidation to the winemaker who should be ready to crush them immediately.

VERAISON   The stage just before full ripeness of grapes. The grape has reached its maximum size and weight but is not completely ripe. From this point the sugar content increases and the acidity decreases. Between veraison and ripeness the appearance of the skin hardly changes and this makes it very difficult to judge the right time of picking. The picking time is nowadays determined after laboratory analysis of grape samples.

VERMOUTH   The name given to a dull, dry or sweet, red or white wine, that has been fortified to 17% alcohol and flavoured with a mixture of aromatic herbs, spices and fruits. The word 'vermouth' is derived from the German *Vermut*, the name of a plant known as 'wormwood' in English. It has a somewhat bitter taste and so the wine is frequently used as an aperitif. In addition to wormwood, gentian, angelica root, elecam-pagne root, centaury leaves, germander leaves, cloves, nutmegs, orange peel, *calamus aromaticus* and other flavourings are used. The whites and tawnies are usually less sweet than the reds.

VESSELS   In general, vessels are any hollow receptacles for liquid and can be of any shape and made of any material. When applied to winemaking a 'vessel' refers to a receptacle which will hold a must or wine and can be closed in such a manner that the wine will not suffer contamination or spoilage. It can be a barrel, bottle, bucket, cask, jar, tank or tub etc.

The materials from which winemaking vessels can be made are restricted to oak, glass, high-density polythene, stoneware and stainless steel, which are all inert, having no reaction to the acids or to the fermentation. No metal other than stainless steel should ever be used. Non-resinous woods, although not inert, may be in contact with wine without harm being caused. Oak, of course, is of positive assistance in maturing wines. Resinous woods should not be used, as they will produce a resinated flavour which is considered unpleasant by most people, even though it is harmless.

The shape of the vessel is of no importance in relation to the process of fermentation provided the opening into it can be effectively sealed by a closure with provision for the escape of gas either by its own mechanical construction or the fitting of an air lock. However, for hygienic reasons and ease of use, the vessel should be of such a shape that it can be thoroughly cleaned inside without difficulty. It should also be of such a shape as to permit of easy handling and be capable of storage in the space available, matters which are individual to each winemaker.

The vessels can be of any size subject to two qualifications. For fermentation they should be of a capacity of one and a half times or more the quantity of wine being produced. After fermentation has ceased they should preferably be of such size as to be filled completely.

Although shape and size are of little importance, except as previously stated, some are generally more suitable for certain purposes than others. (*See* PULP FERMENTATION, SECONDARY FERMENTATION, STAINLESS STEEL etc.)

VIN DE GOUTTE   French for a wine made from the *moût de goutte* or free-run juice.

VIN DE PRIMEUR   Wine that is drunk the same year that it is made—as soon as three months from the vendange.

VINE   Vines are any plants with slender stems that trail or climb, such as hops and melons. The vine used for winemaking is the grape vine, *Vitis vinifera*.

VINEGAR   From two French words *vin aigre* meaning sour wine.

When vinegar bacteria attack low-alcohol wines they reduce the alcohol to acetic acid and turn the wine sour. Today, the word is used for various acetic acid solutions, usually with a prefix—wine vinegar, cider vinegar, spirit vinegar, malt vinegar etc. Malt vinegar is actually acetified beer or ale and until recent times was called alegar.

There is little doubt that vinegar has been known as long as fermented liquor. Hippocrates is said to have used it medicinally, and it was offered to Jesus on the cross as a drink that was unpleasant. We no longer use it as a drink, preferring it as a condiment, for pickling vegetables and fruit, and in the preparation of chutneys and sauces.

In the first instance the production of vinegar was no doubt unintentional and unwanted, but later it was deliberately produced by inoculating poor wines, ciders, beers and solutions of diluted alcohol with the Acetobacter. The vinegars from wines carry something of the flavour of the wine, and those from ciders and beers do likewise. The ones from diluted alcohol, the spirit vinegars, have only the sourness, or flavour, of acetic acid and usually have a higher acid content than the others. Distilled vinegar is usually malt vinegar which has been distilled and retains something of the malt flavour.

If a wine tastes only slightly of vinegar when first noticed, it can be kept as a wine by mixing it with a must of the same type and refermenting it. Otherwise a wine that becomes acetified is best allowed to be fully converted to vinegar as described under vinegar production, and used as such.

VINEGAR BACTERIA, ACETOBACTER There are more than twenty identifiable species of vinegar bacteria, all of which can attack wines and beers and convert them to vinegar. Most of the species and strains cannot develop in wines above 10% alcohol, whilst a few have a maximum tolerance of between 14 and 15%. They are aerobes requiring the presence of atmospheric oxygen, and with it promote partial oxidation of alcohol, resulting in acetic acid of from 3 to 6% by volume. The oxidation process proceeds in ratio to the oxygen available and the temperature, and is essentially according to the reaction

$$C_2H_5OH + O_2 \xrightarrow{\hspace{2cm}} CH_3COOH + H_2O$$

| alcohol + oxygen | acetobacter | acetic acid + water |
| | | (vinegar) |

Acetobacter that occur in wines, ciders and beers of 10% alcohol or below, frequently form a heavy, leathery film or pellicle, on the surface and this is called a 'vinegar mother' or *mycoderma aceti*. Those that occur in wines of from 12 to 14% alcohol are usually found throughout the wine and do not form the typical 'mother'. The two most frequently encountered species are *Acetobacter aceti* which has an optimum temperature of 29–34 °C (86–95 °F) and *Acetobacter oxydans* which has a lower optimum temperature of 20 °C (68 °F). The species *Acetobacter curvum* is normally used as a pure culture with diluted alcohol for the production of 'spirit vinegar'. Two species are not only vinegar-producing organisms but also vinegar spoilage organisms. *Acetobacter rancens* continues the oxidation process and *Acetobacter xylinum* forms capsules containing cellulose.

All acetobacter are carried in the air and can settle in wines, ciders and beers as well as on equipment and vessels. They can also be carried by the vinegar fly which will deposit them on vessels or even in the liquor itself. They can also be on the raw materials, particularly if the latter have been damaged, split, rubbed or pecked by birds. Once they have attacked a wine and tainted it, there is little that can be done in correction. Prevention of contamination is therefore essential and fortunately very simple.

The use of sulphite in a must will inhibit any bacteria present on the raw materials or on the vessels. Covering the fermentation with an air lock will prevent any infection from the air or carried by the vinegar fly and the closing of storage vessels with sound corks and bungs will do likewise. Bacteria, however, may enter the wine during racking, filtering or bottling, but as stated above they need oxygen. Covering a fermentation immediately after racking will cause a carbon dioxide layer to form denying them oxygen. Filling storage vessels or bottles as close to the closure as possible, in other words leaving the absolute minimum air space between wine and closure, will also deny them sufficient oxygen to cause vinegar tainting.

The prevention of vinegar contamination is the wise use of sulphite, keeping vessels covered and keeping air space to a minimum.

Cleanliness in the winery is also a precaution, for wines spilt and not cleaned up are breeding grounds for acetobacter.

VINEGAR FLY, or DROSOPHILA The vinegar fly, more commonly and correctly called the fruit fly, is the *Drosophila melanogaster* which is very widely distributed and is a pest to fruit, especially cultivated figs, grapes and tomatoes. Because they are attracted by the smell of fruit, they find their way into wineries where they can be present in considerable numbers. Despite their presence it does not necessarily result in wines being turned to vinegar, for of their own accord they cannot do so. The danger of their presence is that they may be carrying bacteria picked up from various sources.

Fruit that drops to the ground, starts to decay and is attacked by bacteria also attracts the flies. The small drops of juice that ooze from growing fruit damaged by birds and insects is fermented by wild yeasts. These minute ferments are attacked by vinegar bacteria and the fruit flies paddle in them. These flies will afterwards be carrying the vinegar bacteria and will deposit them wherever they alight. If they have flown into a winery, it will be on the vessels and equipment and in the uncovered wines that the bacteria will be deposited. Wines spilt and not cleaned up provide another supply of acetic acid bacteria for the flies to spread around.

The summer life of *Drosophila* is only from five to eight days, but in winter it is very much longer. Maximum fly activity occurs between 24 and 27 °C (75 and 80 °F) in low intensity light (i. e. not in sunshine) but eggs are deposited at temperatures above 13 °C (55 °F). The female flies are able to retain their eggs in their bodies until conditions and sites are suitable for laying the eggs. This means a life cycle can be started very rapidly; in fact, Middlekauf (1957) observed the hatching of eggs within two hours of being laid. The average hatching time is, however, 24 hours. The rapid hatching time and the fact that a female can lay up to 2,000 eggs in her lifetime accounts for the sudden appearance of the fly in large numbers. It also points the need for the rapid disposal of wastes from winemaking. Fruit, especially soft fruit, discarded after selection, for rot, mould etc., cakes from presses, and strainings from pulp fermentations, all make excellent breeding sites and should not be left in or near a winery.

VINEGAR PRODUCTION   To make a good vinegar a wine may be high in acid or otherwise, but should be dry, low in tannin, and mild of flavour. This is the reason why ciders and ales make such excellent vinegars. Ciders and ales are normally of low alcohol content and can be used direct. Wines should be diluted with water until the alcohol content is around 6%.

For small quantities of vinegar a glass jar or similar vessel can be used. It should only be half-filled with wine, cider or ale and the neck plugged with non-absorbent cotton wool. For larger quantities a cask is preferable. After the tap has been fitted the cask is laid on its side with the bung uppermost and should be filled three-quarters full. Holes are bored in both ends of the cask slightly above the level of the liquor. A glass or polythene tube is inserted through the bung-hole and all holes loosely plugged with cotton wool. The cotton wool is simply to keep the dust and flies out but permit an exchange of air. The use of a cask in this way is known as the Orléans method and is said to produce the best quality vinegar.

If a wine, cider or ale, already attacked by acetobacter, is used, no inoculation is required. To activate a liquor that has not been infected add one part of a good vinegar to five parts of the liquor. The glass vessel or cask should then be kept in a temperature of 21 to 30 °C (70 to 85 °F) and in a short time the 'mother' will appear as a pellicle on the surface and care should then be taken not to disturb it. Acetification should be complete in three months. The lower the temperature, the correspondingly longer the time needed for conversion. By then the acidity should be about 4% which is usual for general use.

The vinegar from a small vessel is racked off into storage jars or bottles, the vessel washed out and more vinegar made in it if desired. From a cask, the vinegar is drawn off by the tap into storage jars or bottles until the cask is three-quarters empty. It is then refilled with more liquor through the tube without disturbing the 'mother' and another batch made. By this means several continuous batches can be made in the cask.

The jars or bottles of vinegar should be filled as full as possible and sealed. This is to prevent attack from *Acetobacter rancens*. The fresh vinegar is harsh, but improves with storage during which it should clear. If it remains hazy it can be cleared by filtration and bottled. Alternatively a tablespoonful of milk can be added to each gallon and mixed well. After allowing time for the vinegar to clear and form a deposit, it is racked into bottles. The addition of about 150 ppm sulphite is made to keep it clear and prevent further activity of bacteria. Alternatively it may be pasteurized.

VINEGAR SPOILAGE   As wine is only one step in the process of the decay of vegetable matter, so vinegar is another. As there are organisms that destroy wine so there are organisms that destroy vinegar.

Acetobacter rancens, if permitted access to oxygen, will continue the oxidation of alcohol past the acetic acid stage, finishing with carbon dioxide and water. It will therefore spoil any vinegar exposed to air and in which it is present. Sulphite at 150 ppm and the exclusion of air are the controls.

Acetobacter xylinum forms the so-called 'blacksmith's apron'. It consists of capsules containing cellulose, which clog the pipes and equipment of commercial production. In the Orléans method it will block the tap and feed tube as well as build up inside the cask. Maintenance of a temperature of 38 °C (100 °F) during acetification is the control.

Anguillula aceti is a worm in vinegar, that, held against the light, looks like a thread of cotton 1·5 mm long. It is capable of living in the highest concentration of acetic acid in vinegar and feeds on the acetobacter. Sulphite used at 150 ppm will prevent and/or kill it.

VINEGAR TAINT   Acetobacter will produce a vinegar taint in wine and then continue to convert it to vinegar, but there are other organisms that can produce a vinegar taint or smell in a wine.

The heterofermentative lactic acid bacteria, in addition to producing lactic acid, alcohol, carbon dioxide and glycerol from dextrose, also produce acetic acid. This gives the wine a vinegar taint and smell but the lactobacillus does not convert the wine to vinegar.

Sometimes a wine can smell of vinegar although it does not taste acid. This is the result of fermentation by certain species of wild yeast, especially *Hansenula*, which produce large amounts of the ester, ethyl acetate. The wine smells of vinegar but again the yeasts do not cause the conversion to vinegar.

The normal use of sulphite will prevent these taints.

VIN GRIS   French for an extremely pale rosé wine.

VINIFICATION, VINOSITY and VINOUS   Vinification is the process of converting juices, saps or extracts to wine. Thus a must that has been properly fermented becomes vinous, or, expressed in another way, becomes wine-like, or has assumed the qualities of wine. Its vinosity is the depth or degree of its vinous qualities. Vinosity and vinous also refer to the 'wine-like' smell and taste of an alcoholic beverage.

VIN NOUVEAU   French for a young wine from the last vendange; i.e. a wine less than one year old.

VINOMETER   A means of testing the approximate alcohol content of a dry wine, but not wines containing residual sugar.

The vinometer consists of a capillary tube with a scale and one end opened out, funnel-shaped. Wine is poured into the funnel until it passes through the capillary tube and drips. The vinometer is then inverted and the column of wine in the capillary tube watched as it falls. The surface of the column will pause, or stop, and the scale is read at this point which will indicate the alcohol content. In practice the vinometer is vague and inaccurate.

VINTAGE   The word vintage originally meant and generally still means the gathering of the grapes, the gatherer being called a vintager. Thus a vintage wine is one of a specific year or, more accurately, a specific gathering.

Commercially, a wine stated to be a '1964 vintage' is a wine produced only from a gathering of grapes in 1964. A finished wine that is a blend of wines of more than one gathering is a non-vintage wine, but frequently a year is stated if the bottle contains 75% of the wine of that year and 25% of other years. The word vintage in no sense means 'an old wine'. Wines that are only a few weeks old are still vintage—this year's vintage.

VISIBLE FERMENTATION   For some time after the must has been yeasted there appears to be no activity. This is known as the lag phase during which the yeast is rapidly reproducing itself to reach the critical concentration of cells. As this concentration is reached, carbon dioxide gas will rise through the must and may at first form a ring of small bubbles around the circumference of the surface. Then as the number and size of the gas bubbles increase they will burst on reaching the surface, causing a twinkling or sparkling effect. Sometimes there is frothing. The rise of gas is the visible sign of fermentation, and the 'visible fermentation' is that which commences with the first visible signs and ends with the last. In other words visible fermentation is simply, as its name denotes, the stage of fermentation which can be seen.

VITAMINS   These are complex compounds essential to all forms of life. Those that are required by wine yeasts are normally present in grapes, except vitamin B_1 (thiamine). This vitamin is required by yeast during reproduction and without it a fermentation can stick. Pure fruit juice probably contains just sufficient, but if there is likely to be a deficiency because of dilution or from any other cause, thiamine should be added at the rate of 2 to 3 mg per 5 litres. No harm is caused by adding it when it is not strictly necessary to do so.

Ascorbic acid (vitamin C) can be used as a reducing agent which prevents oxidation (browning) in a must. It can also be used as an anti-oxidant in place of sulphite in wines of high acidity in which bacterial action is largely suppressed by the acidity. Malo-lactic fermentation can then develop and the acidity can be reduced by about one-third; the latter being an advantage in wines of high acidity.

VITICULTURE   The cultivation of *Vitis*, the grape vine. The natural order of Vitaceae has four genera that bear edible fruit. One of these four is *Vitis* with two sub-genera: *Muscadiniae* with only three species and *Euvites* with over forty species of true grape vines. Of the near fifty species about 35 are North American, 12 are Asian and only one is native to Europe.

Vines existed long before man appeared; and the oldest known fossil is of *V. sezannensis* that flourished in the sub-tropical forests of the Lower Eocene epoch in what is now eastern France. The earliest known cultivation of the grape vine was in the area south of the Black Sea and west of the Caspian between 8000 and 6000 B.C. It was probably one of the first plants to be cultivated and was *Vitis vinifera silvestris*, the wild species that can still sometimes be found growing in the eastern Mediterranean region. From these earliest plantings have stemmed the many cultivar used for winemaking through the centuries. Within the last hundred years, more and more hybrids have been bred by crossing and re-crossing *V. vinifera* with *V. amurensis*, *V. berlandieri*, *V. monticola*, *V. repestris* and others, so that fewer and fewer cultivated grape vines remain pure *V. vinifera*.

The most commonly used cultivars for winemaking are:

For white wines: Aleatico, Chasselas, Chardonnay, Chenin Blanc, Folle Blanche, Frontignan, Furmint, Grüner Veltliner, Gewürztraminer, Malvasia, Moscata, Muscadet, Müller-Thurgau, Muscat, Palomino, Pedro Ximénez, Pinot Gris, Prosecco, Riesling, Sangiovese, Sauvignon Blanc, Scheurebe, Semillon, Seyve Villard, Steen, Sylvaner, Verdicchio.
For red wines: Barbera, Bastardo, Cabernet Sauvignon, Carrignan, Dolcetto, Gamay, Grenache, Kardarka, Malbec, Merlot, Nebbiolo, Petit Syrah, Pinot Noir, Poulsard, Ramisco, Sangiovese, Seibel, Shiraz, Trebbiano, Zinfandel.

The different cultivars perform better in some situations and climates than in others and research continues by hybridizing to find the best varieties for each location. The American vines, *Vitis labrusca* and *Vitis ruparis*, produce wines with a poorer flavour than *Vitis vinifera* cultivars. Nearly all the vines grown in Europe, indeed throughout the world, are nowadays grafted on to American root stocks or hybrid root stock with an American parent.

The method of cultivation varies with the cultivar, the location and the climatic conditions. Frequently, vines are grown on hillsides facing south-east, south or south-west at heights varying between 100 and 1,000 metres, often on soil too poor to support other plants worth growing. The vine enjoys a well-drained soil, a fair rainfall and a warm, humid atmosphere. (*See* HEAT SUMMATION.) Each year the fruit-bearing shoots must be pruned since the fruit is borne on shoots from the previous year's wood.

In cooler climates the vine shoots are supported on wires running between a half-metre and a metre parallel to the ground. The vines are planted about a metre and a half apart in rows a metre and a half apart. In warmer climates the vines are often grown over pergolas that are head high. The former method takes advantage of the heat reflected from the soil, especially the stony soil so much preferred. The high cultivation enables air to circulate freely and prevent the vines from becoming too hot.

Vines need some four years to develop sufficiently to bear fruit for wine and can live to 100 years and more. Many growers consider 30 years to be the optimum life of a vine, however, and after grubbing them up, leave the ground fallow for a few years to recover. When this occurs, the Wine Control Authorities in most of the wine growing countries (except the United Kingdom) insist on the planting of superior cultivars. (*See* CLONE.)

In addition to annual pruning, vines need regular spraying during the growing season (*see* MILDEW) and cultivation with the addition of some fertilizer during the dormant period. Modern methods make use of mechanical sprayers and cultivators and experiments are being made in suitable locations with mechanical harvesters.

Apart from phylloxera and mildew, the vines are at risk from frost, especially at flowering time and from birds at harvest time. Nevertheless, more and more people around the world are planting vines from which to make their own wine. Every wine growing country now has colleges of agriculture with a viticulture department and there are a number of colleges specializing in teaching students the craft and science of viticulture. At least one in each country is conducting research into the most suitable cultivars for the different parts of the country. Helpful advice can always be obtained from these official sources.

VODKA A colourless and tasteless spirit which is very near to being neutral in its characteristics. It is, therefore, the most suitable spirit to use when fortifying wines whilst retaining the natural flavour of the wine. It is also eminently suitable to use with a sugar syrup for topping up bottles of sparkling wine after disgorgement.

VOLATILE ACIDITY and VOLATILE ACIDS That portion of total acidity that becomes volatile, i.e. evaporates at comparatively low temperatures. Formic, butyric, propionic, and other fatty acids are by-products of alcoholic fermentation, but the main volatile acids are acetic acid and ethyl acetate. The soundness and the keeping quality of a wine can be indicated by the volatile acidity. Small amounts of acetic acid are formed during alcoholic fermentation and will be present in sound wines. This is not deleterious, but an appreciable rise in volatile acidity during storage indicates bacterial spoilage and the wine needs the addition of sulphite to produce 100 to 150 ppm sulphur dioxide.

It is also thought, although not clearly established, that a high pH and formic acid are associated with a mousy flavour.

WATER   In its pure form, as from distillation, water is a colourless, odourless, tasteless compound of hydrogen and oxygen, which is of near neutral acidity/alkalinity. Waters, other than distilled water, carry dissolved chemicals which give them an acidity or alkalinity in varying degrees. This can have an effect on the finished wine when water has been used in the must unless the acidity is properly adjusted at the must stage. Fruit (and other ingredients) recipes for wine rarely take this factor into account, and it is one reason why wines made to the same recipe but in different districts can be of different quality.

Of the varying types of water that could be used for wine:

(1) Distilled water is not advised because it contains no dissolved chemicals which, apart from their affect on acidity, provide trace elements necessary for the full functioning of the yeast and which can affect the final bouquet and flavour.

(2) Rainwater is also not advisable as it can carry undesirable chemicals, especially soot, from the polluted atmosphere, that can have adverse effects on the finished wine. It can also contain bacteria.

(3) Spring and well water can carry both desirable and undesirable chemicals, and whilst some will produce excellent wine, others will not.

(4) Tap water is clean and pure and is without doubt the best and safest water to use, but adjustment of the acidity of the must should be practised. The chlorination of tap water will have no effect on a wine if the water is boiled before use.

In districts where the tap water is hard, carrying a high proportion of calcium carbonate (chalk), it is advisable to boil the water and allow it to stand before use. A chalky sediment will be deposited at the bottom and the water can be siphoned off or poured from the deposit which is thrown away. This does not remove all the chalk from the water and it would not be advisable to do so. For reasons not yet scientifically explained, wines appear to derive some benefit from hard water.

WAX   Commonly used by many winemakers for sealing asbestos, concrete, inferior woods, polythene and other partially porous materials. Paraffin wax is mostly used but this is often heated and mixed with cerevaisin wax to ensure the adequate sealing of fine pores. The material to be sealed is first cleaned, then the melted wax is brushed on and allowed to harden. Several coats are usually required. The wax is inert to the acids and alcohols of wine and imparts no flavour. The wax surface should be renewed each year just prior to being used.

Wax of a different kind is also present on some fruits in the later stages of ripening and if kept for a period after picking. A colloidal dispersion of the wax in which has been dissolved some pigment will produce haze in a finished wine. This is especially noticeable in some plum wines in which the haze appears as a faint 'bloom'. The haze will not clear, nor will it settle down as a deposit even after fining, and the only method of removal is pressure or suction filtering through very fine filters. Two or more filterings may be necessary to produce a clear and brilliant wine and a period of maturation must follow.

WEEPER   A term applied to a bottle of wine which shows signs of a porous cork allowing wine to seep through, or shows that the wine is seeping, or has seeped, between the neck of the bottle and the cork. If allowed to continue the bottle becomes on ullage, micro-organisms will attack the seepage and the wine will become contaminated and spoilt. Such bottles should be recorked immediately the seepage is noticed.

If a bottle has been weeping unnoticed for some time, it is preferable to drink the wine rather than recork the bottle, since the wine would deteriorate.

WHITE WINE   *See* PRESSING GRAPES.

WILD FERMENT   A wild ferment is a spontaneous fermentation by a must without yeast being added by the winemaker. It is caused by wild yeasts or other micro-organisms which were: (1) present on the raw material; (2) present in the fermentation vessel due to improper cleaning or sterilization before use; (3) airborne and settled in the must during preparation, and whose action in the must was not inhibited by the use of sulphite.

A wild ferment could produce a good quality wine but most wines that are so made are of very poor quality, difficult to clear, difficult to rack, low in alcohol or with off-flavours.

A good quality wine yeast should always be used.

WILD YEAST   *See* YEAST.

WINE   The word wine is derived from the Greek word *oinos* and is used with two different meanings, both referring to products that are chemically similar.

Amateur winemakers use the word to refer to the product of any fruit juice or vegetable extract that is fermented into an alcoholic liquor.

The commercial wine trade, however, insists that the word has traditionally referred to, and can therefore only refer to, the product of fermented fresh grape juice.

This is, of course, true of the Continental countries where their laws have so defined it, but these laws were passed to protect the country's wine industry, not just to define the meaning of the word. It is also true, that until the present century when science gave answers to many of the secrets of wine production, the product of the grape was generally superior to the products of fermentation of other vegetative extracts.

Even so, the commercial grape wines were not always of the overall standard of commercial wines today. Witness to this was the use of coloured glasses to hide the murky appearance of the wine, and the extensive use of herbs and spices, or the making of mulls, punches and toddies, to hide the vinegar taint and other off-flavours.

The *Shorter Oxford Dictionary* suggests that the word 'wine' comes from the Old English *win* which came from the Latin *vinum*. In turn it is thought probable that *vinum* or similar words such as the Greek *oinos* had a common Mediterranean source. Perhaps they were derived from the Sanskrit word *vena* which meant 'drink offering'. Such a *vena* was the Vedic liquor, used as an essential part of the ancient sacrificial offerings, that was made from the juice extracted from the plant, Soma, by crushing it between two millstones. It became a 'golden nectar, the drink of the gods'. It was an ambrosia, supposed to defeat death for all who drank it, and symbolized immortality. It appears, however, that only the priests were allowed to drink it and not the worshippers!

If this derivation of the word 'wine' is accurate, then it is correctly used by the amateur winemaker of today.

Wine is the alcoholic product of the fermentation of vegetative extracts, juices and/or saps which contain acids, oils, salts and sugars. Chemical changes continue during maturation. Whether or not the wine produced is unpalatable or a pleasing drink with body, bouquet, colour, flavour, quality and strength is the result of a combination of factors. Chief of these are:

(1) The type of species of vegetative pulp, i.e. the particular variety, or combination of varieties, of apple, grape, blackberry, parsnip or whatever is used.
(2) The chemical content of the soil in which the plants grew.
(3) The weather during growth.
(4) The actual and particular state of ripeness or growth when gathered.
(5) The care with which it was handled.
(6) The speed with which it was processed.
(7) The care with which the must was prepared, balanced and treated.
(8) The manner of conducting the fermentation.
(9) The frequency and correctness of racking.
(10) The method of blending and maturing, and the duration of the maturing.
(11) The weather at the time of mashing and then at the time of racking.
(12) The manner of uncorking, decanting and serving.
(13) The company and food with which the wine is consumed.

The bulk of wine is water which is said to vary from 66 to 90% but the lower amount is obviously that of very heavily fortified wines. Unfortified wines would normally contain not less than 80% and possibly up to 90% water.

The alcohol content of wines are normally accepted as:

Light and table	8 to 12% volume
Social or medium	12 to 15% volume
Heavy or dessert	16 to 20% volume
Fortified	over 17% volume

The fortified wines are ones in which fermentation has been stopped at a particular stage by a large addition of alcohol, or ones which have had alcohol added after fermentation.

Many and varied are the wines that are made. Some are extremely good, whilst others are extremely bad, with by far the majority in the very middle—just average. A few are only short lived, others are very long lived (the exceptions, for many, many years), but whatever the life potential, all will die and decay at some time. A good wine is one that is attractive to the eye by colour and clarity; pleasing to the sense of smell by aroma and bouquet; intensely clean on the palate, accompanied by a mellow, smooth texture and subtle flavour that has ordered the derangement of youth but shows no sign of decay or its approaching end.

To be appreciated a wine has not necessarily to be great. Any ordinary, sound wine, provided it is suited to the mood of the company and to the food, can be thoroughly enjoyed and remembered.

WOOD Originally wines were produced, stored, served and drunk from earthenware vessels or skins. Later for the practical reason that the vessels did not break or damage so easily, the wines were produced in wooden vats and stored in wooden barrels, butts, casks, tuns etc. Many different woods were used at first to make the vessels but the use of one became dominant.

Softwoods have open texture, lack of strength, and decay comparatively quickly and so proved unsuitable. Resinous woods produced a flavour in the wine that was considered unpleasant and unwanted except in a Greek wine called Retsina. This wine is still made and has the taste of the fir cone. It is an acquired taste and is not generally appreciated by other than Greeks with cultivated palates.

Non-resinous hardwoods were successfully used, with oak becoming preferred to all others. Redwood was used in America as well as oak. Oak was close grained and not too porous, resisted moulds and decay for a long time and had the strength to resist damage. Some other hardwoods, such as chestnut, had these attributes and were sometimes used, but oak also assisted the maturing of wines and produced a better quality wine than other woods.

Different oak casks, however, produce different results for reasons not yet understood. Of several casks, one may always produce better wine than others.

The porous nature of wood assists maturation by permitting limited oxidation by air. The oxidation must not be allowed to continue, how-ever, until the wine over-oxidizes and spoils. The smaller the cask the quicker will over-oxidation occur.

Oak also contributes to the quicker maturing of wine in other ways not fully understood. It is probably due to the content of the oak which includes tannates and hydrochloric acid, helping to produce a better balance in the wine and causing chemical changes. This is instanced by the similar maturing of the same wine if stored in oak cask and in a glass vessel to which oak chippings have been added. The wine does not ma-ture similarly when stored in a glass vessel without the oak chippings.

With improved techniques and greater knowledge, some quality wines are being produced commercially without the aid of oak, by creating the correct balance in the must and by controlled oxidation. Glass-lined tanks and tanks of stainless steel and other modern materials are slowly replacing oak.

Spoons made from non-resinous woods have long been used for stirring musts prepared in the home. But modern materials such as plastics are taking over.

Small presses for home use have been and still are being made with solid hardwoods, but resin-bonded, exterior grade plywood is stronger and more durable. The type of wood used for the ply is of little conse-quence as the press after completion is coated with two or more coats of polyurethane. Solid wood presses, even of oak, benefit from coating with polyurethane.

WOODY A wine that has taken on the smell of wood from being too long in a large cask or stored in a small new cask is said to be 'woody'. The wine has an unwelcome, but not unwholesome, smell of sound oak and should not be confused with corkiness.

YEAST Yeasts are one of the lowest forms of life. They are a mono-cellular organism or single-celled plant, so small that they can only be seen individually under a high-powered microscope. The usual size of a wine yeast is about 8 × 7 microns (8/25,000th of an inch × 7/25,000th) and it is estimated there are in the region of 500 million cells in 250 ml of an active ferment.

Yeasts are distinguished from moulds in that they usually maintain a cellular growth and rarely form mycelium. It is, however, believed that yeasts are derived from moulds, because the latter form yeast-like cells under suitable conditions and these cells often cause alcoholic fermenta-tion. Further, some yeasts produce asco-spores closely resembling those of some moulds.

As with other fungi, yeast cells contain no chlorophyll with which to utilize sunlight for energy and have to obtain their energy by other means. The cell outer membrane is unable to absorb molecules over a certain size, so much of their metabolism takes place outside the cell by the action of enzymes. To live actively, yeast requires a moist or liquid environment, so that the enzymes can diffuse out and create utilizable food which diffuses in.

Yeast is a class name in which there are many families, sub-families, genera, species, varieties and strains. The spore forming yeasts are included in the family Endomycetaceai which has four sub-families. One of these sub-families is Saccharomycoideae with three tribes. Of these three tribes one is *Saccharomyceteae* among which are *Saccharomyces cerevisiae* and *S. cerevisiae* variety *ellipsoideus*, frequently referred to as *S. ellipsoideus* only. These are sugar fungi, the *S. cerevisiae* including bakers' and brewers' yeasts and *S. ellipsoideus* being the wine yeasts. The latter are called *ellipsoideus* because the cells are oval to plump sausage-shape but with a typical short oval outline. They multiply by budding. On the side of the cell a small bud appears and grows until it is large enough to separate and become an individual cell. The cells can also produce spores which are spherical.

All yeasts have different shapes and/or multiply by different means. Examples of this are: *Hansenula*—long oval-shaped cells and spores which are hat-shaped; *Schizosaccharomyces* (fission yeasts)—cells divide through the middle and split into two separate cells; *Candida*—long cylindrical shape up to 13 microns in length and forms mycelium; *Kloeckera apiculate*—lemon-shaped cells.

As small as they are, the various yeasts are identified and classified by their size and shape, method of reproduction, and by their functions, particularly the fermentation of the various sugars.

From all the fantastically vast number of yeasts, only the *Saccharomyces cerevisiae* and its variety *ellipsoideus* (selected wine yeasts) are capable of producing a strong fermentation which will produce good wine. All other yeasts, even if they can produce alcohol, are inhibited in the higher concentrations. They are called 'wild yeasts' by the winemaker, and range from the useless, through those of little use, to the positively harmful.

Wine yeasts The first evidence of a yeast growth in a must is a slight haziness. Then a greyish-white sediment begins to form, followed by the production of gas. Froth or foam may then form on the surface. The fermentation of most juices properly balanced and under favourable conditions is complete, or almost complete, in approximately three weeks. The yeast cells then sink to form a deposit called the lees.

Wine yeasts vary considerably in their sedimentation. Some form a fine grained powder that is easily disturbed making racking difficult close to the lees. Others form a coarse, granular and heavy sediment that does not rise. Wines made with these yeasts, of which Champagne is the most notable, clear quickly and less wine is lost with the lees. Attributes of *Saccharomyces ellipsoideus*, the selected wine yeasts, are:

(1) They resist a higher concentration of sulphur dioxide than the spoilage organisms.

(2) They require oxygen for reproduction only, being able to live and cause fermentation without air, i.e. are anaerobic, while most spoilage organisms require oxygen (air) to live.

(3) They can ferment sugars to produce a higher concentration of alcohol than can be tolerated by most spoilage organisms, and the production of this alcohol is the basis of wine.

They are sugar fungi and rely upon simple sugars to provide them with energy. To do so they secrete enzymes to change sucrose (white sugar) and/or maltose (malt sugar) to glucose and fructose. Other enzymes are secreted by the yeast and ferment the glucose and fructose to carbon dioxide gas and ethyl alcohol whilst releasing energy to be utilized by the yeast. The fundamental action of the yeast is to provide itself with this energy and the carbon dioxide gas and ethyl alcohol are simply the by-products from obtaining it.

To assist the yeast to obtain energy, it has to have other food generally referred to as 'yeast nutrients' and the maximum activity is then achieved in a low-acid solution kept warm. Although yeasts require oxygen to be able to reproduce themselves, there is sufficient dissolved in a must for a yeast crop to be produced that will fully ferment a light table wine. For the fermentation of heavier wines, further oxygen is required and this can become available to the yeast as a result of stirring, straining and racking.

Selected wine yeasts are, or should be, pure strains of yeast bearing the name of the wine or region from which they were first isolated. This does not mean that they will make a wine of their particular name type irrespective of ingredients or technique, but that they are more suitable for making wine of a similar kind to their name type. In other words some yeasts are more suitable for certain types of wine than others because they normally cease working at specific concentrations of alcohol; between 8% for light wines and 18% for the heavy. Further advantages are their sedimentary qualities and their suitability for different techniques of production.

There is still much discussion on whether the different strains of selected wine yeasts differ very much in their effect on the flavour of a wine. Mestre and Mestre (1946) found that selected pure cultures of *S. ellipsoideus* gave faster fermentation producing more alcohol than the wild yeasts on the grape skins, but did not convey the characteristic flavour of their name type. This partly confirms the opinion of some European oenologists that better flavour and bouquet are obtained by the use of mixed cultures. Wahab (1949) showed that sterilized musts fermented by ester-forming yeasts, such as the *Hansenula*, produced wines of different bouquet and flavour if the fermentation was completed by selected wine yeasts. Further it was shown by Schulle (1953) that

Zygosaccharomyces with selected wine yeasts produced a higher yield of alcohol than the selected yeasts on their own. Despite this Mestre and Mestre also found that the selected yeasts gave more consistent and satisfactory results.

All this offers some explanation of why a wine from a wild fermentation by wild yeasts can occasionally produce a supreme wine. It also suggests that excellent wine of distinctive bouquet and flavour could be produced under controlled conditions by mixed cultures of wine yeasts and other yeasts at present regarded as unsuitable. The difficulty is in the selection of the particular micro-organisms required and the considerable danger of spoilage in uncontrolled ferments. It is therefore advisable to use only proven selected strains of yeast. A selection of selected wine yeasts and their suitability is given below:

Light table wines	Beaujolais, Bernkasteler, Graves, Hock
Medium wines	Burgundy, Bordeaux, Sauternes, Steinberger
Heavy wines	Madeira, Malaga, Marsala, Maury, Port, Taragona, Tokay, Sherry
Oxidized wines	Madeira, Sherry
Sparkling wines	Champagne, Perlschaum
High temperature fermentation	Tokay

There is also available a 'General Purpose Yeast' which is a culture of several types mixed and is suitable, as its name suggests, for general use.

Bakers' yeast is sometimes used to ferment wine, producing a rapid fermentation and an alcohol content comparable with many selected yeasts. A possible disadvantage of using it is the likelihood of its producing a rather flocculent deposit which makes racking the more difficult. This does not always occur.

Brewers' yeast can also be used for winemaking but frequently adds a bitter flavour due to residual hop flavour. It produces a wine of a low-alcohol content.

All the yeasts mentioned can be obtained in a dormant state in the form of granules, paste, powder, tablets, on agar jelly or in distilled water. Whichever form is used it should be activated in a starter bottle before being added to a must. Even so there is a lag phase before visible signs of fermentation are seen in the must. To add the yeast to the must in a dormant state so protracts the lag phase that the must can become contaminated by spoilage organisms. The aim should always be to obtain as rapid a ferment in the must as possible.

Wild yeasts   In winemaking all yeasts other than the selected yeasts are called 'wild yeasts'. They may contain strains of *S. ellipsoideus* or *cerevisiae* capable of producing wine and occasionally wild ferments do produce excellent wines, but, in general, wild yeasts produce a poor ferment, off-flavours and soft loose sediment, unless they completely spoil the wine!

Studies of the spores on grape skins have shown that on green grapes, they were mainly moulds. Wild yeasts appeared as the grapes ripened and the last to appear were the true wine yeasts. These latter did not always appear and when they did they were always greatly outnumbered by undesirable micro-organisms. On grapes allowed to stand after picking, the undesirable micro-organisms rapidly increased. Such comprehensive studies of other fruits have not been made, but there is not much doubt that the same findings would apply to both the fruits and the plants.

Amongst the wild yeasts are many species and strains of *Saccharomyces* other than *cerevisiae*. Some of these have been the cause of wines becoming cloudy after they have been bottled brilliantly clear. Zygosaccharomyces and Pichia have also been responsible for the same effect. These yeasts will ferment only liquids low in sugar.

Most of the *Hansenula* form films on wines of low-alcohol content and form large amounts of esters, chiefly ethyl acetate. The ethyl acetate has a strong odour and makes wine unpalatable. Storage can result, however, in quite pleasing bouquets being developed.

The *Candia mycoderma* (sometimes erroneously called *mycoderma vini*) is loosely known as 'flowers of wine' as it produces a chalky-white film on the top of low-alcohol wines. Able to use ethyl alcohol as a source of carbon it is strongly oxidative, oxidizing alcohol and acids to carbon dioxide and water.

In addition to those mentioned, there are many other genera that form films, produce excess esters and unwanted flavours or cause a wine to go cloudy.

YEAST ENERGIZER/NUTRIENTS *See* NUTRIENTS.

YEAST STARTER BOTTLE/YEAST STARTER SOLUTION *See* STARTER BOTTLE.

YESO A Spanish word for gypsum (calcium sulphate) used when plastering Sherry. (*See* CALCIUM SULPHATE.)

YOUNG The term 'young' has different meanings according to the context in which it is used.

(1) A wine capable of developing with further maturity is called 'young', irrespective of its actual age, until it has developed its full qualities.
(2) A wine that remains fruity and lively despite its age, or lack of age, is said to be 'young'.

Thus there are wines which are drunk 'young' because they quickly acquire their own qualities and deteriorate with keeping. *Vins de primeur* are included in this category. Most dry white wines also fall into this category and should be drunk 'young' within 3 to 5 years of fermentation. A few red wines are best drunk 'young', but most improve with maturity.

ZINFANDEL   The name of a grape variety popularly used for making red wine in California.

ZYMASE   Although this word is the very last in the winemaker's alphabet it is almost the most important. Without zymase there would be no alcoholic fermentation and no wine. Yet the word was coined fewer than 100 years ago by a man named Edouard Buchner who lived between 1860 and 1917. Buchner discovered that it was possible by grinding the cell walls of the yeast to produce a pressed juice that was able to cause fermentation in solutions containing sugar. He named the substance in the pressed juice which had this power, zymase. Some ten years later Harden and Young found that this yeast juice could, by dialysis, be separated into two parts neither of which by itself was able to cause fermentation. Their investigations showed that fermentation is dependent not only on the true enzyme but also on a substance which they described as co-enzyme.

The complete zymase complex is known as holozymase which consists of co-zymase and apo-zymase. The apo-zymase actually causes fermentation but is itself activated by the co-zymase which acts as a hydrogen transmitter or carrier. It takes part in the transformation of the fructose and glucose into alcohol and carbon dioxide, by accepting hydrogen atoms from one molecule and transmitting them to another; this process is known as dehydrogenation. Subsequently it was discovered that apo-zymase is not an individual enzyme itself but a complex of many enzymes including phospherylase, phosphatase, aldolase, mutase and carboxylase. In addition there are many minor enzymes all of which play some small part in the conversion of a must into wine. The zymase complex is secreted naturally by sugar fermentative yeasts, so clearly, good quality wine yeasts should always be used. With modern techniques, more and more enzymes of the complex have been isolated and identified. They have been renamed according to their function. Zymase is now the enzyme that causes the reduction of acetaldehyde to alcohol.

The actual transformation of sugar into alcohol and carbon dioxide in the presence of the zymase complex as at present understood is as set out in the diagram under the heading FERMENTATION OF SUGAR TO ALCOHOL.